Unleashing Your Language Wizards

A Brain-Based Approach to Effective Editing and Writing

John T. Crow

Florida Southern College

PEARSON

Boston   New York   San Francisco
Mexico City   Montreal   Toronto   London   Madrid   Munich   Paris
Hong Kong   Singapore   Tokyo   Cape Town   Sydney

To my wife, Connie—my bedrock, my true North, my inspiration.
A person could not want for a better friend or partner in life.

Vice President, Editor-in-Chief: Aurora Martínez Ramos
Editorial Assistant: Jacqueline Gillen
Vice President, Marketing and Sales Strategies: Emily Williams Knight
Director of Marketing: Chris Flynn
Marketing Manager: Amanda Stedke
Production Editor: Janet Domingo
Editorial Production Service: Lynda Griffiths
Composition Buyer: Linda Cox
Manufacturing Buyer: Megan Cochran
Electronic Composition: SchneckDePippo Graphics
Cover Designer: Linda Knowles

For Professional Development resources, visit www.pearsonpd.com.

Between the time website information is gathered and then published, it is not unusual for some sites to have closed. Also, the transcription of URLs can result in typographical errors. The publisher would appreciate notification where these errors occur so that they may be corrected in subsequent editions.

Printed in the United States of America

10 9 8 7 6 5 4 3 2 1   13 12 11 10 09

   www.pearsonpd.com   ISBN-10:   0-137-02003-1
ISBN-13: 978-0-137-02003-4

Contents

Preface

Learning how to write well is not an easy task. Students work on this skill in varying amounts of time from second grade through high school. If they go on to college, they typically complete one or two more courses devoted primarily to developing composition skills. Despite this large investment in time and effort, however, many students still do not write very well. Something is wrong here; we should be getting a better return on our investment.

Part of the problem, of course, is that students no longer spend much time reading professionally written and edited material for pleasure, so they are not exposed to as much well-written material. This decrease in exposure, however, has not been accompanied by a decrease in expectations: Society still demands good writing skills in academic and business/professional circles.

In academics, for example, knowledge is often displayed in written form. Students with poorly developed writing skills are at a distinct disadvantage. If they cannot express themselves properly, their grades will probably suffer no matter how well they know the subject matter. High-stakes testing at all levels of education has, of course, raised the ante considerably.

The National Commission on Writing in America's Schools and Colleges (p. 3) conducted a survey in 2004 of 64 major U.S. corporations. The following quote sums up the results: "People who cannot write and communicate clearly will not be hired and are unlikely to last long enough to be considered for promotion" (p. 5).

Blaauw-Hara (2006) recounts the situation very nicely:

> Despite how we may feel politically and emotionally about valuing students' native dialects and the desirability of myriad patterns of speech and writing, the work world—and, indeed, most of the world of higher education not directly involved in language studies—that awaits our students upon graduation or transfer does not share such values. (p. 166)

A revolution in the way we teach writing has already begun. Groundbreaking books by Rei Noguchi, Constance Weaver, Jeff Anderson, and Amy Benjamin have fired some important first shots. This book, written for preservice as well as in-service teachers, joins the battle, but from a fresh perspective.

Divide and Conquer

Writing consists of two equally important (albeit somewhat overlapping) skill categories, areas that I refer to as *sentence management* and *concept management*. Vicki Spandel developed a very popular instructional approach—6 Trait Writing®—that we can use to further define these two areas. Table 1 assigns each of the 6 Traits to its appropriate category.

This book takes dead aim at the left side of Table 1. It presents effective, interactive, classroom-tested ways to infuse these sentence management skills into the curriculum in ways that are very much in keeping with natural human learning. This brain-based writing approach takes advantage of the knowledge about spoken and written English that students—standard English learners (SELs), standard English speakers, and advanced English language learners (ELLs)—already possess. This information, tucked away in subconscious areas of the brain, consists of what I metaphorically call **Language Wizards**: special bodies of knowledge about language (English in this case) that must be in place in order for speakers to communicate. Specifically, this text taps into three Wizards—**Grammar Wizards, Sentence Wizards,** and **Rhetorical Wizards**—using what students already know as a resource, connecting that knowledge to what students need to know in order to express themselves clearly and maturely when writing. As you will see, these Wizards provide an enjoyable, pragmatic, engaged-learning approach to the teaching of sentence structure, sentence fluency, and rhetoric.

Table 1 6 Trait Writing® Breakdown

Sentence Management	Concept Management
Conventions	Ideas
Sentence Fluency	Organization
Voice	
Word Choice	

English Speakers

Today's classrooms often contain a variety of English speakers. The Wizard approach outlined in this book addresses all of them:

- *Standard English Learners (SELs):* Students who, by circumstance of birth and/or environment, grow up in a community where a so-called non-standard dialect of English is spoken. Included in this category would be speakers of Ebonics (often called Black English), speakers of Hispanic English, speakers of regional dialects (rural, southern, northern, etc.), and others.

- *Standard English Speakers:* Students who, by circumstance of birth and/or environment, grow up in a community where so-called standard English is spoken.

- *English Language Learners (ELLs) or English as a Second Language (ESL) Students:* Students whose first language is not English. Here we must acknowledge a simple truth: If you are teaching classes that have both native speakers and beginning or intermediate non-native speakers, you have two groups with which to work. No single approach to acquiring English skills is going to meet the needs of both groups of students. Many years of classroom experience have shown, however, that *advanced non-native speakers* will profit greatly from the Wizard approach.

I will refer to these groups as needed. Unless otherwise specified, however, everything in this book applies to all three groups of students.

In This Book

This book is divided into four sections. Each chapter begins with a true–false "pretest" and ends with discussion questions, the first of which is to see whether you want to reevaluate your answers to the pretest. The answers are provided at the back of the book. The chapters break down as follows:

Part One: The Grammar Wizard

- Chapter 1 gives a classroom example—a microcosm that demonstrates why traditional grammar teaching is not effective. It also provides a more fully developed definition of what grammar actually entails, introduces you to the Grammar Wizard concept, and briefly explains the importance of properly focused and presented grammar instruction.

- Chapter 2 shows classroom-tested demonstrations that will acquaint your students with their Grammar Wizards—and you with yours.

■ Chapter 3 examines the brain-based learning movement, human memory, natural versus rote learning, and the natural learning process. It concludes with a listing of 12 basic brain-based learning tenets, showing how traditional grammar pedagogy violates each.

■ Chapter 4 outlines the Grammar Wizard Approach: a pedagogical method for presenting grammar instruction that takes advantage of what students already know, albeit subconsciously, tying it to what they need to know when writing.

Part Two: Using the Grammar Wizard

■ Chapter 5 provides Grammar Wizard Tests—techniques students can use to get in touch with their Grammar Wizards, query them, and use the results to resolve specific Standard Written American English (SWAE) problem areas.

■ Chapter 6 presents a collection of activities that facilitate brain-based learning of many of the concepts presented in previous and future chapters.

■ Chapter 7 presents an assortment of constructions for students to place in their grammar toolboxes. When properly used, these structures provide variety and conciseness—key players in the perception of a mature style.

■ Chapter 8 deals with punctuation from a brain-based perspective.

There is some truly good news in all of this for you: You do not have to master the arcane and forbidding traditional grammar approach in order to bring the contents of these sections into your classroom. You, as either a native speaker of English or a very advanced non-native speaker, have Wizards in your head that are even more fully developed than those of your students. And they are just sitting there, waiting for you to tap into them.

If you already know traditional grammar, that knowledge will stand you in good stead: the same concepts (and often terminology) apply. If, however, you do not know traditional grammar—if you find it confusing, if you have never really been exposed to it, or if you are afraid of it—relax! These sections will help you gain insights into the inner workings of English by showing *you* how to query *your* Grammar Wizard to figure out all sorts of things about English—painlessly.

Part Three: The Sentence Wizard

■ Chapter 9 presents an extended example of a method that tackles the seemingly intractable problem of comma splices, fragments, and run-ons, providing a completely specified Wizard Approach lesson in the process.

This novel approach to sentence boundary errors truly works: Students actually "get" it.

- Chapter 10 delves into sentence variety and complexity. It examines Sentence Beginners, Sentence Interrupters, and Sentence Expanders—patterns that students already know when they read, but may not use when they write. The chapter helps you show students how to learn to read like writers (how to "unpack" text to see what makes it work), and then how to incorporate their findings into their writing.

Part Four: The Rhetorical Wizard

The goal of this section is to explore how to help students leverage their existing subconscious knowledge of the rhetoric of spoken English to make mechanical and structural choices that reflect their engagement, their emotion, and their personalities in a clear and expressive manner.

- Chapter 11 begins with a general exploration of the concept of rhetorical choices, registers, and code switching. It then focuses on punctuation and word choice from a rhetorical perspective. It shows how various choices can change the voice, the tone, or the impact of one's writing and how our students' intuitions about English can be used to build their skills.
- Chapter 12 deals with structural issues: given versus new information, placement of constituents, active versus passive voice, fragments, sentence length, and voice.

For your convenience, a glossary has been placed at the end of this text. It contains acronyms and definitions of terms that I have used throughout this text.

Looking Ahead

I have presented workshops on various aspects of brain-based writing contained in this book to many groups of K–16 teachers throughout the United States. Here are a few of their anonymous comments, taken from post-workshop evaluation forms:

"I left with clear ideas and practical strategies to help my students write more varied and sophisticated sentences."

". . . simple, direct, and creative ways to include grammar in a meaningful way—and without tears from my students or me."

"I will no longer allow my students to be bullied by grammar. Instead, I will collaborate with my students and apply the John Crow strategies that will liberate all of us."

I invite you to visit BrainBasedWriting.com for supplemental information. The website also has my email address. Please feel free to email me with questions, comments, or suggestions—I would love to hear from you: BrainBasedWriting@gmail .com.

Now, sit back, relax, lower your guard, and open your mind. Let your Language Wizards help you demystify the structure of Standard Written American English and help you turn sentence management from staid, sterile, student-detested lessons into fun-filled, active, student-centered ones.

Acknowledgments

Social conventions dictate that an author's name be prominently displayed on the outside of a book and on the title page. I have followed tradition, knowing full well, however, that this book was most certainly not a one-person project. It could never have become a reality without the extraordinary assistance of lots of people:

- My wife, Connie, without whose patient support, assistance, perspectives, and encouragement this book would not have been possible. Her contribution to the overall effort is incalculable.

- My former boss, Paula Buck, who hired me, championed my causes, acted as a marvelously insightful sounding board for so many ideas, and helped pick me up when I was down.

- My colleagues on the English faculty at Florida Southern College: Alex Bruce, Cat Eskin, Keith Huneycutt, Mary Pharr, Bernie Quetchenbach, Rebecca Saulsbury, Peter Schreffler, Claudia Slate, and Margaret Taylor. They were all wonderfully cooperative and collegial as they helped many of these concepts take shape.

- Florida Southern College's President Anne Kerr and Vice President Susan Conner, who supported me at every juncture.

- My freshman comp students at Florida Southern, who provided in-flight corrections and inspired me in countless ways.

- My friend Amy Benjamin, who encouraged me to pursue my dreams.

- Patricia Goonen, Elementary Language Arts Supervisor for Orange County, FL, who was so instrumental in helping me launch this venture.

- Tom and Diane Hoemeke, who, in the early stages, buoyed my confidence.

- The editors and marketing people for Allyn & Bacon, a truly superb group of professionals who supported me in ways too numerous to count.

- Reviewers Elise Barnett (University of North Carolina at Chapel Hill), SueEllen McCalley (Avila University), Jennifer Powers (Green Mountain College), James Rycik (Ashland University), Tom Scott (University of Wisconsin–Milwaukee), and Wayne Slater (University of Maryland), who offered very helpful comments and suggestions.

- Lynda Griffiths, copy editor extraordinaire, whose countless suggestions and corrections contributed immeasurably.

- The editors and marketing people for Allyn & Bacon, a truly superb group of professionals who supported me in ways too numerous to count.

Background

True or False?

1. Most high school graduates know that a noun is a person, place, or thing.

2. Most high school graduates are able to identify nouns.

3. Identifying nouns is a valuable skill for writers.

4. The primary role of grammar is to provide rules that help people speak and write correctly.

5. The ability to break sentences down into phrases and words and to label them is an important skill for writers.

6. When readers make judgments about stylistic sophistication, grammar is a primary means for evaluation.

7. All native speakers of English know English grammar very well.

8. Most students cannot acquire Standard Written American English (SWAE) unless they are able to contrast the grammatical structure of their writing with society's expectations for SWAE.

PC?

We have, in this country, been working for a long time to eliminate prejudice. We often go to considerable lengths to ensure that our language and actions are politically correct—generally referred to as being PC. However, there is one type of bias that permeates most educational institutions, and this bias needs to be addressed: Students and, quite often, English teachers have a deep-seated prejudice against grammar. Like many biases, this prejudice is based on misunderstandings:

- For over 150 years, the word *grammar* has conjured up images of boring classes, arcane concepts, rules and lists to memorize, sentences to diagram, and drill-and-kill exercises. In many corners, the mere mention of the g-word elicits moans and groans from students and teachers alike. This anti-grammar prejudice perseveres even though there are much better ways to teach grammar—ways that allow it to transfer to and positively affect student writing.

- To most people, grammar means two things: error correction (speaking or writing properly) and sentence analysis (identifying, labeling, diagramming, etc.). However, grammar means *much* more than that. Grammar is the meaning-making heart and soul of language. This concept is more fully developed later in the chapter.

This biased dislike of grammar is not PC—not *pedagogically* correct. The first four chapters of the book aim to change all of that. Properly presented, grammar—sentence structure—becomes a center point around which to build writing skills. A sound working knowledge of grammar will help your students

- avoid stigmatizing errors,
- develop variety in sentence structure or sentence fluency,
- make better rhetorical choices according to the context of the writing situation, and
- acquire a more mature, sophisticated style.

These early chapters, then, aim to change three things:

1. *Your Attitude:* How you view the role of grammar in language exchanges in general, and in writing in specific.
2. *Your Aptitude:* How you feel about your capability to teach grammar. If you feel that the subject is just too complicated or boring, if you never got it (or hated it) when *you* studied grammar (if you ever did), you will feel much better prepared after reading this section.
3. *Your Approach:* How you incorporate grammar instruction into your **English language arts (ELA)** classroom.

Processional Caterpillars

A French entomologist is said to have conducted an experiment with processional caterpillars, pesky creatures found mainly in Europe. These caterpillars are so named because, wherever they go, they march in a line—bumper to bumper, so to speak—unthinkingly following the one in front. The scientist took a flowerpot, filled it with dirt, and placed food in the center. He then carefully placed the caterpillars around the rim of the flowerpot and watched as they, true to character, began to march around the rim, unquestioningly following the leader. They marched like this for seven days and seven nights, round and round the pot—sustenance a mere few inches away—until they began to fall off of the flowerpot, exhausted and dying.

When I read about this piece of research, I was struck by a startling similarity: Those processional caterpillars sounded just like traditional grammar teachers! For the past 150 years, generations of teachers have been blindly following in the footsteps of those before them, unquestioningly trying to teach grammar just like their predecessors did—to students who hate it—until they finally collapse, exhausted by the futility of their efforts.

Sustenance, in the form of truly enlightening information from the fields of linguistics and human cognition, is now within easy reach. Such information will allow English teachers to better impart the knowledge that their students need in order to improve their writing skills—and to do so in a manner that is much more interesting, fun, and effective.

A Classroom Example

In every freshman composition class that I teach, I ask my students on day one to give me the definition of a noun. They all respond in almost perfect unison: "It's a person, place, or thing." Occasionally someone will add, "Or an idea." Do they know what they are talking about or are they merely parroting what they have heard?

To find out, I write three words on the board:

beautiful
beautify
beauty

I ask the students to raise their hands if they can, with a high degree of confidence, tell me which of these three words is a noun. The best response I have ever gotten is a 25% show of hands. I then ask students to raise their hands if they don't have a clue. Hands from the remaining 75%+ invariably go shooting into the air. Something is seriously wrong here!

I then write three more words on the board:

grape

apple

banana

I tell the class that all three of these words are nouns and ask them to tell me what single letter they could add to the end of all three words if they wanted to. The class quickly agrees: –s. And, I ask them, what happens to the words when that letter is added? They inform me with great confidence that the words become plural—more than one. I then ask the class what this piece of information allows us to say about nouns in general. They usually tell me that nouns are words to which we can add an –s in order to make it plural. I now introduce two more nouns and ask them to double-check their conclusion:

man

woman

We decide that nouns are words that can be made plural, *usually* by adding –s.

We then go back to the original three words:

beautiful

beautify

beauty

I ask the class if an –s can be added to *beautiful* → *beautifuls*. No way, they inform me. I cross it out.

Next, I ask if an –s can be added to *beautify* (ignoring the spelling change)? Yes—*beautifies*. Does that make it mean more than one? No. I cross it out.

Can an –s be added to *beauty*? Yes—*beauties*. Does that make it mean more than one? Yes. Bingo!

Suddenly, within the space of 2 to 3 minutes, I have transformed the entire class—both native and non-native speakers—into a roomful of noun-identifying geniuses.

I do not share this example because I believe that the ability to identify a noun from a list of decontextualized words is an important skill. It isn't. Instead, I present it as a microcosm of what's wrong with traditional grammar pedagogy (TGP). The students knew the definition of a noun— it had been hammered into their heads repeatedly for years. However, the definition was *not connected to what they already knew about English*, so most of them could not *apply* this knowledge to a language-related task. This demonstration—this sad tale—could be repeated over and over again, switching out the traditional grammar teaching point, but producing the same discouraging results.

Student Reactions

Processional caterpillar grammar teaching is ineffective: Most teachers hate it, most kids hate it, and it doesn't transfer. We will examine why TGP fails and how to replace it with a different approach—an approach that has been thoroughly classroom tested, an approach that is *much* more successful (not to mention *fun*).

Let me share with you a few of the many comments about grammar that my students have made on anonymous evaluation forms from freshman composition courses—both developmental and regular sections—across several semesters. The form simply asks the students to comment on what they liked about the course:

- "Made grammar and writing easy enough for me to understand it. I'm usually terrible at English."
- "I finally for once understand grammar."
- "I've learned a lot about grammar and language—things that have changed some of my views entirely."
- "In high school I had a lot of trouble learning grammar. This is the first time I have fully understood and even enjoyed it."
- "I learned more [about grammar] in four weeks than I learned in the past four years."

Keep in mind that the students were not asked to make comments about any specific aspect of the class—they voluntarily wrote about the grammar component. I can assure you that, when I was teaching traditional grammar, I *never* got these kinds of remarks.

What Is Grammar?

As stated earlier, when most people hear the word *grammar*, they conjure up two images:

1. *Error Correction:* Grammar is determining whether the subject agrees with the verb; whether the pronoun is in the proper case; whether a sentence is a fragment, a run-on, or a comma splice; and so on. In other words, grammar is error correction.

2. *Sentence Analysis:* Grammar is breaking sentences into their constituents and labeling each one (subject, predicate, direct object, indirect object, participial phrase, etc.). Sentence diagramming is a tool that has been traditionally employed to demonstrate how things hang together.

Grammar is, indeed, all these things; however, it is so much more. Grammar is the meaning-making center of language; it is what allows us to string words together in meaningful utterances.

Klammer, Schulz, and Volpe (2007, p. 45) provide a very vivid demonstration of the meaning-making power of grammar. Look at the following "Jabberwocky"-like sentence containing several nonsense words:

The *winfy prunkilmoger* from the *glidgement mominkled* and *brangified* all his *levensers vederously.*

In this example, the words that carry most of the meaning of the sentence, the **content words**, are nonsense words. However, the words that have relatively little *meaning* but that are required by the *grammar* of English, the **function words**, are left intact. The sentence is readable and, in a limited sense, understandable—one could ask and answer questions such as the following:

1. "What kind of *prunkilmoger* are we talking about?" "A *winfy* one."
2. "What did the *prunkilmoger* do?" "It *mominkled* and *brangified* all his *levensers.*"

The authors then provide a second sentence that reverses the situation: The content words (nouns, verbs, adjectives, and adverbs) are real, but the function words are nonsense:

Glop angry investors *larm blonk* government harassed *gerfritz* infuriated *sutbor pumrog* listeners thoroughly.

This version is absolutely nonsensical. When the *grammar* is removed from the sentence, it becomes little more than a list of unrelated words. These two versions of the same sentence are a dramatic demonstration of how grammar lies at the heart of meaning in English. Words have their individual meanings, but without grammar, we cannot tie them together into meaningful utterances.

An additional, vitally important function of grammar involves style: It is a *primary means* by which we judge whether a piece of writing is stylistically mature and sophisticated or simplistic and childish. The following two sentences illustrate this fact:

Version 1: It is difficult to buy a car. I want a sports car. I want a big engine. I want leather seats. I cannot afford one.

Version 2: Buying a car is difficult: I want a sports car with a big engine and leather seats, but I cannot afford one.

Notice that the vocabulary does not change between the two versions.[1] In fact, nothing but *grammatical devices* were used to transform version 1

---

[1] Vocabulary certainly plays an important role when readers judge the sophistication of a passage; however, grammar is at least as important—and probably more so.

into version 2—devices with which your students are very familiar. And the effect is stunning: Version 1 sounds as if it were written by a third-grader at best; version 2 was clearly written by a competent adult writer. If you were an employer, which of these authors would you want working for you?

Hancock (2005) captures the essence of grammar much more clearly with his definition: "*Grammar* is the natural, inherent, meaning-making system of the language, a system that governs the way words come together to form meanings. . . . A popular idea of grammar—and one that we are discarding—is that grammar is the set of prescriptive rules that limit the language we have available" (p. 6).

Traditional grammar pedagogy concentrates on the prescriptive rules (the trees, as it were) while completely missing the very heart and soul of what grammar truly is (the forest). Without grammar, we would not be able to combine words and phrases into anything much more complicated than a grocery list.

Traditional Grammar

Before we begin, let's define our terms:

- **Traditional grammar** is an approach to the analysis of the English language. Standard terms (subject, verb, direct object, clause, parts of speech, etc.) are part and parcel of traditional grammar, as are rules for so-called "standard" English (subject-verb agreement, pronoun forms, verb tense usage, etc.).
- **Traditional grammar pedagogy** (**TGP**) is how the concepts and rules of traditional grammar have been taught in the classroom.

As a method for analyzing sentence structures, traditional grammar has, for the most part, served us well: It has allowed us to capture and codify many of the rules that underlie native speaker proficiency. Although the system is not perfect (what system is?), the perspective it has provided for the past 200 years is, for the most part, sound. However, classroom presentations of traditional grammar have proven not to be very effective. My intent, therefore, is not to create some fancy new way to analyze writing. Rather, my aim is to show a fresh, brain-based way to present traditional grammar concepts in the classroom—a way that ties new concepts to existing knowledge, and a way that shows students how to leverage what they already know in order to master the intricacies of Standard Written American English (SWAE). So I will be using traditional terms and concepts for the most part, but the teaching approach will be decidedly different.

The Grammar Wizard

Every semester I ask my students to tell me what they consider to be their weakest area in writing; the large majority name grammar as their primary problem area. But they're wrong. They do have grammar problems— problems that cause them to make errors that are simply unacceptable in academic or business/professional circles, but the grammar that they *know* and get right *far* outweighs the grammar that they get wrong. While it is true that nobody speaks written English, the grammar of spoken English is, with surprisingly few exceptions, the same as the grammar of written English. These students are in amazing control of spoken English grammar—and have been for years.

Native speakers and advanced non-natives come into the classroom with more grammar knowledge locked up in their brains than is contained in any book or collection of books ever published. This phenomenal body of knowledge, something I refer to metaphorically as one's **Grammar Wizard**, is functioning at a subconscious level inside the brains of all of your students. No matter what grade you teach, your students' Grammar Wizards have had years of training—primarily in an oral environment— before arriving in your classroom. These Wizards are capable of amazing language feats; they crackle with activity whenever your students are speaking or listening, reading or writing. However, we humans take Grammar Wizards for granted—we are blissfully unaware of their presence and of the magic that they perform.[2]

In future chapters, I will show you classroom activities that demonstrate to your students that they *do* have highly functional Grammar Wizards, and I will develop ways to help your students take advantage of some of the unconscious knowledge that is locked up in their brains. For now, however, let's just acknowledge its existence.

What Students Already Know and Don't Know

Look at the following sentences:

> According to research, sentence variety really works. It creates a favorable impression by adding maturity and sophistication to your writing.

---

[2]Many computer scientists have a much greater appreciation of the Grammar Wizard. They have been trying for decades to program machines that can analyze and understand human language—with very limited success.

Most students could not tell you that the first sentence begins with an adverbial prepositional phrase or that the second one contains a gerund phrase as an object of the preposition *by*. But they *can* read and comprehend these statements without a problem (assuming they know the vocabulary), and, at least in the later grades, they *can* make similarly patterned sentences by changing the topic and the words that are being used. In other words, their Grammar Wizards are in control of the grammar structures that comprise the sentences. The students just don't know that they know.

In the TGP classroom, one of the main objectives is to get students to the point where they can label every word and/or phrase in a sentence and explain its function. The sample sentences might be analyzed as shown in Table 1.1. Very few students could perform such an analysis, no matter

Table 1.1 Traditional Grammatical Analysis

Word	Part of Speech	Function
According to	Preposition	
research	Noun	Object of the preposition
sentence	Noun	Adjectival modifying "variety"
variety	Noun	Subject of the sentence
really	Adverb	Adverb modifying "works"
works	Verb	Verb (intransitive)
It	Personal pronoun (3rd person sing.)	Subject of the sentence
creates	Verb	Verb (transitive)
a	Indefinite article	Adjective modifying "impression"
favorable	Adjective	Adjective modifying "impression"
impression	Noun	Direct object
by	Preposition	Adverbial modifying "impression"
adding	Gerund	Object of preposition
maturity	Noun	Object of gerund
and	Coordinating conjunction	
sophistication	Noun	Object of gerund
to	Preposition	Adverbial modifying "adding"
your	Possessive pronoun	Adjective modifying "writing"
writing	Gerund	Object of "to"

how much traditional grammar they studied. In fact, many English teachers could not perform this analysis, nor could many very successful professional authors. And yet, as stated earlier, students readily *understand* and can *produce* such sentences. Obviously, traditional grammatical analyses do not mesh with native speaker intuitions (i.e., Grammar Wizards) very well: A writer does not *require* this type of knowledge in order to write competently.

To Teach or Not to Teach

If students already know so much grammar, why bother to teach it? Before answering that question, we have to examine a fundamental issue. Two basic rationales exist for teaching grammar:

1. *Grammar as an End*: We must expand students' understanding of the language they speak. Because language is such an essential part of our everyday lives, well-educated people should be consciously aware of its inner workings.

2. *Grammar as a Means to an End*: We must equip students with the tools and knowledge they need in order to express themselves clearly and effectively, especially in a writing environment. It is our duty as educators to give all students equal access to **Standard Written American English (SWAE)**. The simple fact is that most students cannot acquire SWAE without being able to perform some sort of grammatical analysis of what they have written vis-à-vis what SWAE requires.

Should we teach grammar? Absolutely. An understanding of grammar is an enormously useful tool in the composition classroom. Not only can students learn to spot and repair areas that do not conform to societal expectations but they can also learn to write in a style that leaves at least a neutral, if not a positive, impression on the reader.

Although I heartily endorse motive 1 in general, years of teaching writing have convinced me that motive 2 is the absolutely indispensable one. Therefore, those areas of sentence structure that do not readily make a specific contribution to the improvement of writing will not be covered in this text. The intent is not to teach students to be able to break sentences down and analyze each and every constituent. Rather, it is to equip students with the specific knowledge they need in order to improve their composition skills.

In his ground-breaking book on grammar as it pertains to the writing classroom, Noguchi (1991) summed up the situation very well: "Paradoxically, maximizing the benefits of grammar instruction to writing requires teaching less, not more, grammar. This means making grammar instruction both less expansive and more cost-efficient" (p. 16). I couldn't agree more.

Discussion Questions

1. Review your answers to the true–false questions at the beginning of this chapter. Do you want to change any of your answers?

2. How has your idea of grammar been altered since reading this chapter?

3. If someone asks you to define grammar, how would you respond?

4. How would you define one's Grammar Wizard?

5. The traditional grammar definition of a noun (a person, place, or thing) does not work very well in practice. Why is the Grammar Wizard definition of a noun (a word that can usually be made plural) so much more effective?

6. What is the difference between traditional grammar and traditional grammar pedagogy?

7. This chapter builds a case for including grammar in the composition classroom. Do you agree or disagree? Defend your answer.

8. What is the difference between being able to *understand* or *produce* a sentence and being able to *analyze* it into its constituent parts? Is it possible to be able to do one without the other? Explain.

9. Explain why the following analogy is fitting:

   Understanding a sentence is to naming its parts as driving a car is to labeling the parts of the engine.

10. In your own words, explain the difference between teaching grammar as an end and teaching grammar as a means to an end.

## chapter 2

Meet Your Grammar Wizard

True or False?

1. All students who are advanced non-native English speakers have phenomenal facility with English grammar.

2. If we did not know grammar, we would not be able to process sentences that contained more than 7 or 8 words.

3. Native speakers use language well, but have little to no conscious knowledge about *how* it works.

4. A sentence can be absolutely grammatical and be absolutely nonsensical at the same time.

5. Most passages can be easily read even though the letters in each word are scrambled—as long as the first and last letter of each word remain in place.

6. Students can learn how to query their existing grammar ability to correct many sentence-level problems that pop up as they write.

7. One essential role of grammar is to create patterns that aid the brain as it processes language.

8. In English, adjectives appear before a noun in any order.

Non-Native versus Native

I began my composition teaching career in **English as a second language** (**ESL**) sections of freshman composition. I was impressed with the fact that I could have discussions with my non-native students about sentence structure and why some things worked and others didn't. Several years later, I was switched to native speaker sections. I was absolutely astounded at their lack of knowledge about how English works. As I began to read the literature and look at the available textbooks, I understood why: If grammar was being taught at all, it was still being taught in the same way as it had been many, many years ago when I (and my parents and their parents before them) was in school. I was amazed. My advanced non-native students understood the structure of English, had a good "feel" for the language, and could talk about it—abilities that I was able to take full advantage of in the composition classroom. However, even though my native-speaking students had a more highly developed "feel" for English, I couldn't exploit this enormously valuable resource because they lacked even rudimentary knowledge about sentence structure.

I later discovered a book that dealt with native speaker competencies in the writing classroom: Rei Noguchi's (1991) *Grammar and the Teaching of Writing: Limits and Possibilities*. Noguchi opened my eyes to exciting pedagogical concepts that became a driving force in my teaching life. And so the Grammar Wizard Approach was born.

English Speaker Competencies

The value of the phenomenal resource that native speakers and advanced non-native speakers bring with them into the classroom cannot be overstated. There is an astonishing wealth of information locked up in those brains—information that can be very valuable for resolving writing issues at many levels. As educators struggle to help students acquire Standard Written American English (SWAE), these intuitions provide an excellent framework into which to connect and upon which to anchor brain-based grammar instruction.

In this chapter, you will learn classroom-tested ways to introduce students to their Grammar Wizards (i.e., ways to make them become aware of and appreciate their competency in English grammar—and you of yours!). As you continue to read, keep in mind that students have *fun* doing these activities: How often have you associated *fun* with *grammar*?

As you will see, these activities work with all three groups of English speakers that you might find in your classroom: standard English learners (SELs), standard English speakers, and advanced English language learners

(ELLs).[1] (See the Glossary at the end of this book for definitions of these three groups.)

Meet Your Grammar Wizard

I inform my students very early in the semester that they are grammar experts. They have, locked up in their brains somewhere, a body of knowledge I refer to (metaphorically) as their Grammar Wizards. Grammar Wizards have phenomenal knowledge about and control over English grammar. This revelation is often greeted with more than a little skepticism. Many students have been chastised for years because of their poor grammar; in fact, most of them consider grammar to be their major weakness in writing. So, the first job is to convince students that they truly *do* know a lot about English grammar. Here are several classroom activities that you can use to acquaint students—both native and advanced non-native—with their Grammar Wizards. Do the first one without fail—it provides a perfect segue (as you will see) into *chunking*, a concept that is very useful when trying to explain why certain writing conventions exist.

Word List Demonstration

Ask your students to get paper and pencil ready. Tell them that you are going to read a list of 10 words—straight through, one time, *as quickly as possible*. Their job is to write the list in the exact order that you present it. They are not allowed to begin writing until you finish reading the entire list and say "Go!" (Try it yourself, if you wish—read the following list one time, look away, and recreate it.)

Word List 1

1. the	5. people	9. wanted
2. to	6. the	10. news
3. about	7. hear	
4. storm	8. some	

After the class has had a couple of minutes to attempt this task, tell them what normally happens: People generally get the first few words correct, they fade out in the middle of the list, but they make a comeback at the end, getting the last couple of words. Most students will smile and shake their heads in agreement—that's exactly what happened to them.

---

[1] As was stated in the Preface, if you have a mixture of native English speakers and beginning or intermediate ELLs in the same classroom, no single approach is going to meet their needs—you have two (or more) different sets of problems with which to deal.

Next, inform the class that the previous list was a warm-up to get them accustomed to the task at hand. Ask them to prepare for another list of 10 words that you are going to read as quickly as possible. The same rules are operative: No writing until you finish reading and say "Go!," and they are to write the words in the exact order that you read them.

Word List 2

1. some	5. hear	9. the
2. people	6. the	10. storm
3. wanted	7. news	
4. to	8. about	

Suddenly everyone is a word list genius! After explaining that *the same 10 words* were used in both lists, ask your students to explain why the second list was so much easier to remember. You will get similar responses each time—something like "The words just fit together" or "The words made a sentence." Your questions should be, "*Why* did the words fit together in this list but not in the first list? *Why* did these words make a sentence?"

Discussion What students almost never say, but what you must be quick to point out, is that the second list allows their knowledge of *grammar* to come into play:

- The first list is their brains on random information.
- The second list is their brains on grammar.

If they didn't know English grammar, the second list would be *just as hard to remember as the first one.* However, as soon as grammar is introduced into the task, their brains become word processors that the finest computer scientists have yet to emulate.

This word list demonstration is an excellent way to introduce the concept of *chunking* to the class. Not only is the explanation truly interesting to the students, but the phenomenon of chunking is also extremely useful as an explanatory device—primarily for punctuation, but also for a few other writing conventions.

Chunking

When our brains receive language, either by listening or reading, the words are initially stored in **short-term memory (STM)** (also referred to as *working memory*). There are two notable characteristics of STM:

1. It is temporary. Information stored there begins to fade out in five seconds or so unless rehearsed.

Figure 2.1 Short-Term Memory Schematic

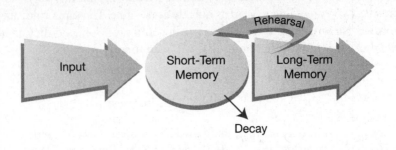

2. It is finite. George Miller pioneered work in this area in 1956 when he published his well-known article that supported the hypothesis that STM is capable of holding approximately seven (7 ± 2) pieces of information. (More recent research [Huitt, 2008] places that number at 5 ± 2, depending on one's age.) Any task that requires you to place more unrelated items in STM results in memory loss due to overload.

Figure 2.1 shows a schematic of short-term memory.

Word List 1 is clearly beyond the limit of STM. Most people cannot accomplish the task successfully. Word List 2, however, is not a problem. The ability to *chunk* the data is the difference. **Chunking** is defined as the process by which our brains combine individual items of information into single, meaningful "units."

Let's examine Word List 2 to see what happened in your brain when you heard or read the words, using Miller's more generous estimation of short-term memory capacity:

Word List 2

1. some
2. people
3. wanted
4. to
5. hear
6. the
7. news
8. about
9. the
10. storm

■ When your brain heard *some*, it stored it in the first "slot" of STM:

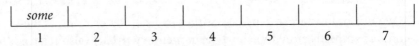

■ When it heard the second word, *people*, your Grammar Wizard kicked into action. It recognized the two words (*some people*) as a noun phrase, so you were able to combine them; now two items were chunked into a single unit. As a result, an additional "slot" was made available in STM to receive more information:

some	people					
1	2	3	4	5	6	7

some people						
1	2	3	4	5	6	7

■ Your Grammar Wizard was able to chunk the next word, *wanted*, with *some people* into an element that we call a clause (subject + predicate). Now three items occupied a single "slot" in STM, freeing up the other "slots" for additional input.

some people	wanted					
1	2	3	4	5	6	7

some people wanted						
1	2	3	4	5	6	7

■ The next word, *to*, did not chunk, but the following word, *hear*, allowed all the words to be chunked into a more complete clause: *some people wanted to hear*. Now five items became one item; the remaining six "slots" became available.

some people wanted	to					
1	2	3	4	5	6	7

some people wanted	to	hear				
1	2	3	4	5	6	7

some people wanted to hear						
1	2	3	4	5	6	7

■ And so it went for the remaining words in the list. When the list was finished, the Grammar Wizard was able to chunk all 10 words into a single element—a complete sentence—leaving plenty of STM "slots" for additional information, had there been any.

In contrast, Word List 1 did not allow chunking to occur:

Word List 1

1. the
2. to
3. about
4. storm
5. people
6. the
7. hear
8. some
9. wanted
10. news

None of these words could be combined into meaningful phrases (or chunked), so each one occupied one precious "slot" in STM:

the	*to*	*about*	*storm*	*people*	*the*	*(etc.)*
1	2	3	4	5	6	7

The result, of course, was overload, and loss of information.[2]

In normal conversational or reading activities, the brain extracts meaning from the chunked data and sends it to a more permanent storage area. That's why you are able to recall the gist of what was said earlier in a conversation but cannot recall the exact words—the temporary nature of STM means that the exact wording faded away quickly.

If we humans were unable to chunk, STM limitations would mean that sentences would have to be restricted to seven words or less, so, for example, you wouldn't be able to process this rather long and complicated sentence that you are reading right now—the exact structure of which you probably have never been exposed to in your life—because your STM would have overloaded long ago.

Grammar is central to the chunking process. As you will see, the brain is a *pattern-seeking device*. Grammar is a *pattern-generating device*. So, they make excellent partners! Your Grammar Wizard is that body of knowledge that is primarily responsible for your ability to perform this rapid-fire, extraordinarily complex process without conscious effort.

Explain the concept of chunking to your students, drawing the seven slots on the board and showing them graphically how it occurs—much as I have done on these pages. In future writing classes, you will be able to explain some problem areas simply by saying things like "You need to show the reader where to chunk," or "The reader won't be able to chunk this information properly," or "The reader will want to chunk here, but it's not the right place." We will revisit this important concept in Chapter 8, Brain-Based Punctuation.

Phrase Building Demonstration

Write two words on the board, with plenty of space in between:

his   dogs

- Ask the students to tell you where to insert the word *big* in the phrase. They will instruct you to put the word between *his* and *dogs*. Ask whether

---

[2] Anyone who was able to recall the entire 10 words from Word List 1 probably used some sort of mnemonic device to aid storage and retrieval. A mnemonic device is the creation of a pattern that the brain can use to organize the storage of the information in longer-term memory. That same pattern can then be used to retrieve it.

it is possible to say *big his dogs* or *his dogs big* in English; the entire class will quickly and unanimously reject the alternatives.

- Then ask them, one word at a time, to add the following words to the existing phrase; place each on the board in its proper place according to the students' instructions:

  > black
  > three
  > German shepherd

  The students will, of course, come up with the following phrase:

  > his three big black German shepherd dogs

- Now try a couple of other word orders; your students will reject them. Examples:

  > *big his black German shepherd three dogs[3]
  > *his German shepherd three black big dogs

- Finally, and most importantly, ask the class the following question:

  > Imagine that I am a student from Tibet who is studying English and is having trouble with phrases like these (a truly difficult task for non-natives). How would you explain to me the rules that you use to create these phrases? What is the knowledge that you possess that allows you to make such rapid-fire decisions with absolute precision?

  The response, of course, is that your students don't know. And so you say, "Meet your Grammar Wizard. *You* know what sounds right; *your Wizard* knows the 'rules' that are operative—the guiding principles that allow you to make these decisions effortlessly and to recognize quickly and easily when these guiding principles are violated."

Discussion   This is one of countless thousands of areas in English where your students know what's right, but they don't know why. Something either sounds right or it sounds wrong—that's the best that most people can do.

Your students' Grammar Wizards grew as they acquired English. The Wizards operate subconsciously—the knowledge is *implicit*, not *explicit*. We rely on our Grammar Wizards all the time to form sentences that we want to utter or write and to understand (and judge) sentences that others utter or write.

---

[3]Throughout this book an asterisk (*) is used to mark ill-formed phrases or sentences. A question mark preceding a phrase or sentence indicates that it is questionable.

Colorless Green Ideas Demonstration

In 1957, Noam Chomsky revolutionized linguistics with *Syntactic Structures*, the book that introduced transformational grammar. Transformational grammar is of no value as a teaching approach (nor was it ever intended to be), but Chomsky did provide some neat evidence for the existence of a grammar component in the brain that allows us to make grammatical judgments separate from other language judgments. He used the following pairs of sentences, as can you in class:

1. Colorless green ideas sleep furiously.
2. Furiously ideas green sleep colorless.

Your students will agree that the first one is grammatical, even though it is meaningless (except in some surreal or poetic world). The second one is complete nonsense—it is both meaningless *and* ungrammatical.

Discussion The first three words of Sentence 1 above, *Colorless green ideas*, meet all of the requirements for a noun phrase pattern; the last two words, *sleeps furiously*, fit the pattern for an English predicate. So this sentence chunks. *Furiously ideas green* doesn't conform to any grammatical pattern in English; adding *sleep colorless* doesn't help at all. Sentence 2 above does not chunk. Because it chunks, the first sentence is easier to remember, to repeat, and to type than the second one.

Thus, we see that an utterance doesn't have to have meaning in order to be "chunkable." The sole requirement is that the words match *patterns* for grammatical constituents that the Grammar Wizard recognizes.

Movement Demonstration

Write the following sentences on the board:

He burned the house down.
He burned down the house.

Ask your students whether there is any difference in the *meaning* of these two sentences; they will agree that there is not. Then ask them to substitute *it* for *the house* and tell you what they discover. Once again, they are unanimous in their decision. The first sentence allows the substitution:

He burned it down.

The second sentence does not:

*He burned down it.

When you ask the students to explain what's wrong with the second sentence, they will, of course, be clueless—as they should be. Tell them to say hello once again to their Grammar Wizards.

Discussion This demonstration shows yet another area where English speakers know what is right, but they do not know why—a sure sign that the Grammar Wizard is involved. Because much of our knowledge about language is subconscious, linguists say that it is *acquired*, not *learned*. They therefore talk about native speaker *intuitions*, since there is no body of conscious information upon which to draw.[4] If students can learn to trust this resource and learn how to query it, many problem areas in SWAE become much easier to resolve and a more sophisticated writing style becomes more accessible.

Letter Scrambling Demonstration

Show your students the following paragraph and ask them to raise their hands when they begin to understand what it says (adapted from Rawlinson, 1976):

> Gamamrr of kwlenogde yuor of bcuseae prltay is tihs. Porbelm wouthit it raed slitl can you and mses taotl a be can rset the. Pclae rghit the at be ltteer lsat and frist the taht is tihng iprmoetnt olny the; are wrod a in ltteers the oredr waht in mttaer deson't it, rscheearch to aoccdrnig.

Let them struggle for a minute or two, and then show them the following version:

> Aoccdrnig to rscheearch, it deson't mttaer in waht oredr the ltteers in a wrod are; the olny iprmoetnt tihng is taht the frist and lsat ltteer be at the rghit pclae. The rset can be a taotl mses and you can slitl raed it wouthit porbelm. Tihs is prltay bcuseae of yuor kwlenogde of gamamrr.

Suddenly it all begins to fall into place for them. Tell your students once again to thank their Grammar Wizards.

Discussion The only difference between the two versions is that the first one has all of the words in reverse order. When the words are listed backwards, grammar knowledge is removed from the processing equation. Without the Grammar Wizard, one cannot begin to make sense of the passage. As soon as the words are in proper order, however, one's knowledge of grammatical patterns, in combination with other areas of knowledge, allows the passage to be read relatively easily.

---

[4]Advanced non-native speakers have, often through a combination of study and exposure, built up a considerable body of unconscious but valuable knowledge about English.

Table 2.1 Sentence Breakdowns

Structure	Sentence 1	Sentence 2
Subject	I	I
Verb	saw	saw
Noun phrase	a car	a friend
Prep. phrase 1	with a broken windshield	of mine
Prep. phrase 2	next to the donut shop	from Los Angeles

Reversal Demonstration

Show the following sentences to your class:

1a. I saw a car with a broken windshield next to the donut shop.

1b. I saw a car next to the donut shop with a broken windshield.

2a. I saw a friend of mine from Los Angeles.

2b. *I saw a friend from Los Angeles of mine.

Ask the class to explain why the reversal absolutely fails to work in the second instance but is acceptable in the first one. They will, of course, have no idea; their Grammar Wizards are once again involved in the decision.

Discussion Sentences 1a and 1b are similarly constructed, as shown in Table 2.1. The components of the sentence, therefore, are not the issue. All we can say for certain is that our native speaker intuition clearly rejects Sentence 2b but is comfortable with Sentence 1b.[5]

I do not use all of the demonstrations in this chapter with any one class. Do two or three of them, and your students will begin to understand and appreciate that storehouse of knowledge about English grammar that I refer to as their Grammar Wizards. Invariably, students are delighted to discover that they know so much about grammar. They are then ready to discover how to query their Grammar Wizards for answers to language-related problems that pop up as they struggle to learn standard written English.

---

[5]A strict follower of SWAE rules will point out that Sentence 1b contains a misplaced modifier. However, since the semantic component clearly attributes proper modification, the vast majority of readers would not notice it at all.

Where Is My Grammar Wizard?

You have seen plenty of evidence to support the existence of a body of knowledge in your brain that allows you to operate in an environment where English is the means of communication. Furthermore, you have seen that you are not consciously aware of its operation. Therefore, your Grammar Wizard clearly exists somewhere in your subconscious memory. In the next chapter, we will, among other things, briefly explore how memory is structured in the human brain so that you will be able to better understand how this Wizard (and other Language Wizards) operates. We will spend the next few chapters learning how to tap into it and unleash its power during the writing process.

Discussion Questions

1. Review your answers to the true–false questions at the beginning of this chapter. Have you changed any of your answers?

2. Why is it important to convince student writers that they already know a great deal about English grammar?

3. What is meant by the concept of chunking, and why is it important for student writers to know about it?

4. Why would chunking be impossible without a solid foundation in the grammar of English?

5. A person is not prepared to teach English to non-native speakers just because that person is a native English speaker. Why is this statement true?

6. Students often think that they are very weak in grammar. What would a non-native speaker who is struggling to learn English think of her or his grammar abilities?

7. Would it be possible for efficient communication to take place without grammar? Why or why not?

8. Read the following string of letters out loud one time. Then turn away and attempt to repeat them.

    LSDN BCT VF BIU SA

    Now look at the footnote and repeat this task with the string of letters that you see there (Sousa, 2001, p. 111).[6] Why is the second list of letters so much easier to remember?

9. What evidence supports the existence of a Grammar Wizard?

10. Why are you able to accurately structure phrases and sentences in English, but you cannot explain *how* to do it?

---

[6]LSD NBC TV FBI USA

Traditional Grammar Pedagogy and Brain-Based Learning

True or False?

1. The brain is well designed for formal classroom learning.

2. Your memory for facts is stored in a different "place" in your brain than your knowledge about skills.

3. The best way to improve a student's grammar skills is through unstructured exposure to good writing.

4. Traditional grammar instruction is the poster child for how *not* to teach something in a natural, brain-friendly manner.

5. Students learn more efficiently when listening attentively to the teacher than they do when interacting with the teacher and their peers.

6. The teaching of grammar has been ineffective because of the way in which it has been taught.

7. Natural learning is often enhanced by elements in the environment of which the individual is not aware.

8. Your Grammar Wizard is a collection of facts that you have learned across time.

9. Lectures supported by reading have been shown to be the least effective way to feed the natural learning process.

Traditional Grammar Pedagogy— Historically Speaking

Traditional grammar pedagogy (TGP) has had a stormy past in educational circles. As early as 1936, the National Council of Teachers of English (NCTE) began to question the value of teaching grammar: "Every scientific attempt to prove that knowledge of grammar is useful has failed" (quoted in Weaver, 1996, p. 10). Things really came to a head, however, when, in 1963, NCTE published the famous Braddock report, an analysis of past empirical studies of grammar instruction. Anti-grammar proponents have made the following quote famous:

> In view of the widespread agreement of research studies based upon many types of students and teachers, the conclusion can be stated in strong and unqualified terms: the teaching of formal grammar has a negligible or, because it usually displaces some instruction and practice in actual composition, even a harmful effect on the improvement of writing. (Braddock, Lloyd-James, and Schoer, 1963, pp. 37–38)

Hillocks reached a similar conclusion in 1986:

> None of the studies reviewed for the present report provides any support for teaching grammar as a means of improving composition skills. If schools insist upon teaching the identification of parts of speech, the parsing or diagramming of sentences, or other concepts of traditional grammar (as many still do), they cannot defend it as a means of improving the quality of writing. (p. 138)

The result of the broad dissemination of these studies is that the pendulum swung too far. Grammar instruction was, for the most part, dropped from the English curriculum in favor of a whole language approach: The students were to learn Standard Written American English (SWAE) by reading and writing. A total abandonment of grammar instruction, however, has produced students who lack the tools needed to analyze and discuss SWAE in order to learn how to create it.

In *The War Against Grammar*, an excellent historical analysis of grammar teaching, Mulroy (2003) comes to the following conclusion: "formal instruction in grammar deserves a careful second look. As an academic practice, the teaching of grammar has a long and honorable history; the arguments used to justify its abandonment do not withstand much scrutiny" (p. 23).

Traditional Grammar Pedagogy has become so thoroughly ingrained in the educational psyche that it is usually seen as the only possible way to cover "sentence management" in the classroom. It isn't. However, before we explore more effective approaches, we need to examine a relatively new movement in education: brain-based learning. The philosophical underpinnings of this movement will help you see why TGP doesn't work and shed some light on better ways to help students improve their writing skills.

Brain-Based Learning

In *Brain-Based Learning: The New Science of Teaching & Training*, Eric Jensen (2000) urges us early on (page 5) to keep the following basic brain-based principle in mind. The italics are in the original:

> *The brain is designed for survival, not formal instruction.*

This nine-word sentence speaks volumes. It encapsulates the very foundation of what many consider to be the most important educational movement ever—brain-based learning. Let's explore brain-based learning, especially as it pertains to the grammar classroom.

In the 1990s, Renate and Geoffrey Caine published a series of books that established and developed the brain-based learning movement. The basic premise of this movement is that the most efficient way for educators to feed the learning process is to do so in a manner that, as closely as possible, replicates the environment in which our brains learn naturally. Thus, teachers need to have some basic understanding about how humans acquire knowledge.

Consider the following scenario: Imagine Gardener A and Gardener B. Gardener A is clueless about what plants need in order to grow. He has no idea about soil, water, sunlight, and nutrients. Gardener B understands the growing process. She knows that plants require an environment that provides good soil, water, sunlight, and nutrients in order to prosper. If both gardeners are given identical plants, one will prosper, while the other will probably fail. (Occasionally, conditions occur that are perfect for plant growth without any intervention. Gardener A will then do well, but he will be lucky, not skilled.)

This situation is analogous to the classroom. If Teacher A knows nothing about how humans learn, he is not in as good a position to feed the learning process as is Teacher B, who has some basic understanding of what's involved. The brain is, of course, the organ that is solely responsible for learning. So the more we, as teachers, know about how the brain learns, the better prepared we will be to create conditions and materials that are conducive to its efficient functioning. As Jensen (2000, p. 3) put it, "If you want to maximize learning, you'll first want to discover how 'nature's engine' [the brain] runs."

You do not have to be a master of the inner workings of the brain in order to use brain-based learning concepts in your teaching:

- First, our understanding about how the various parts of the brain actually process information is minimal.

- Second, we are not in control of this processing. Even if we knew exactly how everything functions in the brain, we would still be faced with the formidable task of how to alter that functioning so as to enhance it.

- Finally, the brain is a phenomenally interactive organ. We might be able to make generalities about left-brain and right-brain processing or about certain functions being centered in specific areas. However, everything in the brain is so extraordinarily interconnected, and there is so much activity going on at any point in time, that it is almost impossible to cleanly separate the functioning of one area from another. It's like asking a man who was injured by a chain saw to isolate which saw-tooth hit him first.

So, before we begin our exploration, a caveat: If, for example, you are reading brain-based learning material that starts talking in detail about what the amygdala does or how information is passed on to the hippocampus, skip all that unless you find it personally interesting. Much of it is relatively useless information insofar as classroom applications are concerned.

Types of Memory

In contrast to how the various parts of the brain function, various *types of memory* are well established and well supported by research; furthermore, understanding the basics is of definite benefit to classroom teachers. So let's begin our analysis of how the brain learns by examining how information is stored.[1]

The most basic breakdown of memory is into short-term (STM) (also known as working memory) and long-term memory (LTM). You might remember from Chapter 2 that *short-term memory* is that facility we have for holding a very small amount of information for just a few seconds. We need to act on information in STM—a newly looked up phone number is a prime example—as quickly as possible.

Long-term memory (LTM) is that facility we have for retaining a seemingly infinite amount of information for a long time—even up to a

---

[1]Human cognition in general and the functioning of memory in specific are very complex subjects. The discussion here is limited to those areas that you need in order to make your instructional efforts more brain-based and, therefore, more effective.

Figure 3.1 Memory Schematic

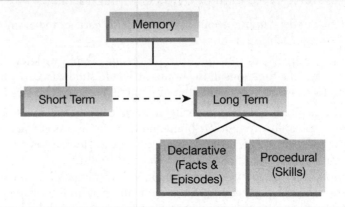

lifetime. Long-term memory can be further divided into declarative memory and procedural memory.

Declarative memory involves facts. Your ability to recall somebody's birthday or the capital of California are examples. Also your ability to recall what happened at your last birthday party or what you were doing when you heard the news about 9-11 entails declarative memory.

Procedural memory involves skills. Your ability to drive a car without consciously attending to the details is a commonly used example. Riding a bike or playing the piano are further examples of procedural memory usage.

Schematically, memory can be broken down as shown in Figure 3.1.

That declarative and procedural memory exist as discrete brain functions is well supported:

- There is a type of amnesia (Korsakoff's psychosis) in which damage to the brain has resulted in the loss of declarative memory ability. For example, in a study conducted by Lai and colleagues (2006), instructions for performing the same task (declarative) had to be given day after day to patients suffering from this type of amnesia, but once the patients got past the instructional stage, their ability to perform the task (procedural) improved across time. In other words, information normally stored in declarative memory (*what* they were supposed to do) was lost, but information stored in procedural memory (*how* to do it) was retained—they got better at the task.

- Patients with Parkinson's disease exhibit opposite symptoms. They normally have good memory for facts and episodes, but are unable to learn new skills (Blakemore and Frith, 2005).

- Brain scans show activity in different parts of the brain depending on whether people are recalling facts or performing a skill (Blakemore and Frith, 2005).

Figure 3.2 Memory Schematic—Grammar Wizard

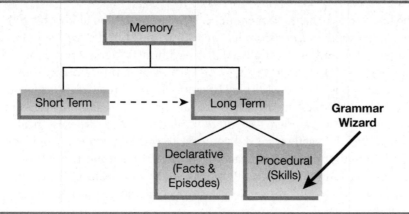

Your Grammar Wizard

The previous chapter introduced you to your Grammar Wizard. Figure 3.2 shows where is it "housed" in this memory schematic. The Grammar Wizard has all of the characteristics of procedural memory:

- You do not consciously control the functioning of your Grammar Wizard.
- You are not consciously aware of what your Grammar Wizard "knows" (i.e., how it arrives at the decisions that it makes).
- Your Grammar Wizard acquired its knowledge naturally in home, street, and school environments, almost exclusively from unstructured spoken language input—with little conscious effort on your part. In other words, you acquired this knowledge by *doing*, in a manner similar to the way you learned to ride a bike.

Compare the Grammar Wizard with other skills that you possess, and you will see the similarities. Take driving, for example: As you are driving down the highway, you often do not think about the act of driving. If, however, traffic gets heavy or some potentially dangerous situation arises, you concentrate more of your efforts on the act itself. The situation is analogous to language-related events. When you are speaking, for example, you are able to form sentences in English using procedural memory (i.e., without consciously attending to the details involved in their construction). In contrast, if you have studied a foreign language as an adult, you know what it is like to form sentences using declarative memory: Consciously applying newly learned grammar rules to create utterances is a painfully slow, intense mental process. If you are properly exposed to that foreign language across time, however, more and more of that grammar knowledge that you have learned declaratively becomes procedural, lightening the conscious mental load considerably.

Natural versus Rote Learning

The brain uses all types of memory as it accomplishes an almost magical feat. It is able to *learn* from its environment—both declaratively (facts and episodes) and procedurally (skills)—without any conscious effort on your part. We will refer to this type of learning as *natural learning*—the cognitive opposite of *rote learning* (memorizing and rehearsing), a facility with which we educators are much too familiar. As an example of natural learning, suppose I were to ask you to recall details about the last meal you consumed: Exactly what did you have to eat? Did you enjoy the food? With whom did you eat the meal? Where were you sitting? I could continue asking you very specific questions about your mealtime experience, all of which you could answer very easily. Let's explore your knowledge about this event:

- Were you born with detailed knowledge of your most recent meal experience?

- Did you know exactly what was going to happen to you at this meal when you went to bed the night before?

- Did you, at any time after the meal, rehearse the events in the off chance that someone might ask you to relate them?

The answer to each of these questions is obvious: No, in all three cases. So, if you weren't born with the knowledge, and you didn't know it the day before, but you do know it now, then you learned it. If no rehearsals were involved, then you did not learn it by rote—you learned it naturally.

Wouldn't it be fantastic if we, and our students, could learn everything this easily and thoroughly! However, given our current level of knowledge about the brain and natural learning, we cannot accomplish this feat, nor can we hope to in the foreseeable future. But both logic and research tell us that, as professional educators, the closer we can come to creating an environment that *facilitates* natural learning, the more successful we will be. Let's take a look at natural learning to see how it functions.

The Natural Learning Process

The human brain has evolved as an organ that specializes in learning:

1. It receives unstructured data—information from all of our senses.

2. It then finds patterns in that data. Three examples follow to illustrate the power of patterns in brain processing:

   a. In Figure 3.3, note how you perceive a triangle that is, in reality, not there. Your brain reacts to the patterns that the little Pac-Man figures impose and "creates" this nonexistent triangle. So powerful is this perception that you can actually see lines, as if an opaque triangle were resting on top of the other images ("Optical Illusions").

b. Figure 3.4 shows an even more compelling illustration of the pattern-generating power of your brain. Look carefully. Are Square A and Square B different colors (Adelson)?

The answer is no—Square A and Square B are the identical shade of gray! Figure 3.5 is the same image with two bars running through it. The bars do not change colors from top to bottom; run your eyes down the bars and you will be able to see that the two squares are, indeed, the identical color.

That the two squares are the same color can be further verified by examining a digital image of Adelson's Illusion using a photo editing program like Adobe PhotoShop. PhotoShop has a tool that will tell you the exact color of the spot that the cursor is pointing to. Computers know everything as numbers; colors are no exception. Colors are measured by how much red, green, and blue they contain. Figure 3.6 shows the result of PhotoShop analyses of squares A and B. When the cursor is in square A (top half of Figure 3.6), PhotoShop shows that the color consists of 121 red, 121 green, and 121 blue units. The second half of Figure 3.6 shows that, when the cursor is in square B, the color breakdown is *identical*.

Why is the perception of different colors so powerful here? The brain knows how shadows affect objects, and it recognizes the checkerboard pattern of the squares. Pattern extraction also facilitates *economy of effort:* If your brain had to examine every square millimeter (or pixel) of every visual image that you encountered, the processing load would quickly increase to the point of overload. Your brain, therefore, samples the environment, makes inferences, and produces the images that you perceive. So powerful is the pattern-seeking, economy-of-effort facility of the brain that it can alter reality. In order to make everything orderly (i.e., to regularize the obvious patterns that exist), your brain imposes a logical perception on you, and thus is born a classic optical illusion.

c. A final example of the powerful attraction of patterns for the brain can be drawn from first language acquisition. A toddler may start off using the irregular past tense of a verb correctly. Let's use *went* as an example. The child might say things like "Daddy went" and "Where Mommy went?" This word may be a part of the child's active vocabulary for

Figure 3.3 The Kanizsa Effect

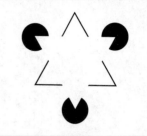

Source: http://commons.wikipedia.org/wiki/Optical_illusion?uselang=de

Figure 3.4 Adelson's Illusion

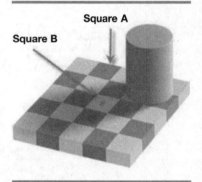

Source: http://web.mit.edu/persci/people/adelson/checkershadow_downloads.html. ©1995, Edward H. Adelson. These checker-shadow images may be reproduced and distributed freely.

Figure 3.5 Adelson's Illusion Exposed

several weeks or months. One day, however, the child drops *went* in favor of *goed*, a form of the verb the child *has never heard an adult utter.* What happened? The child has discovered a pattern: English verbs, apparently, form their past tense by adding *–ed*. This pattern is so compelling that the child throws out what he has consistently heard in his environment in favor of a nonexistent form that fits the pattern. (Let's see behaviorism explain that!)[2]

_____

[2]The child will, of course, self-correct across time. He will realize that there are exceptions to this pattern, and will reacquire *went*, as well as other irregular verb forms, without adult intervention.

Figure 3.6 Adelson's Illusion and PhotoShop

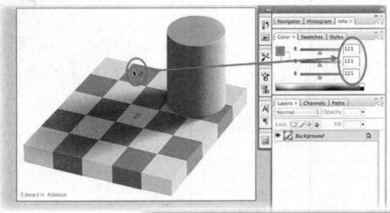

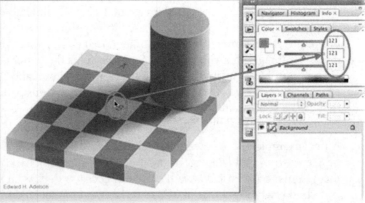

The brain is a *pattern-seeking device*. As was stated earlier, grammar is a *pattern-generating device*. They fit together hand in glove.

3. The next step after pattern recognition in the natural learning process is crucial: The brain then begins to incorporate the newly perceived patterns into the existing networks of information that it has stored, losing old connections (synapses) and creating new ones as required.

4. Experiences are broken down and stored in different parts of the brain. The visual portion is stored in one area, the emotional portion in another, the source of the memory in another, the factual content in another, and so on. When we remember an experience, therefore, we must re-create it from various regions of the brain (Wolf, 2006). Wolf states, "Because memories are reconstructed, the more ways students have the information represented in the brain (through seeing, hearing, being involved, etc.), the more pathways they have for reconstructing and the richer the memory."

5. New connections (i.e., new synapses) need to be reinforced before they can become permanent. Meaningful, varied repetition—**elaboration**—is usually required in order to refine the new pattern and to strengthen the connections that exist in the brain.

Thus, we see that, in natural learning, the brain interacts with unstructured, multi-modal input and, through pattern extraction and networking, structures itself. As Walsh (2005) notes, "The brain is the only organ in the body that sculpts itself from outside experience" (p. 25). Or, in the words of Wallis and Dell (2004), "The brain, more than any other organ, is where experience becomes flesh."

Depth of Processing

We humans are not in control of how much of our brains' resources allocate to a specific task—our brains handle that chore based on the demands of the task. Craik and Tulving (1975) conducted a classic experiment that sheds light on this process. Each participant was asked one of three questions before viewing a word:

1. Is this word written in all caps?
2. Does this word rhyme with _____? (Example: *cat*)
3. Does this word fit in the category of _____? (Example: *bird*)

The participant responded yes or no. This process was repeated through 60 words. After completion, the experimenters gave participants a surprise test that examined the incidental learning that took place during the experiment. They asked the participants to state whether each word in a new list of words was one of the 60 words to which they had been exposed. Figure 3.7 shows the outcome.

Figure 3.7 Incidental Learning Results

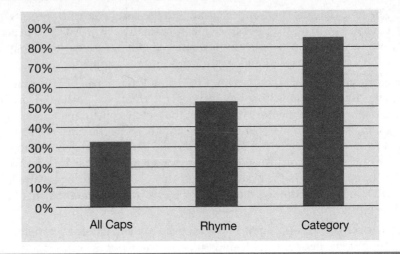

The results support the concept of *depth of processing*. The first task ("All Caps") required very superficial processing—the appearance of the word. The second task ("Rhyme") required a deeper level of processing—the sound of the word. The third task ("Category") required the participants to process the word for meaning—clearly the most complex analysis of the three. The more challenging the task, the more resources the brain was forced to devote to it, producing a significant incidental effect on retention—without requiring greater conscious effort from the participants. The lesson here is clear: Classroom exercises and activities that allow your students to get by with shallow processing will not be as effective as those that require a deeper level.

Methods of Presentation

In his excellent text on natural learning, Sousa (2001) notes that, according to brain-scan research, information is normally transferred to long-term memory when people are sleeping. Therefore, any attempt to see if students truly understood and retained what you are teaching is pointless until at least the next day.

Sousa provides very vivid data (see Figure 3.8) that illustrates the power of natural learning techniques on long-term retention. The graph shows the effect that various methods of presentation had on retention after 24 hours, rounded to the nearest 5 percent (p. 95). As you can see, the *way* you

Figure 3.8 Retention of Material after 24 Hours

35

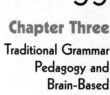

Chapter Three
Traditional Grammar
Pedagogy and
Brain-Based
Learning

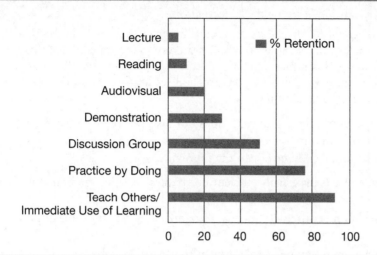

Source: Based on Sousa (2001, p.95).

structure your presentation has a tremendous effect on longer-term retention. Notice that, as you move down the list of instructional activities, one thing is evident: Each of the activities requires a *deeper level of processing* than its predecessor. Keep in mind that even though students may retain information or concepts after 24 hours, research clearly shows that they still need meaningful elaboration across time in order to strengthen retention.

Natural Learning and Traditional Grammar Pedagogy

From this brief overview of the learning process, we can easily see four things that are wrong with traditional grammar pedagogy:

1. *Patterning*: TGP does not take full advantage of known patterns. The TGP definition of a noun, for example, completely ignores the existing pattern that most nouns can be made plural.

2. *Networking*: Because TGP creates explanations that are external to the existing body of knowledge that speakers already possess, incorporating the information is difficult. Using the noun example again, the "person, place, or thing" definition does not readily integrate into what students already know about English. That nouns can be made plural—a so-called operational definition—connects beautifully with prior knowledge and is, therefore, much more effective.

3. *Rote Learning*: TGP requires a lot of rote memorization. The brain is, indeed, capable of memorizing information by rote; it is also spectacularly capable of losing that information.

4. *Presentation*: TGP classes are typically teacher-centered lectures followed by shallow drills and exercises. Research shows repeatedly that this scenario is not conducive to natural learning or to long-term retention. In fact, Figure 3.7 shows that lectures and reading are the two *weakest* producers of long-term retention.

It is no surprise, then, that TGP does not result in retention and does not transfer very well to writing.

In summary, we have seen the following:

- The brain is maximally efficient in a natural learning environment. This facility is what keeps us at the top of the food chain.
- The brain is extremely *adept* at recognizing patterns and making connections.
- The brain is comparatively *inept* at rote learning tasks.

And so we can see why Jensen's (2000) italicized statement, given earlier in this chapter and repeated below, is of such vital importance to teachers:

The brain is designed for survival, not formal instruction.

If you can structure your classroom efforts so that they conform as closely as possible to a natural learning environment, you will be much more effective.

Brain-Based Learning Tenets and Traditional Grammar Pedagogy

Research *clearly* and *repeatedly* supports the superiority of natural learning over rote learning. Here is the question we must answer next: What factors are conducive to natural learning?

In their groundbreaking book *Making Connections: Teaching and the Human Brain*, Caine and Caine (1994) posited 12 basic principles that underlie the natural learning process.[3] Traditional grammar pedagogy violates most of them. In fact, I would consider TGP to be the poster child for how to structure an educational environment that is *not* conducive to brain-based learning. Table 3.1 (pages 38 and 39) contrasts the ideal natural learning environment with the typical TGP classroom. As the table shows, TGP is not very compatible with natural learning. It works with a

---

[3]More information on the 12 principles that underlie brain-based learning is available at www.cainelearning.com/principles.html.

few students because they have a natural proclivity for languages—they can create their own connections; it does not work very well, however, for the large majority of students.

Moving On

We have spent a fair amount of time so far examining what is wrong with grammar instruction in its present form. The next chapter develops and demonstrates an approach that is much more brain-friendly; much more enjoyable for teachers and students alike; and, as a result, much more effective: the Grammar Wizard Approach.

Discussion Questions

1. Review your answers to the true–false questions at the beginning of this chapter. Have you changed any of your answers?

2. Discuss the implications that Eric Jensen's (2000) italicized quote has on the English classroom:

   The brain is designed for survival, not formal instruction.

3. Long-term memory is divided into two types: declarative and procedural. When teaching, we want some types of information to go into declarative, and other types to go into procedural. Provide some examples of each.

4. What are some things that you, as a teacher, can do to help move the learning that occurs in your classes from rote to natural?

5. Why has natural learning outperformed rote learning so consistently in research?

6. Provide an example, other than ones in this book, that shows how patterns facilitate learning.

7. From a brain-based learning perspective, why has traditional grammar pedagogy been, for the most part, ineffective in the classroom?

8. One of the 12 basic tenets of brain-based learning is that the search for meaning is innate. Provide an example of something that you learned naturally, other than the ones in this book.

9. Why is it crucial for teachers to keep in mind that learning is enhanced by challenge and inhibited by threat?

10. Figure 3.7 shows different types of instructional methods. Discuss why each method is more successful than the previous one in producing long-term retention from two perspectives:

    a. *Brain-Based Learning:* Which of the 12 basic principles suggested by Caine and Caine (1994) are incorporated in each (see Table 3.1)?

    b. *Depth of Processing:* How does each method require deeper levels of processing?

Table 3.1 Brain-Based Learning and TGP

#	Caines' Basic Principles	Natural Learning	TGP Classroom
1	All learning engages the entire body.	The entire person is actively involved in and responding to multiple inputs in an integrated fashion.	The teacher talks while the students sit and listen.
2	The brain is a social instrument.	Students (i.e., humans) learn more effectively when their social nature is engaged—when they *interact* with the teacher and with each other.	The typical TGP classroom is teacher-centered: students sit quietly in their assigned seats. Information flows from the teacher to the student. Period.
3	The search for meaning is innate.	The brain has evolved to extract meaning from the environment. When students are interested and engaged in what's going on, the innate desire to discover meaning is triggered.	Students are turned off by the teacher-centered classes and by mind-numbing drill-and-kill exercises. This lack of interest deprives students of powerful brain functions which, in turn, hinders the natural drive to make sense out of what's going on around them.
4	The search for meaning occurs through patterning.	We have already discussed how the brain uses patterns.	TGP often fails to take advantage of existing patterns, as previously discussed.
5	Emotions are critical to patterning.	Natural learning occurs maximally when individuals feel confident and competent.	Rather than impressing students with how much they already know about English and then building on that knowledge, TGP typically informs them that their language is wrong, that they speak a lesser version of English. As a result, those very students who need confidence building the *most* get it the *least*.
6	The brain processes parts and wholes simultaneously.	Making sense of the environment entails the processing of vast amounts of information that comes flooding in from everywhere. Natural learning occurs when individuals see the *big picture* and how the individual parts relate to it. Only then can patterns be connected into the network of existing information efficiently.	In the English classroom, the *big picture* is the language abilities that the students already possess. TGP virtually ignores this area, working instead in areas external to this immense body of knowledge.

Table 3.1 Brain-Based Learning and TGP (continued)

#	Caines' Basic Principles	Natural Learning	TGP Classroom
7	Learning involves both focused attention and peripheral perception.	Learning occurs by paying conscious attention to details. However, learning is enhanced by contextual elements that individuals are often not aware of. A rich context, therefore, enhances learning.	TGP often provides an impoverished context in which to operate. Language is often decontextualized and examined in an almost sterile environment. Such an analysis is acceptable as a beginning point; however, TGP all too often stops there.
8	Learning is both conscious and unconscious.	Deeper-level learning requires a period of reflection. Elaboration is, therefore, an inherent requirement: Material must be recycled through the curriculum, thereby providing students with time to self-monitor, reflect, and adjust.	TGP normally develops a teaching point, works with it briefly, and never returns to it again. Reflection and meaningful elaboration are often nonexistent.
9	The brain is capable of natural learning and rote learning.	Rote learning is used to store isolated information; natural learning integrates information, calling into play higher-order brain functions in the process.	We examined the inherently rote nature of TGP earlier.
10	Learning is developmental.	Human beings do not develop in lockstep fashion according to some externally imposed metric. Individual differences in experience and maturation create an uneven pace for learning.	Errors are natural signposts along the path of the developmental process, an important factor that TGP ignores entirely. We will return to this essential concept in future chapters.
11	Learning is enhanced by challenge and inhibited by threat.	When an individual feels threatened, the brain goes into defensive mode, a state that is not very conducive to learning. When properly challenged, however, the brain rises to the occasion by going into learning overdrive.	TGP is by its very nature threatening. The concepts are difficult to grasp, much less to master; the terminology can be foreboding; and the approach often involves varying levels of humiliation about the language students have naturally acquired from their environment.
12	Each brain is uniquely organized.	Brain-based learning leads to differentiated instruction.	TGP is primarily deductive, relying on repetition and practice. Students with different learning styles are forced to conform to a single approach.

## chapter 4

The Grammar Wizard Approach

True or False?

1. Grammar lessons have to be either deductive or inductive—they cannot be both.

2. The students in your class could resolve a lot of problematic issues in their writing by examining what they already know about English.

3. Brain-based writing concepts are so easy that students will retain them on first exposure.

4. In many situations, students should be praised for their problem areas, not criticized.

5. Standard Written American English (SWAE) is neither more logical nor more efficient than other dialects of English.

6. Sentence-level exercises in most grammar books give students the opportunity to identify errors before repairing them.

7. Many punctuation issues can be resolved by examining how we would speak the same sentence.

8. Traditional grammar shows the logic behind required conventions.

Now that your students have gotten in touch with their Grammar Wizards, and you have a better understanding of natural learning, let's deal with the next question: How does the notion of Grammar Wizard help teach concepts that students will understand and remember as they struggle to master Standard Written American English (SWAE)?

The Grammar Wizard Approach is based on eight basic principles. These principles should inform all of your grammar teaching—from lesson planning to classroom activities to assessment.

Basic Principle 1

Don't cover *the material—let students* uncover *it.* Students should be given the opportunity to *uncover* or *discover* how things work via **inquiry-based** lessons, an approach that helps students tap into the knowledge they already possess. Only after they have tried to figure things out on their own should teachers explain the teaching point(s) being covered.

An inquiry-based approach has three parts:

1. Data for students to analyze
2. Questions to guide the analysis
3. A discussion of the operating principles, thereby answering the questions in #2

Example   Let's look at the *who/whom* decision, a distinction that has, in most situations, disappeared in informal English but is still expected in very formal writing environments and occasionally pops up on high-stakes tests. The three parts of an inquiry-based approach are given in Figure 4.1. Answer the *questions* (in Part 2) that pertain to the *data* in Part 1. After answering the questions, read the *discussion* (in Part 3) that follows.

The advantages of an inquiry-based approach are several:

- The requirement to sort things out for yourself is much closer to *natural learning* than trying to remember information that someone else tells you, which is closer to *rote learning*. An inquiry-based approach allows the brain to invoke higher-order thinking processes—processes that it uses daily as it derives patterns from a variety of sources. Even if students are unable to come up with the solution, the process of *trying* to do so makes them much more receptive to the solution than simply hearing it. Curiosity is the brain's aphrodisiac.

- Requiring students to access their existing knowledge of language helps them interconnect new information (the teaching point) with old (their

Figure 4.1 The Three Parts of the Inquiry-Based Approach

Part 1: Data to Analyze (Inductive)

Underline the correct pronouns and fill in the relationship column for each of these items:

#	Sentence	Relationship
1a.	Who passed the test? (He/Him) did.	who/_____
1b.	Who passed the test? (They/Them) did.	who/_____
2a.	Whom did you invite to the party? I invited (he/him).	whom/_____
2b.	Whom did you invite to the party? I invited (they/them).	whom/_____

Part 2: Questions to Guide Analysis (Inductive)

1. *Who* is associated with what two pronouns?
2. *Whom* is associated with what two pronouns?
3. The above information shows one letter that can help you decide when making the *who/whom* decision. What is it?
4. What does the above information tell you to do when you need to decide?

Part 3: Discussion (Deductive)

Whenever you need to make the *who/whom* decision, answer the question that is being asked with either *he* or *they*—something that your Grammar Wizard can do easily. If your answer ends with *–m* (*him* or *them*), then use the *–m* word (*whom*). If it doesn't, don't.

Who versus Whom

Although the *who/whom* distinction is dying out, it still exists in certain contexts.

Notice the difference in meaning of each of the following:

- *Who am I to ask?* (What right do I have to ask?)
- *Whom am I to ask?* (To what person should I direct my inquiry?)

Although both of the following sentences violate the same rule, only one of them would be considered malformed by the vast majority of English speakers:

- *Who should I invite to the party?*

Only the Grammar Gestapo would object to this usage of *who* today, even though the *–m* Test clearly shows that **whom** should be used

- **To who should I give the book?*

Everyone's Grammar Wizard rejects this sentence.

existing language competency). It also helps them build confidence in their knowledge of spoken grammar—much of which is compatible with the requirements of SWAE.

- Inquiry-based teaching accommodates a wider range of learning styles than lecture-based. Steps 1 and 2—trying to figure out what's going on— is *inductive*. Step 3—listening to the solution—is *deductive*.

Research strongly, albeit somewhat indirectly, supports the combination of inductive and deductive approaches. In a seminal book that synthesizes educational research, Marzano, Pickering, and Pullock (2005) provide support for combining the two modes: "Thinking in real life is probably never purely inductive or deductive. Rather, scholars assert that reasoning is often more 'messy' and non-linear" (p. 105). They also support the type of inquiry-based instruction we have discussed: "Inductive strategies require a well-orchestrated set of experiences so that students might infer accurate and appropriate principles from which to generate hypotheses" (p. 105).

Richard Felder (1993) notes, "Research shows that of these two approaches to education [inductive and deductive], induction promotes deeper learning and longer retention of information" (p. 287). He goes on to say, however, that some students learn best through an inductive approach wheras others do better through a deductive approach. Inquiry-based teaching provides both.

Basic Principle 2

Help students learn how to query their Grammar Wizards. Whenever possible, provide ways that allow students to tap into their existing knowledge of English to solve problems that arise because of differences between informal and formal styles. I call these queries *Grammar Wizard Tests.* They should be introduced by using an inquiry-based approach as outlined in Basic Principle 1. (Chapter 5 is devoted exclusively to Grammar Wizard testing. Others examples are scattered throughout additional chapters.)

Example Here is the Grammar Wizard Test that would follow the example from Basic Principle 1:

Grammar Wizard Test for *who/whom*—The *–m* Test: Determine whether to use *who* or *whom* by pretending to answer the question with *he* or *they*:

- If the question is answered by a form that does not end in *–m* (*he* or *they*), then use the no *–m* form—*who*.

- If the question is answered by a form that ends in *–m* (*him* or *them*), then use the *–m* form—*whom*.

Basic Principle 3

Learning is **recursive**. Recycle previously covered areas through the semester or school year, adding fine points to these areas when possible. When students initially learn some new feature or characteristic about the grammar of SWAE, it is stored as **declarative knowledge**—new facts. If students are to incorporate the new information into the writing process, that information must eventually become a part of their **procedural knowledge**. That is to say, the information must become a part of their Grammar Wizards—to become "automatic." Such transferring requires time, meaningful exposure, and realistic application. The best way to facilitate this process is to let the information grow cold for a few days and then revisit it, adding refinements and meaningful elaboration in the process.

Example   After playing with the *–m* Test for a while, drop it. Come back to it a few days later, provide a quick review activity, and then play around with the formal convention of putting *whom* after a preposition in SWAE:

- *Who* did you give the book to? (Perfectly acceptable in conversation.)
- *Whom* did you give the book to? (Not acceptable anywhere. This sentence shows the result of proper application of the *–m* Test, but it is neither informal nor formal.)
- *To whom* did you give the book? (Perfectly acceptable in SWAE.)

In a future writing assignment, you might ask students to try to add a preposition + *whom* to their compositions during the revision phase and have them identify it for you. (Prepositions are covered in the next chapter.)

The point here is straightforward: Keep revisiting grammar issues; keep stirring the pot. This type of varied spiraling of teaching points allows students to strengthen connections and to refine hypotheses— exactly how nature intended it!

Basic Principle 4

Mistakes are a natural part of the learning process. In a natural learning environment (see Figure 4.2), humans learn by over- or undergeneralizing and then by refining their understanding. Why should the writing classroom be any different?

Example   When you cover the semi-colon in a lesson, encourage students to use it when they write, but don't expect all of them to get it right at first. Many of them will misuse it for a period of time as they zero in on its exact usage. Do not penalize them for these initial errors. Instead, praise them for trying, show them what's wrong, and encourage them to continue using semi-colons.

Basic Principle 5

Never teach SWAE as the right way to use language. This point is especially important if you have standard English learners (SELs) in your classroom. Standard Written American English is not superior to the language that students learned while growing up. For one thing, the grammar that they learned informally is identical with formal language grammar most of the

Figure 4.2 Natural Learning Schematic

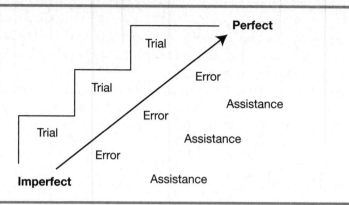

time. For another, the informal language that they speak is *absolutely correct in their everyday interactions with friends and family*. Standard Written American English is not a better way of communicating; it is simply an alternative—one that will serve your students very well in academic and business/professional circles. You want your students to be challenged, but you do not want them to be threatened, to feel inadequate, or to become defensive. We will return to this important point in Chapter 11.

Basic Principle 6

When practicing grammar points, always require students to first identify *whether or not a problem exists.*

Example Let's imagine that you are teaching subject-verb agreement. A traditional grammar exercise might have instructions for an exercise as follows:

> The following 10 sentences contain subject-verb agreement errors.
> Locate the errors and fix them.

Exercises like these omit a *crucial* step in real-life applications: Students are not concerned about whether or not each sentence is well formed—the instructions tell them very clearly that each one is erroneous. In real life, nobody is going to go through student writing and mark all the sentences that contain subject-verb agreement errors; the students must first *find* them on their own and then *fix* them.

If you want to begin working on a targeted teaching point at the sentence level, the instructions should look more like this:

Most of the following sentences contain subject-verb agreement errors.
Locate the errors and fix them.

Be certain that the exercise contains at least *one correctly written sentence*.
Now the students are forced to first decide whether or not a targeted
problem exists before they begin to resolve it. This type of problem identification is much closer to reality: Students must be able to examine their
own writing and find their problem areas before they do any repairing.
Traditional grammar exercises deprive the students of the vital step of first
locating the problem.

Basic Principle 7

Whenever possible, show students the logic *that underlies SWAE requirements.* Seeing *why* something is required will provide relevance, which is
a critical component of effective learning (Sousa, 2001, p. 46). It will also
help students interrelate the teaching point with existing information,
thereby helping them acquire the concept more accurately and with less
conscious effort.

Example A basic rule exists in punctuation (with exceptions, of course):
Always put a comma before a coordinating conjunction (*and, yet, for, so,
nor, or, yet*) that joins two clauses. The reason for doing this is that coordinating conjunctions are used in other capacities all over the place in
English. For example, *and* can join any two elements: *oranges and apples*
(nouns), *bright and bubbly* (adjectives), *to and from* (prepositions), and so
on. When *and* joins two clauses, the comma in front of it signals the end
of a clause, notifying the reader to chunk the previous string of words as
such and to set up for a new clause. (This point is developed more fully in
Chapter 8.) Understanding *why* this comma is required provides a logical
reason for its existence and allows students to interrelate the rule into an
ever-growing web of connections about *how* things work, thereby more
closely resembling natural learning. The recitation of the traditional grammar pedagogy rule ("Always put a comma in front of a coordinating conjunction") is drab and disconnected; the presentation of the rule and the
reason for its existence is much more interesting and interconnected.

Basic Principle 8

Train students to tune in to the signals that they send when they speak.

Example Punctuation is used in writing to show readers where and
how to chunk information. There is a similar requirement in spoken

language. The primary signaling device that we use when speaking is intonation; pauses are a secondary—and not very dependable—signaling device. Students have already mastered the oral system—it's part of their Grammar and Sentence Wizards. Whenever possible, show the relationship between the punctuation they are trying to learn and the intonation that they already know. Chapter 8 gives specifics for how to help your students make the proper associations.

Table 4.1 provides an overview of the Grammar Wizard Approach. I suggest that you review this table often as you do your lesson planning.

Wrapping Up

There is an ancient Chinese saying that encapsulates the Grammar Wizard Approach. I would encourage you to use it as a mantra as you prepare your lesson plans. It goes like this:

Tell me and I will forget.

Show me and I might remember.

Involve me and I will understand.

Amazing, isn't it, how the Chinese had this figured out centuries ago?

Discussion Questions

1. Review your answers to the true–false questions at the beginning of this chapter. Have you changed any of your answers?

2. What is the difference between *covering* the material and *discovering* it? Why is this difference important?

3. Discuss the role of each of the three parts of an inquiry-based lesson:
   a. Data to analyze
   b. Questions to guide the analysis
   c. Discussion

4. How is an inquiry-based approach both inductive and deductive?

5. How would you define a Grammar Wizard Test to a teacher who has not read this chapter?

6. You teach a mini-lesson on when to use a colon. In the next set of essays, you see more colons than ever before, but some of them are used improperly. How should you react?

7. Historically, SWAE has been considered to be the most efficient, most logical form of English. What effect does that attitude have on student confidence and willingness to write?

8. Most of the instructions for traditional grammar exercises omit a step that is *always* required in real life. What is that step and how can you easily include it in your classroom exercises?

9. Although some requirements in SWAE are not logical, many are. Why should you, as a teacher, go out of your way to present the logic of a particular requirement?

10. Punctuation in writing often correlates with intonation in speaking. Discuss how each serves the same purpose from a processing perspective.

Table 4.1 Grammar Wizard Approach Overview

Traditional Approach	Grammar Wizard Approach	Examples
Provide rules to memorize.	Provide analyses that take advantage of native speaker intuitions.	Nouns are words that can be made singular or plural.
Explain how something works and then provide exercises.	Let students attempt to derive the operating principle(s) before showing them how something works.	Provide students with carefully selected language data. Guide students with questions that will help them analyze the data and derive the operating principles. Then tell them how it works.
Review previously covered concepts rarely, if ever.	Learning is recursive. Provide review exercises that augment concepts from previous chapters.	Introduce participles in one lesson. Revisit them later, looking at alternative placements for stylistic variety. Review participles again later on from a punctuation perspective.
Work with one concept at a time. Period.	Work with one concept at a time, but provide exercises that incorporate all of the concepts studied to date.	Provide essay-level exercises that incorporate all of the previous grammar points.
Teach grammar from the perspective of right versus wrong.	Teach formal written English as another way of expressing oneself, as a complementary dialect.	Stress the point that nobody speaks written English. Students already have many "voices" that they use in different social situations. Formal written English is another one that they are trying to add.
Rarely require students to *identify* errors (e.g., every sentence in every exercise contains the targeted grammatical problem).	Make error identification a primary task in all exercises, more accurately reflecting the reality of editing one's own writing.	■ In sentence-level exercises, always provide at least one sentence that is well formed. Thus, for every item in an exercise, students must first see if it is incorrect. ■ Provide essays that mirror real life: Students have no idea what types of errors they might encounter (except that they will have been previously covered)
Make virtually no attempt to show students the *logic* of grammar or punctuation—why things are the way they are from the reader's perspective.	Show students *why* punctuation and grammar conventions are necessary.	■ Give students some minimal understanding of the reading process so that they can better understand what is required to facilitate it. ■ Provide students with opportunities to experience what it is like to read material that violates a targeted convention.
Ignore spoken conventions that are used in place of punctuation.	Train students to listen to their spoken language to help decide where punctuation belongs.	Model the changes in pitch, intonation, and speed that a speaker uses to signal the end of an introductory element (i.e., train students to "hear" where a comma belongs).
Put students on the defensive.	Challenge but do not threaten.	Teach SWAE as a register, not as the correct way to speak in all situations.

## chapter 5

Grammar Wizard Tests

True or False?

1. Grammar Wizard Tests are ways to assess what students know about grammar.

2. Parts of speech in English are clear-cut categories: nouns are nouns, verbs are verbs, and so on.

3. From a logical perspective, a written apostrophe is usually unnecessary.

4. Because prepositions are difficult to define, they are difficult to teach.

5. A possessive noun ending in –'s sounds the same as a plural noun ending in –s. Therefore, one's Grammar Wizard is unaware of the distinction between plural and possessive.

6. We should do whatever we can as teachers to prevent students from making errors.

7. Viewing the same teaching point from a variety of perspectives is superior to repetition.

8. If a teaching point is presented via a brain-based approach, students will retain it immediately.

What Are Grammar Wizard Tests?

A **Grammar Wizard Test** is a logical way for students to query their existing knowledge of grammar—acquired in an informal, oral context—in order to resolve issues that arise as they learn to master the details of formal English (i.e., Standard Written American English).

Grammar Wizard Tests are good not only for students but also for teachers. Many English teachers today, both preservice and in-service, have had little to no training in sentence structure and, as a result, feel insecure about teaching it. If you feel less than confident about your knowledge of English grammar, this approach will relieve much of your insecurity. As you learn about these Grammar Wizard Tests, you will see not only how to present the concepts to students but also how to access your own native- or near native-speaker competency. Both you and your students will discover that you know a lot more about grammar than you ever thought.

How Do I Present Grammar Wizard Tests?

Before we begin to explore the power that is hidden away in one's Grammar Wizard, let's establish a brain-based routine for presenting the material to your students.

Initial Presentation

I strongly suggest that you present *every* language-related lesson in an inquiry-based manner, as described in Chapter 4. Most often, doing so takes perhaps 5 minutes longer than a more traditional presentation; the payback in student interest and teaching effectiveness more than makes up for this modest investment of classroom time. Space precludes including an inquiry-based presentation for every point in this book. So, for every teaching point that you incorporate into your lesson plans, think about how you could create the three required sections: (1) data for students to analyze, (2) questions to guide their analysis, and (3) a discussion during which you answer the questions.

Closure

After presenting and practicing a teaching point, engage your students in some sort of **closure activity.** Sousa (2001, p. 70) defines *closure* as "the covert process whereby the learner's working memory summarizes for itself its perception of what has been learned." In a closure activity, students silently review the content of a lesson you have just completed. Sousa suggests the following two types of closure activities:

- *Reflection:* Let's imagine that you have just finished working on noun identification. To initiate a *reflection activity*, you might say, "I'm going to give you two minutes to think about three ways to tell whether a word is a noun. Be prepared to discuss them." Don't allow students to look at any books or notes. Then lead the discussion. Sousa points out that this short activity is useful for three reasons:

  1. Students get a chance individually to reflect on and reinforce the main teaching points that they have retained.

  2. The follow-up discussion serves as a review and reinforcement activity that comes primarily from the students, not the teacher.

  3. Student responses allow you to determine how effectively you have presented the material and how completely students have grasped it (formative assessment).

- *Journal Writing:* Sousa (2001) notes, "Journal writing is a very useful technique for closure because the specific steps help students to make connections to previous knowledge and organize concepts into networks for eventual storage" (p. 149). He recommends that teachers use this strategy several times a week for 3 to 5 minutes. Teachers need only to spot check the journals on occasion. Sousa suggests that you give your students three questions to which to respond (p. 163):

  1. "What did we learn today about _____?"

  2. "How does this connect or relate to what we already know about _____?"

  3. "How can this help us, or how can we use this information in the future?"

Sousa also notes that, if today's lesson is a continuation of a previous lesson, you can have students reread their journal entries as a review activity.

I encourage you to incorporate brief closure activities on a regular basis as you present Grammar Wizard Tests—or any other lesson, for that matter.

Parts of Speech

Although traditional grammar teaches eight parts of speech, English has only four that lend themselves relatively easily to this type of analysis: nouns, verbs, adjectives, and adverbs. Three of the remaining four (pronouns, prepositions, and conjunctions) are, for a variety of reasons, not true parts of speech and will be dealt with in Chapter 9. Interjections, the eighth member, occur so rarely and are so simple to use that they are not included.

Another very important consideration must be taken into account. English grammar was originally written based on Latin grammar. In Latin, parts of speech tend to form nice, tidy categories: Nouns are nouns, verbs are verbs, and so on. In English, however, the boundaries are very flexible. Whether a word is a noun or a verb or an adjective or an adverb depends on *how it functions in a given sentence*. For example, is *rule* a noun or a verb? What about *walk* and *talk*? To illustrate further, here are a couple of the countless thousands of examples that could be listed:

Example 1: *book*

1. The *book* is on the table. (noun)
2. The police *booked* the suspect into jail. (verb)
3. I have yet to hear from the *book* publisher. (adjective)

Example 2: *flies*[1]

1. Time *flies* like an arrow. (verb—the action)
2. Fruit *flies* like a banana. (noun—the insect)

In English, one simply cannot consider *form* (part of speech) and ignore *function* (the role a word plays in a sentence); words change roles as easily as we change clothes. So any discussion about parts of speech must be tempered with the concept that words used as examples might become different parts of speech in different contexts.

Nouns

We have already seen one Grammar Wizard Test for nouns in Chapter 1: If a word can be made plural, usually by adding *–s*, it is functioning as a noun. There are, however, nouns that cannot be made plural. For example, *Ohio* is certainly a noun, but there is only one of it. Here are three other tests, two of which *Ohio* passes:

- Nouns can become possessive by adding *–'s* or *'*. Example: Ohio's governor

- Nouns can be changed out for pronouns. Example: Ohio is a beautiful state. → *It* is a beautiful state.

- Nouns fit in the following blank:

  a /an /the _____.

  Examples: a book, an apple, the car. (Ohio fails this test—one cannot say *the Ohio.)

> **Form versus Function**
>
> In class one day, we were going over a story when a student raised his hand. "I thought you said only nouns fit in a blank after *the*. But in the story, the author talks about burying *the dead*. Isn't *dead* an adjective?"
>
> After congratulating the student for an excellent question, I reminded him that words change how they act all the time in English. Although *dead* is most often used as an adjective, in this instance, it was functioning as a noun. In other words, it's day job is as an adjective, but, like most English words, it can have other side jobs.

So, when is a word functioning as a noun? When it passes any one of the preceding noun tests in the environment in which it finds itself.

---

[1]The two sentences that follow comprise a quote from the comedian Groucho Marx.

Verbs

Traditional grammar teaches us that verbs are "action words." However, it is often difficult for students to *see* any action for many verbs (e.g., *believe, remember, hate*). Grammar Wizard Tests are much more effective. See if you can come up with one before reading further: What can happen to a verb that cannot happen to any other part of speech?

- Only verbs can be changed into past, present, or future forms. Example: Yesterday I walked, today I walk, and tomorrow I will walk.

- Only verbs can take an *–ing* ending. Examples: walk → walking

- Only verbs can fill this blank: I can (or cannot) _____.

> ## Form versus Function
>
> In my what-is-a-noun demonstration (described in Chapter 1), I initially used *table, book,* and *chair* as examples of basic nouns. One day, several years later, one of my colleagues correctly pointed out that each word could also easily be a verb: One can *table* a motion, *book* a criminal, and *chair* a committee. I had to think a bit before I could come up with three nouns that do not easily function as verbs in English—*grape, apple,* and *banana*.

Adjectives

Adjectives are a bit harder to pin down than nouns and verbs:

- Only an adjective can be put in this blank: *a/an/the* _____ (any logical noun). Examples: a *beautiful* day, an *enormous* animal, the *white* cat.

- Only adjectives answer *which one?* or *what kind?/color?/size?/etc.*

- Only adjectives can modify (i.e., change one's mental image of) nouns. I taught for many years before I fully understood the concept of *modification*. I suggest that you elaborate on this a bit in the classroom:

  1. If I say "a book," then the listener could picture any nondescript book.

  2. If, however, I say "a *red* book," then I have changed (*modified*) the listener's image: He or she must now envision a book that is a specific color. Thus the adjective ("red") *modifies*, or changes, the image of the noun ("book").

Adverbs

Adverbs, too, are not as easy to pin down as nouns and verbs:

- Only an adverb can, by itself, be put in this blank: *I ran* _____.

- Adverbs answer *wh- questions (where, why, how, when).*

- Adverbs modify (i.e., change one's mental image of) non-nouns. Examples: I ran *quickly*, a *very* big book. Again, the concept of "modification" needs to be amplified for your students:

  1. In the sentence *I ate quickly, quickly* changes the reader's perception of *ate: to eat* is one thing; *to eat quickly* is yet another.

2. In the phrase *a very big book, very* does not go with *book*: *a very book. Instead, it goes with *big*: very big. In other words, *very* does not, by itself, change my image of *book*; it changes my image of *big*, which, in turn, changes my image of *book*.

Pronouns

Before we begin looking at Grammar Wizard tests that involve pronouns, let's correct an erroneous definition. Traditional grammar states that a pronoun is a word that takes the place of a noun. This definition fails in real language usage. By way of illustration, try to substitute *she* for *princess* and *it* for *frog* in the sentence below and you come up with nonsense:

> The beautiful princess kissed the ugly frog. → *The beautiful *she* kissed the ugly *it*.

More accurately, a pronoun *points back to* or *connects to* a noun. (I tell my students that a pronoun is a parasite: It cannot exist unless it can "attach" itself to another noun.) However, a pronoun *takes the place* of *a noun phrase*:

>   She   it
> ~~The beautiful princess~~ kissed ~~the ugly frog~~.

Possessive Pronouns   Let's begin our exploration of pronouns with a very common problem: Students have a terrible time with personal pronouns and apostrophes. In order to help them resolve this issue, an important generalization exists that you should help your students discover—a pattern that traditional grammar pedagogy (TGP) overlooks. I'll show it to you in an inquiry-based format to serve as a reminder of how the approach works (see Table 5.1). This lesson assumes that you and your class have already explored possessive nouns (a topic covered later in this chapter). Fill in the blanks in Table 5.1 with the possessives of the words in the left column. Then respond to the questions before reading the discussion:

Table 5.1 Possessive Pronouns

Word	Phrase
student	The _____ book is here.
teacher	The _____ book is here.
I	_____ book is here.
you	_____ book is here.
he	_____ book is here.
she	_____ book is here.
it	_____ book is here.
we	_____ book is here.
they	_____ book is here.
who	_____ book is here?

Questions

1. The first two words in the "Word" column are what part of speech? Support your answer with a Grammar Wizard Test.

2. What punctuation mark did you use to change these words so that they would correctly fit in the blank?

3. What part of speech are the remaining words in the "Word" column?

4. What punctuation mark did you use to change these words so that they would correctly fit in the blank?

5. Facts:

    a. All of the words in the first column of Table 5.1 had to change into their *possessive* form in order to fit in the blanks.

    b. All of the pronouns are called *personal pronouns* because they all refer to a specific person or people (or a thing in the case of *it*).

6. Based on the analysis, what is the difference between how *nouns* become possessive and how *personal pronouns* become possessive?

7. *Extra Credit:* If you see a possessive pronoun with an apostrophe (e.g., *it's*), the evidence above clearly shows that it is *not* possessive. What is it?

Discussion When nouns (and most pronouns) are changed into possessive forms, we always use an apostrophe ('). *Personal pronouns* are exceptions to the rule: They *never* require an apostrophe to become possessive. Instead, there is a possessive *form* for each pronoun—and your Grammar Wizard knows each form very well. Because personal pronouns have a special form for possessive, marking them with apostrophes is unnecessary. (For example, *his* is already possessive—you don't need any additional marks.) If you use an apostrophe with a personal pronoun, therefore, you are creating a *contraction*. For example, *it's* means *it is* or *it has*.

> Which of the
> following is true?
> 1. A dog knows
>   its master.
> 2. A dog knows
>   it's master.
> 3. Both 1 and 2.

This exception is very confusing. Since all nouns and most pronouns use apostrophes in the possessive when writing, it is logical to want to make possessive pronouns fit the pattern. They don't—they have their own pattern. You *cannot* trust your Grammar Wizard here—*it's* and *its* sound identical, so your Grammar Wizard, trained through speaking, cannot hear the difference. So you have to train yourself to check each occurrence when editing. When word processing, do a search (Ctrl–F in most programs) for "_its_" and "_it's_" (where the underline represents a space) and confirm that each is correct. After a while, your Grammar Wizard will learn how to handle this situation when writing.

The PP Rule For a fun way to introduce and reinforce this concept, you can establish and invoke the *Personal Pronoun Rule* (referred to as the *PP Rule* or the *4P Rule*).

> **Grammar Wizard Test—The PP Rule:** Personal pronouns never form the possessive with apostrophes.

If a student misuses an apostrophe with a personal pronoun—a very common and logical error—all you have to say is that she or he has violated the PP Rule.

Note: Pronouns that do *not* refer to a specific person or thing do *not* have special possessive forms; they behave regularly. Examples: one → one's, everyone → everyone's.

Who versus Whom The Grammar Wizard Test for this distinction is the *–m* test, as explained in the previous chapter.

Whose versus Who's Again, students have to learn *not* to trust their Grammar Wizards here. Both words are pronounced the same—the apostrophe is not an issue in speech, of course. Students can, however, *test* their Grammar Wizards. And, with proper exposure, they can *train* their Grammar Wizards to sense which is which. However, since no such training has occurred in a spoken environment, we teachers have to help out.

- *The PP (4P) Rule:* Personal pronouns *never* form the possessive with apostrophes. Thus, *who's* cannot be possessive; it is a contraction of *who is* or *who has.*
  1. If you can expand the word to *who is* or *who has,* you need the apostrophe. Examples: *Who's (Who is)* going with me? *Who's (Who has)* seen this movie?
  2. If you cannot expand it, you cannot use the apostrophe. Example: *Whose* book is that? (You cannot expand this to *Who is book is that?* or *Who has book is that?)

Its versus It's This is another instance of *not* trusting one's Grammar Wizards because both words sound the same.

- *The PP (4P) Rule:* Personal pronouns *never* form the possessive with apostrophes. Thus, *it's* is a contraction of *it is* or *it has.* If you can substitute either phrase in the sentence, you need the apostrophe. Otherwise, you don't.

Your versus You're First of all, let's get rid of *your's* (and *her's, *our's, their's):
  1. *Your* (and the others) cannot be possessive—it's a clear violation of the PP (4P) Rule (see above).
  2. There is no such thing in English as *your is* or *your has (her is/her has,* etc.). *You're* is a contraction of *you are.* If you can substitute *you are* in the sentence, you need the apostrophe. Otherwise, you don't. It's that simple.

Pronoun Case The *case* of a pronoun refers to its form: should it be *I, me,* or *my/mine? They, them* or *their/theirs?* Two Grammar Wizard Tests take care of this issue most of the time:

> **Grammar Wizard Test—Strip It Down:** If two or more people are used, remove everything except one of the pronouns and let your Grammar Wizard decide.

Examples

1. Is it *He gave it to <u>him and me</u>* or *He gave it to <u>he and I</u>?* Strip it down to one pronoun. You would never say **He gave it to he;* likewise, you would never say **He gave it to he and I.*

2. Is it *Joe and <u>me</u>* went to town or *Joe and <u>I</u> went to town.?* Strip it down and the answer becomes obvious: *Me went to town is clearly wrong.

> **Grammar Wizard Test—Make It Plural:** Substitute *we* or *they* for the people who are involved and your Grammar Wizard will know what to do.

Examples

1. Is it *He gave it to <u>him and me</u>* or *He gave it to <u>he and I</u>?* When you try to substitute *we,* the answer is obvious: *He gave it to <u>us</u>.* So <u>*he and I*</u> is out.

2. Is it *Joe and <u>me</u>* went to town or *Joe and <u>I</u> went to town?* When you substitute *we,* the answer is, once again, obvious: <u>*We went to town.*</u> Therefore, <u>*Joe and I*</u> is the right form.

Prepositions

A preposition has always been a difficult "part of speech" for traditional grammar to define. A dictionary definition looks something like this:

> **preposition:** a function word that typically combines with a noun phrase to form a phrase which usually expresses a modification or predication. (Merriam-Webster)

Definitions like these only confuse the issue. Handbook definitions are not much better:

> **preposition:** relate nouns or pronouns to other words in a sentence: *about, at, down, for, of, with.* (Fowler, Aaron, and Okoomian, 2001, p. 256)

Here is the interesting part: Your students have been using prepositions for years—thousands upon countless thousands of times—with only occasional problems. Their Grammar Wizards are in excellent control of this concept of English. Your job, once again, is to get them in touch with what they already know.

Several "tricks" have been used very effectively. Here are a couple of them:

Figure 5.1 Prepositions—Mouse and Box

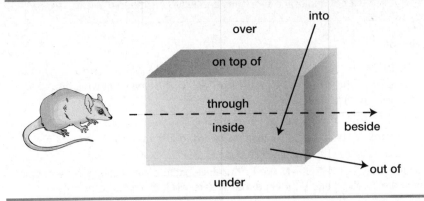

- Prepositions show what a mouse can do to a box: run *over* it, *around* it, *beside* it; be *on top of* it, *next to* it, *under* it; and so on (see Figure 5.1).
- Prepositions show what an airplane can do to a cloud: fly *through* it, *around* it, *above* it, *below* it, and so on.

My favorite approach came from a workshop ("The Inner Game of Grammar") that I did with Amy Benjamin, a brilliant teacher and consultant. Amy uses the following approach: Before students enter your classroom, place the picture in Figure 5.2 (or one like it) on their desks. They naturally begin to try to find the hidden objects. After a few minutes, ask them to begin telling you where the objects are, and write on the blackboard the *prepositional phrases* that they use to describe the location. Example: The whale is *near the gate*. Keep two guidelines in mind:

1. Don't allow students to begin a phrase with a word (preposition) that has already been used.
2. If students do not come up with multiple-word prepositions on their own, ask them to do so by saying, "Use some phrases that begin with more than one word, such as *next to* or *on top of.*"

After you have written four or five student responses, circle the prepositions and tell the students that words like these are called *prepositions*. Their Grammar Wizards will know that additional words combine with the preposition to create *prepositional phrases*. For follow-up, have them find examples in their compositions or in the literature that they are reading.

That's it! Your students have now connected the new information (concept of *prepositions*) with what they already know by solving a problem—picture-perfect brain-based teaching (no pun intended).

You will, of course, have to revisit the concept a few times, reminding them, perhaps, of this classroom activity. They will also have some trouble at first recognizing "fancier" prepositions such as *due to, because of,* and *according to,* but this approach is extraordinarily effective as a beginning point—it's fun and fast.

Possessives

As we have already seen, the apostrophe is a troublesome item for most student writers, and for a very good reason: *whenever students have to attend to a language distinction in* writing *that is not attended to in* speech, *that language issue will be problematic.* Because Grammar Wizards are built in an oral environment, written conventions that are not congruent with spoken conventions are not a part of your students' natural arsenal and are, therefore, difficult to acquire. Apostrophes are certainly a case in point:

- Marking possessive nouns is not necessary in speech —whether an *–s* ending signals plural or possessive is almost always taken care of by context.
- Marking contractions is not necessary in speech—context and pronunciation clearly signals when a speaker is using a contraction. Examples: *I'll* vs. *Ill, can't* vs. *cant, won't* vs. *wont.*

It stands to reason, then, that if such markings are unnecessary in speaking, they should be unnecessary in writing—that context would work equally well to allow the reader to know whether a possessive or a contraction is being used.

Although the apostrophe may very often be *logically* unnecessary, there are very real *social* requirements for its usage. Failure to use it properly is stigmatized in most academic and business/professional circles. The delivery of the message may be unharmed by its misuse, but the messenger may very well be damaged by the omission—appearing to be either ignorant or careless.

For the most part, contractions are learned fairly easily by student writers. Possessive nouns are the main problem. Because they unthinkingly run right past them when they speak, they often go unnoticed by student writers. To further complicate matters, the possessive ending (*–'s*) sounds the same as the most common plural ending. So student writers have two issues with which to contend:

Figure 5.2 Prepositions— Hidden Pictures

In this picture, find the heart, duck, chef's hat, potato, sewing needle, scissors, fish, baseball glove, hammer, bird, and artist's brush.

Can you find these Hidden Pictures?

bird · baseball glove · duck · potato · scissors · chef's hat · sewing needle · fish · heart · artist's brush · hammer · whale

Source of graphic: http://highlightskids.com/ GamesandGiggles/HiddenPics/HiddenPicsPrintable/ HPP1220_bunniesGarden.asp. Copyright © by Highlights for Children, Inc., Columbus, OH.

Table 5.2 Plural versus Possessive

Sentence	PPST	Result
The *dog(–s)* tail was short.	*Its* tail	Possessive
The *dog(–s)* slept on the sofa.	*They* slept	Plural
The *dog(–s)* tails were wagging furiously.	*Their* tails	Possessive

1. Is it plural or possessive?
2. If it is possessive, should one use –'s or just an apostrophe?

Step 1: Plural or Possessive?

A student's Grammar Wizard almost always knows whether a noun is being used in the possessive or in the plural. It also knows possessive pronouns from nonpossessive pronouns. If students learn how to take advantage of this knowledge, they can easily distinguish between the plural –s sound and the possessive –'s sound. All they have to do is substitute a pronoun. See Table 5.2 for examples. If the test determines that the target noun is plural, you are finished—an apostrophe is almost always wrong. If the test determines that the target noun is possessive, you have one more step to complete.

> **Grammar Wizard Test for Plural versus Possessive—Personal Pronoun Substitution Test:** Substitute a pronoun. If you substitute a possessive pronoun, then the noun is possessive.

Step 2: Apostrophe + –s or Just Apostrophe?

Once the student has determined that the noun is possessive, the final issue to resolve is whether to mark it with an apostrophe + –s or with just an apostrophe. Once again, the Grammar Wizard comes to the rescue. Here are two ways to make the determination:

> **Grammar Wizard Test for Possessive –'s or –':** If the noun is plural and already ends in –s, only add an apostrophe. In every other case, use apostrophe + –s.

Examples

1. one dog (+–s) tail → *its* (or *her* or *his*) tail = possessive. The noun *dog* is clearly singular, so, according to the rule, the correct form would be *dog's*.

2. several dog (+–*s*) tails → *their* tails = possessive. The noun *dogs* is clearly plural and already ends in an –*s*, so the correct form would be *dogs'*.

3. the boss (+–*s*) wife → *his* wife = possessive. The noun *boss* is clearly singular, so the correct form would be *boss's*.

4. the boss (+–*s*) wives → *their* wives = possessive. The noun *bosses* is clearly plural (we hope!). Since the plural form of *boss* already ends in –*s*, only add an apostrophe: *bosses'*.

5. men (+–*s*) cologne → *their* cologne = possessive. The noun *men* is clearly plural. Since the plural form does not end in –*s*, add an apostrophe + –*s*: *men's*.

Grammar Wizard Test for –'s or –': Say It Twice. Say the noun *before* you make it possessive and then say it after you make it possessive. If you hear an extra –*s* sound, add an extra –'s when you write. If you do not hear an extra –*s* sound, just use an apostrophe.

Examples

1. one dog (+–*s*) tail: *dog* is the basic word. To make it possessive, you would clearly add an –*s* sound, so the correct form would be *dog's*.

2. several dog (+–*s*) tails: *dogs* is the basic word. To make it possessive, you would clearly *not* add an –*s* sound (*dogses tail), so the correct form would be *dogs'*.

3. the boss (+–*s*) wife: *boss* is the basic word. To make it possessive, you would clearly add an –*s* sound, so the correct form would be *boss's*.

4. the boss (+–*s*) wives : *bosses* is the basic word. To make it possessive, you would clearly *not* add an –*s* sound (*bosseses), so the correct form would be *bosses'*.

5. men (+–*s*) cologne: *men* is the basic word. To make it possessive, you must add an –*s* sound, so you must add an apostrophe +–*s*.

This process of determining whether a noun is plural or possessive and, if the latter, determining whether to add –'s or just an apostrophe is rather involved. Keep in mind, however, that we are getting our students in touch with things they *already know*. With practice and meaningful elaboration (see below for an extended example), the entire process will become internalized; that is, it will become a part of the students' Grammar Wizards for SWAE. I would also remind you to include closure activities after new presentations to help students reflect on and internalize new concepts.

Other Grammar Wizard Tests are scattered throughout the remainder of this book in their applicable chapters. They will all be clearly marked as such.

Recursiveness and Elaboration

Again, teaching students how to query their existing knowledge of grammar—getting them in touch with their own personal Grammar Wizards—is an extraordinarily powerful, very brain-based teaching approach, one that will help students see the logic behind SWAE requirements and one that will foster interrelationships with existing knowledge. However, the new knowledge will not transfer over to the Grammar Wizard—it will not become part of the students' procedural memory—unless you provide two other ingredients: *recursiveness* (spiraling) and *elaboration*. Sousa (2001) notes that "extensive research on retention indicates that 70 percent to 90 percent of new learning is forgotten 18 to 24 hours after the lesson" (p. 71).[2] A brain-based teaching approach will help lower these percentages. However, humans learn through repetition and meaningful application, through making errors and learning from them. The remainder of this chapter demonstrates how to incorporate recursiveness and elaboration by examining one area—adjectives and adverbs—in greater detail.

Let's imagine that you have done quick lessons in adjective and adverb recognition. How can you, short of repeating the same material, reexamine these concepts and build on them in varied and meaningful ways? There are two operative principles here, the second of which should be very familiar by now:

1. Whenever you revisit a concept, try to add something to it.

2. Let the students figure out the new additions before you explain things.

The following items are not presented in any particular order, nor am I suggesting that you take the time to do all of them. My point here is very straightforward: If you decide that adjectives versus adverbs are worth spending classroom time on, then you need to plan to return to them in short bursts across the next several weeks. So I am providing examples of things you could add as you revisit this distinction.

-ly Adjectives versus -ly Adverbs

You cannot be confident that a word is an adverb just because it ends in –*ly*. So you may want to have a mini-lesson that elaborates on this point. Table 5.3 shows an inquiry-based way to do so.

---

[2]A significant contributor to this lack of retention is method of presentation. See Figure 3.7 in Chapter 3 for details.

Table 5.3 −ly Adjectives versus −ly Adverbs

_____	Base Word	_____	Base Word
a *heavenly* scent		ran *happily*	
an *hourly* occurrence		act *stupidly*	
a *cowardly* act		*nearly* missed	

Questions

1. Use your Grammar Wizard Tests to find out whether the −*ly* words in Column 1 are adjectives or adverbs. Write *ADJ* or *ADV* in the blank above Column 1.

2. Use your Grammar Wizard Tests to find out whether the −*ly* words in Column 3 are adjectives or adverbs. Write *ADJ* or *ADV* in the blank above Column 3.

3. All of the −*ly* words were formed by adding −*ly* to a basic English word. Fill in the Base Word columns with the basic words.

4. Looking at the Base Words, how can you know whether adding −*ly* to a word will make an adjective or an adverb?

Discussion Explain how adding −*ly* to nouns creates adjectives, whereas adding −*ly* to adjectives creates adverbs. For follow-up activities, you can do the following:

- Examine some −*ly* words in literature selections.
- Divide the class into teams and do a rapid-response competition.
- Send students on a Web scavenger hunt: Search long literary selections for *ly* (*ly* + space) and categorize the results. (Most Web browsers let you search the text in the current window. Ctrl–F initiates the search process.)

Spelling Changes

A few relatively simple spelling changes are required when adding −*ly*. Table 5.4 shows my inquiry-based approach for them.

Questions

1. If the adjective ends in −*y*, what must you do before adding the ending?

2. What happens if the adjective ends in −*ible* or -*able*?

3. What do you add to adjectives that end in −*ic*?

Discussion Have students fill in the second and third columns of Table 5.5 (shown already completed for your convenience).

Table 5.4 Spelling Changes

Adjective	Adverb
serious	seriously
normal	normally
happy	happily
incredible	incredibly
capable	capably
academic	academically

Table 5.5 Spelling Changes Summary

Adj. Ends In	Changes To	Example
–y	–i	easy → easily
–ible or –able	drop the –e	legible → legibly
–ic	add –ally	specific → specifically

Comparatives and Superlatives

Comparative is the form of an adjective or adverb that you use when comparing two things or qualities (e.g., *smarter, more ridiculous, more quickly, less easily*). *Superlative* is the form of an adjective or adverb that you use when comparing three more things or qualities (e.g.; *smartest, most ridiculous, most quickly, least easily*).

- Provide students with a list of adjectives, some of which allow –er/–est (cute–cuter–cutest) and some of which require *more/most* (*important–more important–most important*). They will have a rather difficult time figuring out the rule that is used to determine when to use –er/–est and when to use *more/most*. (The key is the number of syllables. Generally, words that contain less than three syllables allow –er/–est; words that are three or more syllables do not. There are, of course, exceptions, such as *fun*.)

- When adding –er/–est, figure out when to double the final consonant and when not to. You can set up an inquiry-based approach to let the students discover how it works.

Tom Swifties

Here is a fun way to play with adverbs. In the 1920s, a type of humor called Tom Swifties was developed around a cartoon character named Tom Swift. The trick involved using adverbs that had a double meaning that tied into what was being said. Here are a couple of examples:

"I cut my fingernails too far," Tom said quickly.

"Don't try to pull the wool over my eyes," Tom said sheepishly.

See if you can match what Tom said in each of the sentences below with the appropriate adverb from this list:

gratingly	defiantly	innocently	half-heartedly
decidedly	illegally	wickedly	mystically
rapidly	insightfully		

1. "I've had my left and right ventricle removed," Tom said _____.
2. "Don't burn your candle at both ends," Tom said _____.
3. "I have locked onto the target," Tom said _____.
4. "Thanks for shredding the cheese," Tom said _____.
5. "The river has gotten rough," Tom said _____.
6. "Those ants will never get in here," Tom said _____.
7. "All that's left is the front and the back," Tom said _____.
8. "Where can I find a copper figure of Lincoln?" Tom said _____.
9. "How come my clock only tocs?" Tom asked _____.
10. "That bird is sick," Tom said _____.

Close Reading

Close reading is the process of examining well-written material to see what makes it tick. You can look at grammatical structure, punctuation, word choice, and so on, deciding why the author chose to express himself or herself in that manner and, optionally, what would happen if certain changes were made. This is an ideal way for you to combine literature and composition. I will return to close reading activities again and again throughout the book. Take advantage of whatever students are reading for your class or other classes:

- Encourage students to identify adjectives and adverbs as they read, looking for examples of usages that the students feel are especially effective.
- Have students find, with your help at first, examples of the things that you have been covering: adverbs versus adjectives, consonant doubling, and spelling rule examples.

Encourage or even require students to incorporate some of the features as they revise their own writing.

Rome wasn't built in a day; neither are good language skills. However, because these skills not only remove stigmatizing errors but also contribute to a smooth, mature style, the time invested is well worth it. If you can show your students how to use their Grammar Wizards, and then revisit teaching points, elaborating in a variety of meaningful ways, the gain in knowledge will transfer into better writing skills much more effectively than using traditional grammar methods.

Discussion Questions

1. Review your answers to the true–false questions at the beginning of this chapter. Have you changed any of your answers?

2. Explain what a *closure activity* is and why it is important from a brain-based learning perspective.

3. What is the primary difference between a teacher-led review session and a closure activity?

4. What is a Grammar Wizard Test?

5. Explain the difference between the *form* of a word (its part of speech) and its *function*.

6. What is the primary difference between a TGP definition of a part of speech and a Grammar Wizard definition?

7. Students have a difficult time with the distinction between *its* and *it's*.

   a. Explain this difficulty from the perspective of speech vs. writing.

   b. Explain this difficulty from the perspective of the general rule of possessive formation in English.

8. Why is it not necessary to *define* a preposition before you *teach* it?

9. Explain the following statement: The Personal Pronoun Substitution Test proves that one's Grammar Wizard is well in control of the distinction between possessive –'s and plural –s, even though they sound identical in speech.

10. What is the difference between *recursiveness* and *elaboration*? Why are they necessary in almost any teaching endeavor?

Grammar Wizard Activities

True or False?

1. Many grammatical issues can be best explored without first telling the class exactly what you will be covering.

2. Students at all grade levels are already aware that adjectives modify nouns and adverbs do not.

3. The greater the challenge, the more resources your brain utilizes to resolve it.

4. Games can be excellent tools for teaching in ways that replicate natural learning.

5. A pronoun takes the place of a noun.

6. Changing a statement into a questions that can be answered by "yes" or "no" is a good way to determine if the sentence is a fragment.

7. Singular nouns are made possessive by adding –'s; plural nouns are made possessive by adding an apostrophe (').

8. A sentence is a complete thought. A sentence fragment, therefore, is an incomplete thought.

The previous chapter developed ways to help students get in touch with their Grammar Wizards in order to resolve a few specific SWAE problem areas. In this chapter, we will explore general activities that take advantage of Grammar Wizards. These activities are not aimed at any specific structural issue; they are, instead, activities that can be used to demonstrate a wide variety of teaching points.

Brain-Based Checklist

Before we get started discussing specific activities, please examine Figure 6.1. It is a checklist that I use consistently while lesson planning to help ensure that my instructional efforts embody brain-based learning principles. It's not always possible to check off all items. However, the more items I can check off, the closer the activity comes to emulating a natural learning environment.

The last item in Figure 6.1 (recursiveness) is required because of the way humans learn. The brain learns by establishing new connections between nerve cells and these connections need to be reinforced. You should not be surprised or disappointed, for example, if students can readily handle possessives today but falter when they are asked to do it a couple of weeks later. Two things may have happened, both of which are a natural part of learning:

1. Some students may have formed patterns (hypotheses) that are not quite accurate. They need additional exposure and practice in order to refine these patterns until they are on target.

Figure 6.1 Brain-Based Checklist

☐ *Multimodal:* The activity provides input via at least three channels (seeing, hearing, touching, moving, interacting, smelling, or tasting).

☐ *Hands On:* The students learn by doing.

☐ *Problem Solving:* The students have an opportunity to figure out the underlying principle(s) before being told.

☐ *Pattern Based:* The students are able to perceive or derive the pattern(s) that are involved.

☐ *Interconnective:* The students are able to relate what they are learning to what they already know.

☐ *Challenging:* The students are challenged by the task, but it is not threatening.

☐ *Recursive:* The teaching point(s) is (are) revisited in subsequent weeks for review and, when possible, further development.

2. The brain is normally in learning mode during all waking hours. Therefore, it is constantly creating new connections (synapses) and losing ("overwriting") others. So what students learned a couple of weeks ago may have fallen victim to what they have learned since then—both in class and out. They need additional exposure and practice in order to reinforce the connections and to make them more accessible.

Body Grammar[1]

In discussing effective elaboration, Sousa (2001) makes the following statement: "The more senses that are used in [elaboration], the more reliable the associations. Thus, when visual, auditory, and kinesthetic activities assist the learner during this rehearsal, the probability of long-term storage rises dramatically" (p. 117). Body Grammar is the perfect embodiment of a multi-sensory exercise. It is a fun-filled activity that has students up and about, interacting, having a good time, and unwittingly resolving grammar issues in the process.

Materials Type a sentence, putting one word on each line in a very large font—the bigger, the better. Optionally capitalize the first word of the sentence and put a period after the last word, depending on your objective(s). Cut out each word. If you find sentences that work really well, laminate the words so that you can use the sentences in subsequent classes. Let's use the following sentence:

The beautiful princess quickly kissed the ugly frog.

Instructions Tell the students that they are going to make a movie.

- Ask for volunteers. You will need one actor for every word in your prepared sentence—eight actors for our sample sentence. You will also need a director.
- Randomly hand out the words to the actors; the director doesn't get one.
- Ask the students to arrange themselves so that the audience can read the plot of the movie (i.e., the sentence). The director oversees the process of creating the movie and has final say (in gentle consultation with the teacher) in settling any disagreements (often grammar discussions in disguise) that might arise. Once the students have figured things out, they should be standing in front of the class, holding up their words so that the audience can read the sentence correctly.

---

[1]Adapted from a presentation by Wanda VanDeGoor, ATEG Annual Conference, Chicago, IL, 2005.

■ Now tell the director that the movie consists of actors who are stars and actors who play supporting roles. In the princess–frog sentence, for example, you would state that this movie has three stars (three words that are the most important ones in this sentence). Have the director select them, in consultation with the actors and audience. (In my example, *princess, kissed,* and *frog* are the stars.) Students almost always get it right—sometimes after a bit of productive discussion. I say "productive" because, once again, whether they know it or not, when they debate who the stars are, they are often discussing the *grammar* of the sentence. If they have any trouble (a rarity), tell the director that the stars of this movie should form a newspaper headline.

■ Ask each of the stars to take two steps forward.

■ Now ask the director to oversee having the remainder—the supporting cast—indicate who supports which actor by having them place their hands on their star's shoulder. In our example sentence, students holding *The* and *beautiful* will rest their hands on the shoulder of the student who holds *princess, quickly* will touch *kissed,* and *the* and *ugly* will touch *frog.* Rarely, the person holding *The* will want to support *beautiful.* If that happens, you can ask if it is *The beautiful* or *The frog.*

Discussion   That's it—that's the basic exercise. The students have demonstrated—with very little, if any, assistance from the teacher—several concepts that can then be discussed in more detail as desired:

■ Subject, Verb, Direct Object (the "stars" of the movie)

■ Adjectives

■ Adverbs

■ Modification

The students, of course, already "know" these concepts subconsciously; if they didn't, they wouldn't be able to create or understand the sentence. So you can now explain these concepts with tangible examples available to you in front of the class.

Variations   This activity can be used to demonstrate countless features of English grammar. Using the same example sentence, here are a few suggestions:

■ Have more words ready to add, such as *blonde* and *green.* Recruit more actors and have them assume their correct positions. The concept of *adjectives modifying nouns* has just become more tangible for your class.

■ Have the word *very* prepared and bring in another supporting actor. Since there are several places where this one could go, it will generate some discussion. Be sure to point out, however, that no matter where it winds up, it does not support (modify) a noun actor. A basic concept related to *adverbs* has just been demonstrated: They never modify nouns.

- Have a tag question (*didn't, she,* and *?*) and a comma ready. Recruit other actors and have them take the words *didn't, she,* and *?* to the appropriate place. Ask the director if she is happy with the movie. The answer should be "No." Hand the director the comma and ask her to fix the plot. (I'll be discussing tag questions in detail in the next section.)

- Illustrate optional movement of various words and phrases and discuss what the new placement does to the "plot." For example, ask the director to move *quickly* to some other spot in the movie—let's say to the end. Let your director tell you what changes, if any, are needed and how the change affects the flow of the "plot."

- Extend the movie metaphor:

  1. Pronouns are stuntmen (or stunt doubles). Trying to substitute the wrong case of a pronoun (e.g., *him* when you need *he*) is analogous to trying to substitute a male stunt double for a female, an adult for a child, and so on.

  2. Punctuation divides up a movie:

      Period = The End
      Semi-colon = Intermission
      Comma = End of a Scene (Fade to Black)
      Colon = Coming Attraction(s)

- Have students prepare "scripts" (sentences) that their fellow students will make into "movies."

- Use sentences that illustrate all kinds of grammar points—let your imagination run wild!

Brain-Based Checklist Review   Let's briefly examine why this kind of activity is a good brain-based grammar lesson:

- ✓ The activity is interactive and multimodal—students are moving around, reading, discussing, and touching, so their brains are receiving input from a variety of channels.

- ✓ The students are learning by doing—hands on.

- ✓ The students figure out how things work with minimal, if any, teacher intervention. Their brains are involved in problem-solving activities rather than passively listening to the teacher explain subject-verb-direct object, for example.

- ✓ When the teacher provides labels for the concepts (subject, verb, etc.), the students can begin to see the patterns that are involved.

- ✓ The students can easily connect the new information (the concepts) with what they already know (how to form sentences).

- ✓ Since this is a group activity, no single individual is threatened by the task; it is, however, challenging.

Figure 6.2 Challenge and Brain Power

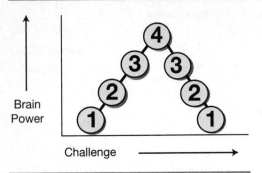

This last point bears amplification. As was noted in Chapter 3, the brain functions best when it is properly challenged. Too little challenge results in boredom; too much challenge can be threatening. There is an optimal point where the brain is maximally engaged. Beyond that point, the brain starts going into defensive mode, devoting more and more of its resources to protection. (See Figure 6.2.)

Tag Questions

Every student in your class uses **tag questions** regularly, primarily to seek verification and/or to "tag" the other person—to let that person know it is his or her turn to speak. I can end every sentence with a tag question, *can't I?* They are very easy to form, *aren't they?* This is how I introduce tag questions to my students, *isn't it?* I give an example of one, *don't I?* (I'll stop now.) And then I start doing orally what I have just done in writing: I end several sentences in a row with tag questions.

Although we can produce them effortlessly, careful analysis shows that tag questions are surprisingly complex structures. The good news, however, is that we don't have to delve into the complexities underlying their creation—we'll leave that for a linguistics class or a class whose primary purpose is to teach grammar. In the Grammar Wizard approach, there is no reason to go into detail about a structure that students have already mastered unless there is a further teaching point to be made. In this case, simply tell the students to let their Grammar Wizards take care of things.

Subject–Predicate Identification
Tag questions can be used to illustrate the concepts of *subject* and *predicate*. Here's how it works: Have students add a tag question to any basic sentence:

Our English teacher always rides a bicycle to school. →
Our English teacher always rides a bicycle to school, *doesn't she?*

Then ask the class what *she* refers to (i.e., what *she* takes the place of). If the students say *teacher* (which is exactly what traditional grammar instructs them to say—a pronoun takes the place of a noun), make the substitution and see how they react:

Our English *she* always rides a bicycle to school.

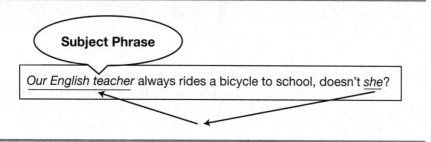

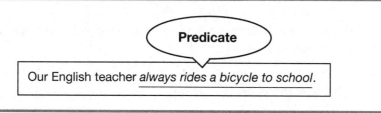

The class will, of course, reject this version and provide the correct one:

> *She* always rides a bicycle to school.[2]

Now tell your students to thank their Grammar Wizards for helping them identify the *subject* of the sentence—the phrase that is referred to by the last word in a tag question. Since the entire subject is more than one word, I refer to it as the *subject phrase*. Although the subject of a sentence can certainly be one word (e.g., *Students* study.), it is usually more than one. (See Figure 6.3.)

Note: The students' first answer (i.e., that *she* = *teacher*) is, in one sense of the word, correct—*teacher* is the so-called *true subject* of the sentence, which is an important concept that we will return to when working with subject-verb agreement.

Once students have identified the subject phrase, finding the predicate is easy. The *predicate* is everything that is left over after the subject phrase is removed from consideration. (See Figure 6.4.) Again note that the predicate is more than one word. It doesn't have to be (e.g., Students *study*.), but it usually is.

Figure 6.4 Predicate Identification

---

[2]This is a good example of what Schuster (2003) calls a "definition that doesn't define."

Students can now easily label the parts of this sentence:

Our English teacher || always rides a bicycle to school.
  Subject Phrase   *Predicate*

Discussion Now the students are ready for some practice. Provide them with sentences to which they add tag questions. Then have them use arrows and lines to show how the pronoun in the tag question takes the place of the subject phrase. They can now draw lines dividing the sentences into subject phrases and predicates. Remember to keep the sentences simple at this point. If you add in additional clauses, there are other complexities to deal with—complexities better saved for follow-up activities. As with anything in language, do a review exercise a week or two later, and then as required.

Variations Body Grammar is an excellent way to present the preceding information to your classes. In the example just given, recruit two actors for *doesn't she*; in addition, have a capitalized version of *she* (*She*) ready. Then, with a modest change of "costume," *she* can come out of the tag question and move over to become a stunt double for an entire group of actors (the subject phrase). You can also use felt boards, magnetic words, PowerPoint, and so on.

Yes–No Questions

Here is another device that can be very useful as a brain-based way of analyzing sentences. Again, your students already know how to form **yes–no questions**—they have been doing it for years. Therefore, you do not have to go into details about the surprisingly complex set of operations that is required; simply illustrate them.

The basic premise is to change a sentence into a question that can be answered by *yes* or *no*. A couple of examples follow:

1. Brad Pitt is coming to my birthday party. → Is Brad Pitt coming to my birthday party?
2. The man in the black suit ate squid for breakfast. → Did the man in the black suit eat squid for breakfast?

That's it. Once you have modeled this device for your students, their Grammar Wizards will handle the rest.

Discussion—Sentences versus Clauses The ability to identify a clause or sentence is a crucial skill for writers if they are to avoid fragments, comma splices, or run-ons. One of the primary reasons why these errors seem to be so intractable in student writing is because traditional grammar pedagogy does such an inadequate job of explaining what a sentence (or clause) is. There are two requirements, according to TGP, that makes a group of words a sentence: (1) It must have a subject and predicate and (2) it must be a complete thought. This definition simply does not work very well for students. Consider the following two examples:

1. Speaker A: Why did you eat lunch?
   Speaker B: *Because I was hungry.*

In SWAE, Speaker B's sentence is a fragment unless it is in quotes. It has a subject and a predicate, but TGP maintains that it is not a complete thought. It doesn't make sense to most students to say that "Because I was hungry" is not a complete thought in a context like this. Both participants clearly understand the part that is required by SWAE in order to make it a complete sentence (i.e., "*I ate lunch* because I was hungry"). Understood elements are allowed in many places in English; what's wrong with one here?

2. The truck kicked up a rock, it broke my windshield.

This is a classic example of a student-generated comma splice. As far as the student writer is concerned, the second sentence is necessary to truly complete the thought begun by the first. The student who wrote the sentence has probably come to the following very rational conclusion: A period is used to mark the end of a complete thought. Since "it broke my windshield" is part of the complete thought, a comma between clauses seems much more logical than a period.

We will deal with fragments, comma splices, and run-ons in great detail in Chapter 9. For now, suffice it to say that students must be able to identify clauses as an initial step in resolving sentence boundary issues, and the traditional definition of a sentence is confusing. As we have seen, sentences can be transformed into yes–no questions. If a group of words does not form a sentence, the transformation cannot be accomplished. Let's again look at the two examples:

1a. Speaker A: Why did you eat lunch?
    Speaker B: *Because I was hungry.*

Attempting to create a yes–no question from the above results in nonsense:

*Was because I hungry?

(It is possible to make any utterance into a yes–no question by using rising intonation. If your students try to form it in this manner, tell them that this form of question does not work as a valid test—they have to move things around to make a true yes–no question.)

However, a version of the above utterance that is acceptable in SWAE becomes a yes–no question very easily:

I ate lunch because I was hungry. →
Did I eat lunch because I was hungry?

The next example behaves similarly:

> 2a. The truck kicked up a rock, it broke my windshield.

A yes–no question would, once again, produce nonsense:

* Did the truck kick up a rock, it broke my windshield?

A repaired version of this sentence, however, lends itself nicely to yes–no question formation:

The truck kicked up a rock that broke my windshield. →
Did the truck kick up a rock that broke my windshield?

Tag questions are not as effective as yes–no questions at helping students spot fragments, comma splices, or run-ons because they can often sound perfectly fine:

Because I was hungry. → Because I was hungry, wasn't I?

The truck kicked up a rock, it broke my windshield. →
The truck kicked up a rock, it broke my windshield, didn't it?

In these examples, the tag questions do not clearly point out that the sentences are not properly formed. Therefore, present yes–no question formation to your students as a good Grammar Wizard Test to check any sentence that they have doubts about; let tag questions handle subject–predicate analyses.

Variations You can use yes–no questions to identify the subject phrase and the verb phrase. However, the operation is a bit more complex, so I prefer to use tag questions, as outlined earlier.

Manipulatives

As has been stated several times over the past chapters, in the typical TGP classroom, the teacher talks while the students listen—there is virtually no movement or interaction, virtually no problem solving. Manipulatives are an excellent way to present grammar points in a more brain-compatible manner.

Discussion A **manipulative** is anything that students can get their hands on and maneuver as they work with the lesson. Examples include index cards, colored blocks, magnetized words, card games, Legos®, and other items. Whenever manipulatives are introduced into the lesson, natural learning is enhanced. Let's revisit our brain-based learning checklist that we developed earlier (Figure 6.1) to analyze why this statement is valid:

1. *Multimodal:* In addition to the TGP norms of seeing and hearing, manipulatives add touching and, often, moving and interacting.
2. *Hands On:* By definition, whenever manipulatives are used in the classroom, students will learn by doing.
3. *Problem Solving:* Properly structured, manipulatives have students solving problems with minimal, if any, guidance from the teacher.
4. *Pattern Based:* Manipulatives are often an excellent way to physically demonstrate patterns.
5. *Interconnective:* Manipulatives are a highly effective method to scaffold instruction. Students are often required to use what they already know as they build toward the teaching point.
6. *Challenging:* Manipulatives are often a fun way to challenge students.
7. *Recursive:* Manipulatives are a great way to present or re-present teaching points.

Variations We have already seen one activity that involved manipulatives: Body Grammar. A few more ideas are presented below to help you start thinking about ways that you can bring manipulatives into your classroom.

Index Cards—Possessives

As was noted in Chapter 5, any time writers must attend to a detail or distinction that speakers can ignore, we can safely predict that the area will be problematic for student writers. Possessives fill the bill perfectly: We do not differentiate between a plural noun and a possessive one when speaking—they both sound the same. Context normally allows listeners to know which is which. In writing, however, we are obliged to distinguish possessives from plurals by that pesky little apostrophe.

This activity is a brain-compatible, fun way to introduce possessive noun formation. Make pairs of index cards—one card for each student in your class. On one card, write a noun; on another, write the possessive of that noun. Be sure to include pairs from each of the following in the overall set:

1. Singular nouns, including at least one that ends with an *–s* (e.g., *boss*)
2. The same singular nouns in the possessive
3. Regular plural nouns
4. The same regular plural nouns in the possessive
5. Irregular plural nouns
6. The same irregular plural nouns in the possessive

Table 6.1 shows a sample list of 11 words (22 cards) that I might use for this exercise.

- Let each of your students draw a card, sight unseen, from the stack.
- Tell the students to form themselves into two logical groups—it's up to them to decide how. Remind the students that this is a *grammar* lesson, so they can ignore *meaning* as they form the groups. After a brief discussion, they should divide themselves into a nonpossessive and a possessive group.
- Have each group of students tell you how they determined membership.
- Once they have correctly formed the two groups, have them pair up so that each nonpossessive noun is matched up with its possessive counterpart.
- Tell the pairs that they are "married" and are now to function as a single unit.
- Now here is the tricky part: Have the pairs once again divide themselves into two logical groups. The only possible choice is a group whose possessive ends in *–'s* and a group whose possessive ends in *–s'*. However, students don't always see this division immediately, so some interesting—and sometimes rather chaotic—discussion takes place. A bit of gentle guidance will help the chaos dissolve into order.
- Finally, have each group report its findings, thereby generating the guiding principles for possessive formation.

Is this activity a good example of brain-based grammar? Absolutely. It is a multimodal, hands-on activity that involves group (i.e., nonthreatening) problem solving to derive patterns that can then be linked to what students already know about English.

Note: Spelling rules often lend themselves to this same type of activity: when to double the final consonant, *–i* before *–e* except after *–c*, and so on.

Table 6.1 Example List of Words for 3 × 5 Cards—Possessive

Nonpossessive	Possessive
boss	boss's
James	James's
John	John's
student	student's
cat	cat's
people	people's
dogs	dogs'
person	person's
students	students'
men	men's
teachers	teachers'

Noun Phrase Building

This exercise is adapted from an activity that Amy Benjamin originated. It is a brilliant way to show your students how to expand noun phrases. Not only does the activity give them hands-on grammar practice but it also shows them how to add concrete details and grammatical sophistication to their writing.

Prepare the following material:

- The smallest size sticky notes (e.g., Post-it® notes)—at least six for each student.
- 5 × 8 cards—one for each student plus one for you. Write a concrete noun in the middle of each 5 × 8 card, leaving room for sticky notes before and after it.

In class, pass out a card and several sticky notes to each student. Tell the students that they are going to build more descriptive noun phrases. Here are some of the things you can play with, using *shoe* as an example. First, build up the left side of the noun phrase.

Determiners Every singular countable noun in English must be preceded by a **determiner**. This concept is very difficult for ELL students to learn, but native speaker Grammar Wizards have absolutely mastered it. There are five categories of determiners. I will give you the traditional grammar names here, but since native speakers have already mastered the concept (albeit subconsciously), I never require students to remember them; rather I simply give them examples:

1. Articles: *a, an,* or *the*
2. Demonstratives: *this, that, these, those,* etc.
3. Possessives: *my, his, your,* etc.
4. Quantifiers: *each, every, many, several,* etc.
5. Numbers (cardinal or ordinal): *one, first, two, second,* etc.[3]

Model the process of choosing a determiner, writing it on one of the sticky notes, and sticking it on the 5 × 8 card in front of the noun. Using the *shoe* example, you might now have *the shoe, my shoe, this shoe, each shoe,* and so on. Have your students do the same, selecting any determiner they desire. They have now formed a simple noun phrase.

Adjectives Further expand the noun phrase. Write an adjective on a sticky note and place it in the correct position on the card. Have students

---

[3] For an interesting contrast of determiners vs. adjectives, go to http://en.wikipedia.org/wiki/Determiner.

do the same thing. Then they can add several adjectives—as many as they want, actually, but I limit them to two to conserve sticky notes. You might now have something like *the beautiful black shoe*. (A fun alternative is to have each student write an adjective on a sticky note without having seen anybody else's noun. Tell them to let their imaginations run wild. Then have the students exchange the sticky notes, which will produce some really fun results, much like the familiar Mad Lib game.)

Adverbs Further expand the noun phrase by putting an adverb on a sticky note and pasting it in front of adjectives: *the very beautiful pure black shoe*.

Now build up the right side of the noun phrase.

Prepositional Phrases Further expand the noun phrase by writing a prepositional phrase on a sticky note and placing it after the noun: *the very beautiful pure black shoe on the staircase* or *the very beautiful pure black shoe in the middle of the room* (two prepositional phrases).

Relative Clauses You can expand the noun phrase further by writing a short relative clause (i.e., a clause that is introduced by *who, which,* or *that*) and putting it in its proper place. Again, the students' Grammar Wizards are in full control of this structure, so all you have to do is model one, such as *the very beautiful pure black shoe that Lisa found in the middle of the room*.

This delightfully brain-based activity allows you to introduce or review several grammatical structures (more than I demonstrated here) while simultaneously showing your students how to add concrete details to their writing. And it accomplishes all of these objectives by tapping into what the students already know about English—it's a perfect Grammar Wizard activity!

Reinforce noun phrase building during the writing process. Tell students to look through their rough drafts for impoverished noun phrases. Ask them to create a better picture for the reader by building up the left and/or right side of the noun phrase.

Reading Rods Sentence-Construction Kit®

This is another activity that was presented by Amy Benjamin as part of "The Inner Game of Grammar Workshop". Reading Rods® are color-coded, interlocking blocks that students can manipulate to form sentences. (See Figure 6.5.) They are marketed by ETA Cuisenaire[4] as a pre-K–12 tool for teaching sight words and grammar. They are truly wonderful manipulatives

---

[4] See www.etacuisenaire.com/readingrods/simple.jsp for details.

Figure 6.5 Reading Rods®

81

Chapter Six
Grammar Wizard
Activities

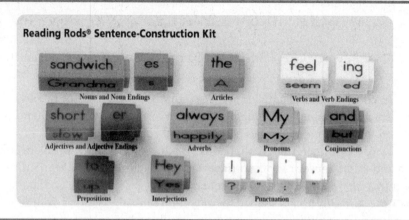

Source: © ETA/Cuisenaire. The Reading Rods® teaching method is covered by U.S. Patent Nos. 6,685,477 and 7,018,210. Other patents pending.

that can be used to illustrate various grammatical conventions to budding elementary and middle school writers.

Amy introduces the rods to her students by simply placing random handfuls at every student's desk before class. However, she doesn't give anybody any yellow ones (verbs). Students sit at their desks and, without any instruction, immediately begin playing with the rods, trying to make sentences. She gives the students a few minutes to struggle before asking them to read their sentences to the class. The students complain that they can't make sentences because they are missing something—they cannot make anything *do* anything. This prompts Amy to introduce the concept of *verb* and distribute yellow blocks to everybody.

I won't go into detail here about how to use these rods to present and play with grammar—the picture speaks for itself. Suffice it to say that Reading Rods® present a terrific, multimodal, brain-friendly, fun-filled way to introduce and play with quite a variety of grammatical concepts and writing conventions.

Velcro Punctuation[5]

The setup for this activity takes a few minutes, but it is worth the time invested:

- Laminate sentences that illustrate various punctuation requirements, leaving spaces for the actual punctuation.

---

[5] Adapted from www.findarticles.com/p/articles/mi_m0STR/is_5_112/ai_96810480.

■ Create a collection of punctuation marks to laminate separately: a period, a semi-colon, a colon, and several commas.

■ Place Velcro circles (readily available at home supply stores) where the punctuation belongs.

■ Stick the other pieces of the Velcro pairing to the back of the punctuation marks.

In class, pin a laminated sentence so that everyone can see it. Have a student (or students) place the punctuation on the pinned up sentence in the proper places. Change out sentences and continue the process.

Here is a fun alternative that adds an additional layer of problem solving and multi-sensory input to the exercise: Take the pieces of punctuation that are required for a given sentence and place them in a container of some sort. Pin up a sentence for everyone to read. Ask for a volunteer to play the game. Blindfold that person and have her draw a piece of punctuation out of the container. Tell the individual what she has selected and guide her to the pinned-up sentence. The student must then feel the length of the sentence, searching for the Velcro that marks the spot where her punctuation mark belongs. She then sticks it on. Allow the class to provide vocal support if desired. The same student can continue drawing and adding punctuation marks until the sentence is completely punctuated or you can ask for one volunteer per punctuation mark.

This exercise transforms punctuation practice into an interactive, entertaining, dynamic activity that, potentially, allows you to check off all seven of the items in our Brain-Based Checklist: It is a multimodal, hands-on, problem-solving, pattern-based, interconnective, challenging activity that, if used as an alternative way to practice, can be recursive.

Games Based on Existing Games

Students love competition! Games are therefore an excellent, brain-based way to reinforce Grammar Wizard skills. Some suggestions follow; however, let your imagination run free!

Grammar Charades

This venerable party classic lends itself nicely to brain-based reinforcement of many possible sentence structure areas. Divide students into teams. Create sentences that contain structures that you have covered in class. Put blanks on the board for each phrase. Let's work through the following African proverb (de Zwann):

A calm sea does not make a skilled sailor.

Depending on what you have covered in class, you might draw the following on the board:

_____ _____ _____
   Subject Phrase   Verb   Direct Object

Or you could break it down further:

A _____ _____ _____ a _____ _____
   Adj.   Noun   Verb   Participle   Noun

Put target words on 3 × 5 cards plus the grammatical slot that it occupies in the sentence.

calm	sea	does
Subj. Phrase	Subj. Phrase	Verb

and so on . . .

Teams take turns. A player draws a word, reads the name of the slot to which it belongs, and acts it out. After the word is guessed, the student writes it in the proper slot. Obviously, words in a given slot may need to be rearranged. If, for example, *sea* was drawn before *calm*, some reordering would be required. The first team to guess the entire sentence wins that round.

Variation Make sure that some of the sentences have at least one grammar problem. The first team to spot and correct the error gets an extra point.

Mad Libs

This time-honored game is a great way to play with parts of speech. The Web has some sites already set up for you:

www.funbrain.com/brain/ReadingBrain/ReadingBrain.html

www.eduplace.com/tales/

http://madlibs.org/

You could also have students write their own stories for their classmates to complete.

Grammar Jeopardy®

The following site has a nice PowerPoint template that you can use to build a Jeopardy® board game and fill in your own categories and questions:

www.jmu.edu/madison/teacher/jeopardy/jeopardy.htm

Remember that the students must phrase their responses in the form of questions that the prompt could answer. Table 6.2 shows some sample categories.

Table 6.2 Grammar Jeopardy Examples

Category Name	Description	Sample Item	Possible Answer
Structures	Parts of speech, subject phrase, verb phrase, predicate, direct object, prepositional phrase, etc.	What the underlined part of the following sentence is called: A calm sea does not make a skilled sailor.	What is the subject phrase?
Errors	Any grammar problem that has been covered in class.	The problem with the following sentence: Jim and me went home.	What is "me" should be "I"?
Bridges	(See Chapter 9 for an explanation.)	Although	What is a swinging bridge? OR What is a subordinating conjunction?
Punctuation	Sentences needing punctuation or an explanation for existing punctuation.	The correction needed in the following sentence: The path to a friends house is never long.	What is "friends" needs an apostrophe?
Spelling	Spelling changes necessitated by adding suffixes (double consonants, $y \rightarrow i$, drop the silent –e, etc.)	Of "running" and "runing," the one that is correct.	What is r-u-n-n-i-n-g?
Apostrophes	Possessive vs. plural, contractions	When to add just an apostrophe to show possession	What is when the noun is plural and ends with –s?
Grammar Toolbox	Gerunds, participles, appositives, etc. (See Chapter 7 for details.)	What the underlined part of the following sentence is called: My friend, a concert pianist, is from Poland.	What is an appositive?
Commas	Comma requirements (sentence correction or requirement explanation)	The comma(s) missing in the following sentence: He who dies with the most toys is nonetheless dead.	What is before and after "nonetheless"?

Hollywood Squares or
Who Wants to Be a Millionaire?

These classic TV game shows lend themselves very nicely to lively sessions of team competitions that provide elaboration for anything you are teaching, including grammar. The following site has templates available for each game, along with instructions:

http://teach.fcps.net/trt10/PowerPoint.htm

Other games can be modified slightly and turned into pleasurable ways to reinforce or review Grammar Wizard concepts. Students will enjoy the time spent doing these games and benefit from the additional brain-friendly exposure.

Discussion Questions

1. Review your answers to the true–false questions at the beginning of this chapter. Have you changed any of your answers?

2. Discuss why Body Grammar is such an excellent example of brain-based learning.

3. Discuss the relationship between *challenge* and *threat* insofar as natural learning is concerned.

4. Why are Tag Questions so effective at introducing the distinction between subject phrase and verb phrase?

5. Why does this text use the terms *subject phrase* and *verb phrase* instead of *subject* and *predicate*?

6. A student comes to you and wants to know whether a sentence that he has written is a fragment. How would you help him test it to find out for himself?

7. How does the TGP definition of *sentence* encourage students to produce comma splices?

8. Defend the following statement: "Whenever manipulatives are introduced into the lesson, natural learning is enhanced."

9. Using a manipulative, draw up a brain-based lesson plan that introduces when to double the final consonant in a word (e.g., *ru<u>n</u>* → *ru<u>nn</u>ing*).

10. When building up noun phrases, what typically goes to the left of the noun?

## chapter 7

Grammar Wizard Toolbox

True or False?

1. If students can understand a structure easily when they read, they can use it easily when they write.

2. Students should learn the names of grammatical structures that professional authors use.

3. Identifying similarities and differences is an effective technique to use when teaching.

4. Students can usually spot dangling participles by rearranging the sentence.

5. Whether to move a structure from one place to another in a sentence is a decision that can only be made in context.

6. Research shows that analogies, whether teacher made or student made, confuse students, so they should not be used.

7. Students already know most of the structures that professional authors use to create a sophisticated style.

Receptive versus Productive

Professional writers, both creative and expository, employ certain gram-matical constructions—tools, as it were—to make their writing tighter, clearer, more concrete, and less cluttered. These constructions, when prop-erly employed, are primary contributors to a style that creates a positive impression on the reader.

Here is the good news: Your student writers, native or advanced non-native, already *know* these structures! When they see them while reading, or if someone uses them while speaking, your students understand the structures effortlessly.

Here is the bad news: Many of these same students tend not to *employ* these structures when they write. In order to understand why this seem-ingly odd state of affairs exists, we have to examine a dichotomy that exists in all facets of language usage. Language skills can be divided into two cat-egories: receptive and productive.

1. **Receptive skills** are needed when we read or listen. We are *receiving* language that is already formed—be it well formed or ill formed. Our primary task in these situations is to *decode* (i.e., to extract meaning from the existing structure and vocabulary).

2. **Productive skills** are needed when we speak or write. We are *producing* language that we must form ourselves. Our primary task is to *encode* (i.e., to wrap our thoughts in language so that they can make the trip from our heads to the heads of our listeners or readers, remaining relatively intact in the process).

Although there is some overlap in the involved skills, the productive side of the coin is clearly the more difficult. It entails choosing the right words and then combining them in the correct mixture of structures so as to get the point across in a manner that is suitable for and acceptable to one's audience. On the receptive side of things, these formidable tasks have already been completed.

Most student writers are in *receptive* control of the structures that successful writers use; many of them are not, however, in *productive* control. They may not know exactly when or how to use these structures, or they may simply not think of using the structures when they write. Whatever the cause, the result is that they do not incorporate them into their writing.

What causes this imbalance between recep-tive and productive control? A major contributor is

Receptive versus Productive

Whenever students talk to me about their foreign language abilities, they invariably inform me that they can read and listen much better than they can speak or write. They really do not have to tell me that. *Receptive* skills are, by their very nature, much less demanding than *productive* ones. It is always safe to assume that a student of a foreign language finds it easier to receive than to produce the language.

the decline in the amount of reading of professionally prepared material. Whereas students several generations ago used to read well-written literature for entertainment, today's students often do not. Instead, they are multiliterate: They surf the net, text their friends, peruse MySpace or FaceBook, play video games, and watch TV. Multiliteracy enables today's students to take advantage of the available technology tools. However, without some assistance from teachers, formal writing ability tends to suffer.

Constant exposure to well-written material has a trickle-down effect on composition skills. Characteristics creep into procedural memory across time, become part of one's Grammar (and other) Wizards, and mysteriously begin to appear in their writing. Since today's students read *less* traditional print texts, we have to do *more* to help them expand their options.

This chapter shows how to present certain structures—those structures that successful authors use to such great effect—to your students. The approach takes advantage of the fact that student writers already *know* these structures receptively. The goals are to make them consciously aware of these constructions and to encourage them to experiment with them when they write. The structures that are covered in this chapter are as follows:

- Participle phrases
- Gerund phrases
- Appositive phrases
- Infinitive phrases
- Parallelism
- Nominative absolutes
- Adjectives out of order

The Joshua Tree Syndrome

Any subject area has terminology that one needs to master in order to be conversant; grammar is no exception. I do not advocate employing traditional grammar *approaches* in the classroom, but I do, for the most part, favor using traditional grammar *terminology*. It is very important for students to be able to recognize and name the structures covered in this chapter. In an excellent book on page layout and design, Robin Williams (no, not *the* Robin Williams) provides a perfect analogy for why I think this skill is important:

> Many years ago I received a tree identification book for Christmas. I was at my parents' home, and after all the gifts had been opened, I decided to go out and identify the trees in the neighborhood. Before I went out, I read through part of the book. The first tree in the book

was the Joshua tree because it only took two clues to identify it. Now the Joshua tree is a really weird-looking tree and I looked at that picture and said to myself, "Oh, we don't have that kind of tree in Northern California. That is a weird-looking tree. I would know if I saw that tree, and I've never seen one before."

So I took my book and went outside. My parents lived in a cul-de-sac of six homes. Four of those homes had Joshua trees in the front yard. I had lived in that house for thirteen years, and I had never seen a Joshua tree. I took a walk around the block, and there must have been a sale at the nursery when everyone was landscaping their new homes—at least 80 percent of the homes had Joshua trees in the front yards. *And I had never seen one before!* Once I was conscious of the tree—once I could name it—I saw it everywhere. Which is exactly my point: Once you can name something, you're conscious of it. You have power over it. You own it. You're in control. (2003, pp. 11–12)

The seven grammatical structures that are covered in this chapter pop up all over the place in the professionally written materials to which our students are regularly exposed, both in English classes and in other content areas. Like Joshua trees for Robin Williams, however, students do not *see* them; they are not consciously aware of their existence. If they can name them when they see them, they are in at least partial control over them, a phenomenon that I refer to as the *Joshua Tree Syndrome*. Learning to identify participles, gerunds, and the like, helps make students aware of their presence in the texts they are reading. This awareness is a source of *meaningful elaboration*, thereby enhancing the transfer to procedural memory and, eventually, to writing.

High-Yield Strategies

Marzano, Pickering, and Pollock's *Classroom Instruction That Works* (2005) identifies nine instructional strategies, derived from a thorough review of empirical research, that will increase instructional effectiveness. Four of them lend themselves very nicely to our efforts:

1. *Identifying Similarities and Differences:* Compare and contrast various structures as you introduce them in class. Venn diagrams and analogies are excellent devices for comparing or contrasting; research supports that they are powerful teaching tools. I incorporate them as elaboration techniques for several of the tools in this chapter.

2. *Nonlinguistic Representation:* Show students graphic representations that embody the teaching points. Or, better yet, have students create their own.

3. *Generating and Testing Hypotheses:* Give students the opportunity to figure out how things work. The inquiry-based method that lies at the heart of the Grammar Wizard Approach assists students in forming hypotheses and testing them.

4. *Reinforcing Effort and Providing Recognition:* Spiral important teaching points from a variety of angles through an assortment of mini-lessons.

Each of the sections in this chapter contains a heading called "Recursiveness and Elaboration." Material within these headings provides additional information and activities that can be incorporated as you revisit and reinforce concepts across the school year.

I encourage you to expand on these instructional strategies in your classroom. I would also encourage you to incorporate closure activities as discussed in Chapter 5.

Participle Phrases

The following explanation is provided as background information for English teachers. Whether or not you choose to present it to your composition students is, of course, your decision. I normally choose not to include it.

Verbs have four forms in English, as demonstrated in Table 7.1. I use *eat* as an example of an irregular verb and *walk* as an example of a regular verb.

There are two additional facts to consider:

1. For regular verbs (such as *walk*), the past participle form (*walked*) is the same as the simple past form (*walked*). For most irregular verbs (such as *eat*), the past participle form (*eaten*) is different from the simple past form (*ate*). To avoid ambiguity, the symbol for simple past is *–ed*, and the symbol for the past participle is *–en*.

2. When used as the main verb in a clause, the present and past participle forms always have at least one helping verb:

   a. *Present Participle:* The helping verb is some form of *to be*: I *am* eating/walking; We *were* eating/walking; She *is* eating/walking.

Table 7.1 English Verb Forms

#	Form	Verb Ending	Example
1	Base or Infinitive	(No ending)	I want to *eat*, to *walk*.
2	Simple Past	*–ed*	Yesterday I *ate*, *walked*.
3	Present Participle	*–ing*	I am *eating*, *walking*.
4	Past Participle	*–en*	I have *eaten*, *walked*.

b. *Past Participle*: The helping verb is usually some form of *to have*:[1] I *have* eaten/walked; We *had* eaten/walked; She *has* eaten/walked.

When a present (*–ing*) or a past (*–en*) participle form is used *without* a helping verb, it becomes a different animal—either a gerund or a participle.

Now let's explore what *students* need to know in order to use participles in their writing. The following activities should be spread over several days. Note that the material is scaffolded, allowing for gradual release of control.

How Is It Used?   Participles have two primary uses:

■ In real life, things happen simultaneously. Participles are a way to show *in a single sentence* that more than one action is happening at the same time. Examples:

> 1a. Jorge walked across the stage. He was smiling from ear to ear. →
>
> 1b. *Smiling from ear to ear*, Jorge walked across the stage. (Both *smiling* and *walking* occurred simultaneously.)

One could, of course, add additional simultaneous actions:

> 1c. *Smiling from ear to ear*, *flashing the victory sign*, and *waving at the people around him*, Jorge walked across the stage.

■ Participles can also be used as simple adjectives in a noun phrase:

> 2. A *snoring* man in the next room kept me awake all night.

Exercise   The following activities facilitate gradual release of control as you introduce participles.

1. Provide students with several examples of sentences containing participles. Then devise a series of questions that will help students discover the "How Is It Used?" information.

2. Have students identify participles in a reading passage—preferably a passage from a common reading.

3. Give students a sentence-combining exercise like 1a., above, ensuring that all of the resulting participles will be *–ing* forms. Be prepared for well-formed solutions that do not use participles.

---

[1]I am ignoring passive voice constructions for the time being. Passive versus active will be covered in Chapter 12.

Not Quite Right
Students may well combine the sentences correctly but not use a participle. Congratulate them on a good sentence, but tell them that they didn't use a *participle*. Since the purpose of this exercise is to get them familiar with participles, I tell them that the solution, although correct, doesn't scratch where I itch.

How Is It Formed?   Participles have two forms:

1. An *–ing* form of a verb—a form that traditional grammar refers to as a *present participle*.
2. An *–en* (or *–ed*) form of the verb—a form that traditional grammar refers to as a *past participle*.

When do we use each one? There is absolutely no need to go into an in-depth explanation. Native speakers rarely, if ever, get confused about which one to use—their Grammar Wizards have this feature under control. For example, your students would never dream of writing *a snored man* instead of *a snoring man*. They would also never fail to distinguish between *an eaten fish* and *an eating fish*.[2]

Exercise   Give students another sentence-combining exercise, but this time mix in present and past participle possibilities. Be prepared once again for well-formed solutions that do not use participles.

More Details   A participle phrase contains the participle plus whatever else you want to add to it to expand it. It can be a one-word phrase:

> 3. *Walking*, we saw lots of scenery; *driving*, we saw nothing but road.

It can also be very involved. Here are a couple of more complex ones:

> 4. <u>Eatinga hamburger that looked like it contained half a cow</u>, the man had grease from one side of his face to the other.
> 5. <u>Excitedat the prospect of making lots of money</u>, people invested large sums in the stock.

Participles are often added to paint a more vivid or complete picture. In the following sentences, note how your image of the baby expands, how it becomes more concrete and more vivid:

> 6a. The baby let us know that she was hungry.
> 6b. Kicking and screaming, the baby let us know that she was hungry.
> 6c. Kicking her legs frantically and screaming at the top of her lungs, the baby let us know that she was hungry.

Exercise   Give students sentences that need more descriptive detail, instructing them to provide the detail with participle phrases. Example:

---

[2]This distinction is problematic for non-natives, often even at the advanced level.

7. The runner crossed the finish line. → <u>Waving her arms and smiling broadly,</u> the runner crossed the finish line.

Problem Area The most common problem with this structure is the so-called *dangling participle*. Here is an example of one:

8a. Flitting from flower to flower, the football player watched the beautiful butterfly.

Obviously, the football player isn't *flitting from flower to flower*. But that's the way the sentence is written. Here's why: The participle phrase contains a verb form, but it does not contain the *doer* of the action; the reader is obliged to *infer* who did it. Therefore, the *doer* is usually going to be the closest noun that could, conceivably, perform the action. Any human is capable of *flitting*, so sentence 8a allows for the resulting comical misinterpretation. Something has to move:

8b. The football player watched the beautiful butterfly flitting from flower to flower.

> **Grammar Wizard Test for Spotting Dangling Participles:** If the participle phrase is placed immediately *after* the noun instead of *before* it, your Grammar Wizard will see the problem immediately.

8c. *The football player, flitting from flower to flower, watched the beautiful butterfly.

There are two varieties of dangling participles:

- *Minor Surgery:* The subject of the participle is somewhere in the sentence. Sentence 8a is a good example. The fix is easy: Move the participle phrase close to its subject.
- *Major Surgery:* The subject of the participle, the doer of the action, is not in the sentence:

9a. *Walking along the beach, seashells were easy to find.

The sentence fails the Grammar Wizard Test for dangling participles:

9b. *Seashells, walking along the beach, were easy to find.

The doer of the action (*walking*) must be somehow inserted into the sentence:

> 9c. Walking along the beach, we found a lot of seashells.
>   (Retaining participle) OR
>
> 9d. Seashells were easy to find as we walked along the beach.
>   (Dropping participle)

Exercise Give students sentences to work with, most of which (but not all) contain dangling participles. Be sure to include both Minor Surgery and Major Surgery sentences.

Recursiveness and Elaboration

As previously discussed, a vitally important component of learning is meaningful repetition. As Marilee Sprenger states, "Although rote memorization may be useful for multiplication and lists of states and capitals, real understanding comes from using elaborative rehearsal that helps the brain make connections" (cited in Allen, 2008). Once a structure has been initially introduced, analyzed, and discussed, you need to incorporate reinforcement and elaboration activities to aid in retention. Each of the following activities provides a way for you to revisit participles, adding something to the concept in the process.

Placement Participle phrases can often be placed in one of three locations in a sentence: (1) before the noun it modifies, (2) after the noun it modifies, or (3) at the end of the sentence. Example:

- *Base Sentence:* The thief waited for darkness.
- *Participle Phrase:* hiding behind a wall

Possible placements are:

1. *Hiding behind a wall*, the thief waited for darkness.
2. The thief, *hiding behind a wall*, waited for darkness.
3. The thief waited for darkness, *hiding behind a wall*.

You can then discuss the rhetorical effect of the movement—that is, how the different placements affect the way the text reads or feels. Also, since language decisions in real life are always made in context, you could discuss different contexts that might logically favor one placement over another. We will return to the placement issue in Chapter 12.

Analogy Give students the following analogical frame and ask them to come up with their own solutions. You can expect a wide variety of answers, leading to some interesting, reinforcing discussion. One possible answer is "penciled in" here.

> A participle phrase is to the noun phrase that it modifies as <u>lipstick</u> is to <u>lips</u>. (Both provide extra detail, making their target easier to "see.")

Graphic Image Ask students, individually or in groups, to come up with a visual representation of their understanding of participles as they relate to the nouns the modify.

Literature Occasionally spend a few minutes doing the following as you are going through a reading selection:

- Point out participle phrases that the author has used.
- Ask students to find participles.
- Ask what would happen if a participle phrase were moved to different positions, knowing in advance that the movement would occasionally create a dangling participle.
- Divide the class into small groups and time them while they scour a given text for participle phrases. The group that finds the most is, of course, the "winner."

Student Writing During revision, ask students to find at least one noun in their compositions that could use more descriptive detail and then ask them to provide that detail by adding one or more participle phrases.

Gerund Phrases

How Is It Used? *Gerunds* are verbs ending in *–ing* that function as *nouns*. They are an excellent tool to use to remove excess words and to add variety to your writing. Example:

> 10a. If you build a house, it will be very expensive. (10 words)
> 10b. *Building a house* will be very expensive. (7 words)

How Is It Formed? This one is simple: A gerund is formed by adding *–ing* to a verb.

Exercise Give students an exercise that consists of sentences such as the above, where two clauses or sentences can be combined into one sentence with a gerund. As we established before, be prepared for legitimate answers that do not contain gerunds, remembering that such answers are not wrong—they are just off target. (See the Grammar Wizard Test on the next page for a way to identify gerunds.)

Problem Area Since most participles and all gerunds end in *–ing*, students confuse them easily. Grammar Wizards, however, definitely know the difference. Students just have to learn how to make the right connections.

Since gerunds function as nouns, one might reasonably expect them to *behave* as nouns—and indeed, they do.

> **Grammar Wizard Test—The *It* Test:** A gerund phrase can be replaced by *it* or *something*.

> 11a. Walking to work every day, Maria lost 10 pounds.
>
> 11b. Walking to work every day caused Maria to lose 10 pounds.

Applying the Grammar Wizard *It* Test will tell you immediately which of the above sentences contains a gerund phrase and which contains a participle phrase:

> 11c. Can you replace the *–ing* phrase with *it* (or *something*)?
>
> Walking to work every day, Maria lost 10 pounds. →
> *It, Maria lost 10 pounds. OR *Something, Maria lost 10 pounds.

Clearly, the answer is no—this phrase fails the *It* Test. Therefore, it is a participle phrase.

> 11d. Can you replace the *–ing* phrase with *it* (or *something*)?
>
> Walking to work every day caused Maria to lose 10 pounds. →
> It caused Maria to lose ten pounds. (It = "Walking to work every day.") OR
> Something caused Maria to lose 10 pounds.

The answer here is yes—this phrase passes the *It* Test. Therefore, it is a gerund.

Exercise Provide students with a passage that contains both gerunds and *–ing* participles. Ask them to find each one and decide, using the It Test, whether the *–ing* phrase is a participle or a gerund.

Recursiveness and Elaboration Each of these activities provides a way to reexamine gerunds.

Roles A gerund phrase can fit in a sentence wherever a noun phrase fits. Revisit gerunds and work with them in a variety of roles or positions. Here are some possibilities:

- *Direct Object:* You should try *studying with a group from class.*
- *Object of a Preposition:* He improved his grades by *studying with a group from class.*

■ *Appositive:* The new technique, *studying with a group from class*, improved his grades. (Appositives are the next tool that we will examine.)

Literature Be on the lookout for gerunds in whatever the class is reading:

■ Point them out yourself at first.

■ Ask students to find or identify them.

■ Ask students to prove to you that an *–ing* phrase is either a participle or gerund phrase by applying the It Test.

Graphic Representations Since gerunds and participles are easily confused at first, ask students to fill in a Venn diagram. Figure 7.1 shows a completed one.

If you present the Verb Endings covered earlier in this chapter to your students, you can ask them to come up with their own graphic representations of this information. Figure 7.2 (on the following page) shows one possibility.

Analogy Give students the following analogical frame and ask them to come up with their own solutions. One possible answer is "penciled in" here.

A gerund is to a noun phrase as a <u>Ford</u> is to a <u>car</u>.
(Gerunds are one type of noun phrase like Ford is one type of car.)

Figure 7.1 Venn Diagram—Participles and Gerunds

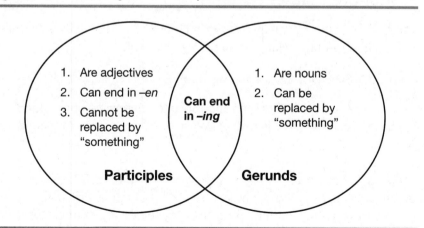

Figure 7.2 Verb Endings

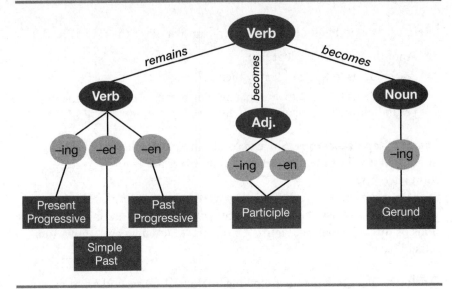

Student Writing Gerunds aren't quite as easy to add to a composition as participles. One can always find a place to add more descriptive detail via a participle phrase; finding a place for a gerund (like the one that begins this clause!) isn't as easy. However, you can encourage your students to look for places where the language could be made tighter by using a gerund phrase (oops—there's another one!).

Appositive Phrases

How Is It Used?
An *appositive* is a noun phrase that *restates* another noun phrase, adding details in the process. Example:

> 12a. My friend, Tom, is a policeman.

In the above sentence, *Tom* is an appositive to *my friend*—both noun phrases refer to the same person. A colleague of mine refers to them as "echoes."

How Is It Formed?
An appositive is nothing more than a noun phrase. It cannot be a clause; otherwise we would call it, well . . . , a clause. It can be a very simple noun phrase, as in the preceding example, or it can be a very elaborate one, with all sorts of attached clauses and phrases. Grammar Wizards can build them without a problem.

Problem Area Many types of noun phrases and clauses exist. Students often have difficulty identifying whether a phrase is an appositive.

> **Grammar Wizard Test—The *Either–Or* Test:** If a noun phrase is an appositive, you can remove either of the two noun phrases and still have a good sentence.

Look at the following example. The question we are trying to answer is whether *who is a policeman* is an appositive to *my friend*:

12b. <u>My friend</u>, <u>who is a policeman</u>, has been working for 20 years.
      Phrase 1   Phrase 2

We can remove Phrase 2 and still have a good sentence:

12c. My friend has been working for 20 years.

However, the sentence falls apart when we remove Phrase 1:

12d. *Who is a policeman has been working for 20 years.

Therefore, Phrase 2 is not an appositive.

With an appositive structure, however, either phrase can be safely removed:

12e. <u>My friend</u>, <u>a policeman</u>, has been working for 20 years.
     Phrase 1   Phrase 2

My friend has been working for 20 years.

A policeman has been working for 20 years.

When one of the phrases is removed, some information is lost, of course, but both sentences remain intact.

Exercise Appositives are a great way of getting rid of sentences with weak verbs. For instance, the first sentence, below, has a weak main verb— a form of *to be*. Such sentences can often be turned into appositives, thus removing the weak verb sentence:

12f. <u>My friend</u> is <u>a policeman</u>. He has been working for 20 years.

My friend, a policeman, has been working for 20 years.

Give students pairs of sentences like the above that can be combined using appositives. Be sure to point out how they are getting rid of sentences with weak verbs, tightening up the language in the process. And once again, be prepared for solutions that produce good sentences, but that do not contain appositives. Ask them to apply the *Either–Or* Test to their answers to verify that they have successfully made the change.

Recursiveness and Elaboration These activities provide a way to reexamine appositives.

Movie Reviews The easiest place to find appositives is in a movie review. The current trend seems to be putting the appositive in parentheses—always an option, of course. Look at the following excerpt from the movie titled *Enchanted*:

> Giselle (delectable Amy Adams) is a princess ejected from her magic kingdom by a curse from her evil potential mother-in-law (Susan Sarandon) in the inspired Disney fairy-tale mash-up *Enchanted*. And when the heroine pops up in New York City, dazed by her transformation from animated cartoon girl to live-action beauty, she's put up for the night by a stranger, a harried divorce lawyer (Patrick Dempsey). But there's a hygiene problem. He's the distracted single parent to a little girl (Rachel Covey), his girlfriend (Idina Menzel) is on his case for more commitment . . . . (Schwarzbaum, 2007)

This short piece has five appositives, all of which are especially easy to find because of the parentheses—a great beginning point for student recognition. Have students find the appositives and see how they pass the Grammar Wizard *Either–Or* Test. As a follow-up activity, ask students to write a review of a movie they like, using appositives to introduce the characters.

Movement Appositives are usually placed after the noun phrase they refer to; however, they can be moved to the front. Example:

> 13a. Cormac McCarthy, *a graduate of the University of Tennessee*, won the Pulitzer Prize for fiction in 2007.
>
> 13b. *A graduate of the University of Tennessee*, Cormac McCarthy won the Pulitzer Prize for fiction in 2007.

Reintroduce appositives by focusing on this optional movement, discussing

- which placement sounds better to your students,
- what changes in focus or emphasis the movement creates, and
- different contexts that might favor one position over the other.

We will revisit the appositive movement in Chapter 11.

Punctuation This rather difficult issue is an excellent way to reintroduce appositives: When should you set them off with commas and when shouldn't you? (The concept, *essential* versus *non-essential*, is discussed in detail in Chapter 8, so I won't go into it here.)

Analogy Give students the following analogical frame and ask them to come up with solutions. One possible answer is "penciled in" here.

> An appositive is to a noun phrase as a <u>definition</u> is to a <u>word</u>.
> (Why? Both provide additional information.)

Literature Again, point out or have students locate examples as they occur in whatever the class is reading.

Composition Encourage students to incorporate at least one appositive during the revision process of an essay they have written. Have them look carefully at all weak verb sentences to see if sentences could be combined using appositives instead.

Infinitive Phrases

How Is It Used? An *infinitive phrase* is a construction that students have absolutely no problem forming. The infinitive is *to + verb*. Infinitive phrases pop up all over the place. They are most easily defined by example:

14. They decided *to bring the issue up for a vote at the next meeting.*
15. *To be a champion chess player* was a dream of hers for many years.
16. He saved his money (in order) *to buy a boat and sail around the world.*

How Is It Formed? Again, formation is so simple that examples explain it all—Grammar Wizards are normally in complete control of the structure.

> **Grammar Wizard Test:** There is no need for a Grammar Wizard Test for this structure—it is easy for students to recognize and use—if they think of it.

Exercise Give students sentences to combine, using infinitive phrases to accomplish the union. Example:

> 17a. He had one ambition. He wanted to marry a rich woman.
> 17b. *To marry a rich woman* was his one ambition. OR
> 17c. His one ambition was *to marry a rich woman*.

Recursiveness and Elaboration This structure is so simple for students to create that there is little need for much recursiveness or elaboration beyond sentence-combining practice. Simply point out infinitive phrases in class readings and encourage students to use them in their writing.

Parallelism

How Is It Used? Parallelism is a very widely used tool in writing. Virtually every professional author, irrespective of genre, uses it over and over to create smooth, flowing prose and to lighten the processing burden on readers.

How Is It Formed? Parallelism is achieved by making each element of a series identical in *grammatical structure*. The most basic example is any simple series:

> 18a. I like to swim, fish, and hike. (Each item is an infinitive.)

Nonparallel versions could be either of the following:

> 18b. *I like to swim, fish, and hiking: (Infinitive, infinitive, gerund—the final item in the series is not in the same grammatical form as the first two.)
> 18c. *I like to swim, to fish, and hike: (The first two items are expressed as *to + infinitive*, whereas the last one is just the infinitive without *to*.)

Parallel structures can be much more complex than the simple series in sentence 1a. All kinds of phrases can be structured similarly; entire sentences can even be made parallel to powerful effect. Words or phrases can optionally be repeated in order to strengthen the parallelism.

Excellent examples of parallelism at several levels, using both identical grammatical structures (required) and repetition (optional), can be found in Martin Luther King Jr.'s phenomenal "I Have a Dream" speech. Here is a brief excerpt with the parallel structures underlined:

> <u>I have a dream that</u> <u>one day</u> even the state of Mississippi, a state <u>sweltering with</u> <u>the heat of injustice</u>, <u>sweltering with</u> <u>the heat of oppression</u>, will be transformed into <u>an oasis of freedom and justice</u>.

<u>I have a dream that</u> my four little children will <u>one day</u> live in a nation where they will not be judged <u>by the color of their skin</u> but <u>by the content of their character.</u>

Problem Area Student errors in parallelism usually occur in series that are contained within a single sentence.

> **Grammar Wizard Test—The *Repeat the Intro* Test:** Repeat the words that introduce the series before each item of the series to locate nonparallel items.

These problem areas can often be made visible to the Grammar Wizard by repeating the understood phrase that introduces the series. Example:

> 19a. The medicine had a bad smell, an unusual color, and tasted nasty.

Repeating the intro, which is an understood element in any series, produces the following weirdness:

> 19b. *The medicine *had a* bad smell, *had an* unusual color, and *had a* tasted nasty.

Here are two more examples taken directly from student papers:

> 20a. Giving money to these countries can ultimately cure diseases, create new international products and it could save your life.
>
> 20b. *Giving money to these countries *can* ultimately cure diseases, *can* create new international products and *can* it could save your life.
>
> 21a. The coach told the players that they should get a lot of sleep, that they should not eat too much, and to do some warm-up exercises before the game.
>
> 21b. *The coach told the players *that they should* get a lot of sleep, *that they should* not eat too much, and *that they should* to do some warm-up exercises before the game.

Exercise Students will be in a much better position to create parallel structures in their writing if they are able to recognize it when they see it in their readings—the Joshua Tree Syndrome. Therefore, two different types of exercises are suggested:

1. Provide examples of parallelism from professional authors. Have students find what makes the structures parallel. Ask them to rewrite the excerpt in a non-parallel (but correct) manner to help them see and feel the difference. Let them also experiment by rewriting the excerpt using a different type of parallelism. An example of both exercises follows:

- *Original Sentence:* If professional writers had to choose a single tool to put in their toolboxes, a single tool to add polish and sophistication to their writing, a single tool to help them present their thoughts in an organized manner, parallelism would undoubtedly be their choice.

- *Nonparallel (correct but not as effective):* If professional writers had to choose a single tool to put in their writer's toolbox, parallelism would undoubtedly be their choice. Parallelism is a device that adds polish and sophistication to writing. In addition, it is a good way to present one's thoughts in an organized manner.

- *Modified Parallel (with synonyms instead of repetition):* If professional writers had to choose a single *tool* to put in their writer's toolbox, a single *device* to add polish and sophistication to their writing, a single *method* to help them present their thoughts in an organized manner, parallelism would undoubtedly be their choice.

2. Give students practice at combining sentences by creating parallel structures. Example:

- *Separate Sentences:* There are three factors to consider when buying a house: How much does it cost? Is the house in good condition? The most important consideration is location.

- *Parallel Combination:* The three factors to consider when buying a house are cost, condition, and—most importantly—location.

Recursiveness and Elaboration   These activities provide a way to reexamine parallelism.

Punctuation   Deciding whether to use commas or semi-colons in series provides an excellent opportunity to revisit parallelism. See Chapter 8 for details.

Literature   Parallel structures abound in literature:

- Point them out occasionally.
- Tell your class that paragraph *X* contains *Y* examples of parallel structure. Then let the students find them.
- Divide the class into small groups and send them on a scavenger hunt for parallel structures in a passage that you just finished reading.

Composition   Ask students during revision to find at least one place where they can put a parallel structure in their writing and have them identify it for you. Be prepared for faulty parallel structures as a result. As was stated earlier, do not penalize the students; instead, praise them for trying, help them repair the problem(s) and encourage them to keep trying.

Error Analysis Keep a collection of faulty parallel structures (anonymously, of course) that your students have created. They make excellent material to use in a repair exercise. For one thing, you could never make up better examples. For another, knowing that previous (or current) students created these erroneous sentences adds a certain weight, a certain note of authenticity to the exercise. (Don't forget to put at least one well-formed parallel structure in the exercise.)

Demonstration The best example of the power of parallelism that I have ever seen originally appeared in *Living, Loving, and Learning* by Leo Buscalia (cited in Noden, 1999). Here is the paragraph, followed by the questions that I ask my students and "penciled in" answers that I expect:

> [1]Remember the day I borrowed your brand new car, and I dented it? [2]I thought you'd kill me, but you didn't. [3]And remember the time I dragged you to the beach, and you said it would rain, and it did? [4]I thought you'd say "I told you so," but you didn't. [5]Remember the time I flirted with all the guys to make you jealous and you were? [6]I thought you'd leave me, but you didn't. [7]Do you remember the time I spilled strawberry pie all over your car rug? [8]I thought you'd hit me, but you didn't. [9]And remember the time I forgot to tell you that the dance was formal, and you showed up in jeans? [10]I thought you'd drop me, but you didn't. [11]Yes, there were lots of things you didn't do. [12]But you put up with me, and you loved me, and you protected me. [13]There were lots of things I wanted to make up to you when you returned from Viet Nam. [14]But you didn't.

1. How does the author introduce every incident that she remembers?
   "Remember the day/time"

2. How does the author present the anticipated result of each incident?
   "I thought you'd"

3. How does the author indicate that the anticipated result did not occur?
   "but you didn't"

4. The author uses a different phrase to signal that she is finished remembering incidences—a phrase that she repeats twice. What is it?
   "there were lots of things"

5. Below are three perfectly good versions of sentence #12. Discuss the different reaction that you have to each version and why the author might have chosen the final version for her letter:

   a. But you put up with me, loved me, and protected me.

   b. But you put up with me, you loved me, and you protected me.

   c. But you put up with me, and you loved me, and you protected me.

   - The first version is a relatively unemotional statement of fact.

■ The repetition of <u>you</u> in the second version emphasizes each individual action.

■ The repetition of <u>and you</u> in the final version adds emphasis and emotion to the statement.

Nominative Absolute

How Is It Used? What a horrible name for a structure that is so easy to form and is so widely used by professional writers! A nominative absolute (also called a noun absolute) is a device that allows the writer to zoom in on one particular detail of an image. Here are a couple of examples:

22. The dog slipped off into the darkness, <u>its tail tucked between its legs</u>. (We zoom in from the dog to its tail.)

23. <u>Her heart pounding furiously</u>, Mary tried to remain hidden in the bushes. (We zoom in from Mary to her pounding heart.)

How Is It Formed? Let's examine the formation via an inquiry-based approach. Table 7.2 provides the *Data to Analyze*. Your students may or may not be able to answer all of the *Questions to Guide Analysis* that follow, but they will engage the students and get them to thinking. You will, of course, answer the questions during the third phase—*Discussion*.

Table 7.2 Nominative Absolute Formation

#	Sentence	Omitted Word
1a.	Mary tried to remain hidden in the bushes. Her heart was pounding furiously.	
1b.	Her heart pounding furiously, Mary tried to remain hidden in the bushes.	
2a.	The dog slipped off into the darkness. Its tail was tucked between its legs.	
2b.	The dog slipped off into the darkness, its tail tucked between its legs.	
3a.	My muscles were aching and my lungs were on fire, but I continued to run.	
3b.	My muscles aching and my lungs on fire, I continued to run.	

Questions for Table 7.2

1. Example 1A is two sentences; 1B is one sentence. What word was removed in order to combine the sentences? Write the word in the right-hand column of Table 7.2.

2. Do the same thing for examples 2A/2B and 3A/3B.

3. All three of the words that were omitted come from the same base word—the same infinitive. What is that base word? Look at the footnote if you need a hint.[3]

4. Traditional grammar refers to this construction as a *nominative absolute*. A better name might be *near clause*. Why do we suggest this name?

5. From the above data, what is the rule for forming a near clause?

6. Why can't the near clauses in the "B" versions be called participle phrases?

7. In each of the "B" versions, the main actor (*Mary*, *dog*, and *I*) is shown from a broad or general perspective. What happens when a near clause is added?

Discussion Here are the main points to hit: Nominative absolutes are normally created by dropping some form of the verb *to be* from a clause. The resulting phrase is not a clause any longer—it has a missing piece. It's close, however: It contains a subject and a part of the verb. So let's call it a *near clause*.

A **near clause** provides a way for the writer to zoom in on one particular feature or aspect of the subject. In example 1b in Table 7.2, for instance, the main clause is about Mary; the *near clause* zooms in on her heart.

Near clauses differ from participles because they contain the subject—the *doer* of the action. Contrast the following:

23a. Her heart pounding furiously, Mary tried to remain hidden in the bushes. (near clause)

23b. Pounding furiously, Mary's heart seemed ready to burst. (participle)

In sentence 1, we see immediately that the *heart* is what is *pounding*—that information is in the near clause. In sentence 2, however, we do not know what is *pounding* until we read further.

Can you always remove a form of *to be* and create a near clause? No. Look at the following example:

24a. The man was trying to save his house. The fire proved to be too strong. →

24b. *The man trying to save his house, the fire proved to be too strong.

---

[3] Hint: Fill in the blank: He *is* a rock star. I want to _____ one also.

The beginning of sentence 3b looks like a well-formed near clause, but it doesn't work in the sentence—something your Grammar Wizard told you as soon as you read it. The combination doesn't work because the near clause is not zooming in on *fire*, the subject of the main clause. Your Grammar Wizard knew that fact implicitly—pretty amazing, actually.

Exercise Provide pairs of sentences, most of which can be combined by using a near clause (nominative absolute). Again, recognize other combining techniques that produce good sentences, but require students to use the target structure during the exercise.

Recursiveness and Elaboration These activities provide a way to reexamine nominative absolutes.

Movement The next time you review near clauses (nominative absolutes), show how they can often be moved from in front of the main clause to after it. Example:

> 25. Perspiration dripping from his face, Max crossed the finish line.
>   OR Max crossed the finish line, perspiration dripping from his face.

Discuss the effect of this movement and possible contexts that would favor one position over the other.

Punctuation Point out that near clauses are always set off by commas. Discuss the logic for the commas from the perspective of chunking.

Literature Find examples in whatever the class is reading:

- Point out how the author always sets the near clause off by a comma.
- Determine if the near clause can be moved to a different position. If it cannot, discuss why not. If it can, discuss the rhetorical effect of the movement and, possibly, why the author chose to put it in its original place.

Composition Again, encourage or require students to incorporate at least one near clause into their writing as they revise.

Adjectives Out of Order

How Is It Used? In English, adjectives normally come before the noun. However, if the writer stacks too many of them in front of the noun, they sound awkward. An adjective train wreck is the result:

> 26a. The big black sleek graceful cat arched its back lazily.

It is possible, however, to place some of them *after* the noun. Example:

> 26b. The big black cat, sleek and graceful, arched its back lazily.

Adjectives out of order accomplish two purposes:

- They allow for more descriptive detail without getting ridiculous.
- They allow the writer to highlight or emphasize certain qualities. The ones that come after the noun are more prominent to the reader.

How Is It Formed?
Formation is easy; the effect is striking. Here are the rules, most of which are already a part of your students' Grammar Wizards:

- Usually, at least two adjectives are required after the noun. Moving a single adjective often sounds silly:

> 26c. *The big black cat, sleek, arched its back lazily.

- The adjectives are almost always joined—usually by *and* or *but*:

> 26d. The big black cat, sleek *and* graceful, arched its back lazily.
> 26e. The big black cat, evil-looking *but* sweet, arched its back lazily.

- They are always set off by commas.

Notice that, for emphasis, adjectives can be out of order even if the noun that they modify has no adjectives in front. Example:

> 27. Maria, small but tough as nails, refused to surrender to the disease.

Exercise
I suggest two steps here:

- Provide sentences that have adjective train wrecks. Have students decide which ones can be moved and then rewrite the sentences accordingly.
- Provide sentences that have bare (i.e., adjectiveless) noun phrases as subjects. Ask students to expand each one with adjectives and adjective phrases, using adjectives out of order in each sentence.

Recursiveness and Elaboration
These activities provide a way to reexamine adjectives that are out of order.

Movement Adjectives out of order often directly follow the noun that they modify. However, they can be added before or after the main clause *as long as there is no other noun in the way*. Examples:

28a. The fire spread, fast and unrelenting.

28b. Fast and unrelenting, the fire spread throughout the building.

29. *The baby stretched her legs, short and chubby.

30. The sun blazed in the sky, remorseless and punishing.

Example #29 doesn't work because *back* gets in the way: It is possible for a *back* to be *sleek* and *graceful*. Notice, however, that #30 is acceptable: No one could call the sky *remorseless* and *punishing*—these are qualities that have nothing to do with the concept of *sky*.

Manipulatives Body Grammar (Chapter 6) is an excellent way to introduce or review adjectives out of order. The Noun Phrase Building process (Chapter 6) is also an excellent way to introduce or reinforce this structure.

Literature Find examples in whatever the class is reading. Briefly discuss the following:

■ Why the author used this structure.

■ How the structure matches the structure provided in the "How Is It Formed?" section.

■ What would happen if the adjectives were placed before the noun they modified?

■ What would happen if the adjective were placed before or after the main clause?

Composition Encourage (or require) students to include at least one example of adjectives out of order as they go through the revision process of something they have written.

Inclusive Activities

In this chapter, the various structures have been organized into tidy sections. In the real world, things aren't so neat. These structures pop up willy-nilly in reading selections, and the opportunity or need to use these tools occur randomly across writing assignments. Therefore, you need to move your students toward more unstructured exposure.

The *I Am* Poem Constance Weaver (1996) introduces an excellent vehicle for combining four of the above grammar tools into a single, nine-line poem—the *I Am* poem (p. 44). I follow her three-step approach:

1. *Present an Example:* Here is an example of an *I Am* poem:

I am

A pair of crutches,

> Helping people in need;   **Participle Phrase**

A towel,

> Soft, warm, and cuddly;   **Adjectives Out of Order**

A story teller,

> My imagination soaring to new horizons;   **Near Clause**

A teddy bear,

> A child's friend in times of need.   **Appositive**

2. *Model the Process:* Create an *I Am* poem together as a class. I tell the students to build one about me, and ask them to feel free to relax and have fun with it. We first make a list of possible things I could be, both serious and silly. Then I start writing what they dictate, choosing phrases from the list of things I could be and adding the required structures.

3. *Assign an Original:* Now it's their turn. For homework, they are to write an *I Am* poem about themselves. I warn them that I will read several of them in class, so if they do not want me to reveal their names or read theirs out loud, they should write a note to that effect on the paper. If some of them don't have the structures exactly right, then they present excellent (anonymous) teaching moments.

Mini-Revisions   Kelly Gallagher (2006, pp. 57–58) suggests an activity that lends itself very nicely to an overall review and application of these grammar tools. This activity also provides an excellent opportunity for you to impress on your students the importance of revision and to provide examples of things that can be done during the revision process:

1. *The Activity:* Tell the students that you are going to perform an action that you want them to capture in a single sentence. Explain that the activity starts after you say "Go," and continues until you say "Stop." Let's say, for example, that (after saying "Go") you walk over to your desk and pick up a book. Then you say "Stop."

2. *The Sentence:* The students now write a basic sentence that describes your action. Have several students read their sentences out loud, noting similarities and differences. Ask students to be sure to bring these sentences with them to class for the next several days.

3. *The Revisions:* Over the next several days, ask students to make specific revisions to their sentences. Here is an example series of events using the following sentence as a model:

> 31a. The teacher walked over to the desk and picked up a book.

■ *Day 2—Simple Appositives*: Instruct students to add a simple apposi-tive—your name, for example—to the sentence. Ask students to read the results. Example:

> 31b. The teacher, Mr. Smith, walked over to the desk and picked up a book.

If students have added structures that are not appositives, help them apply the *Either–Or* Grammar Wizard Test to show that the new struc-tures are not appositives.

■ *Day 3—Complex Appositive*: Ask students to remove the simple appositive and add a more complicated one. Again, spot-check the results, discuss-ing the outcome—not only from a structural perspective but also from a rhetorical one. Notice, for instance, how the following example creates tension and a sense of impending trouble.

> 31c. The teacher, a normally calm and collected man, walked over to the desk and picked up a book.

■ *Day 4—Participle*: Ask students to provide more descriptive detail about the subject of their sentences by adding introductory participle phrases. They may either retain or drop the appositives. As always, spot-check the results. Example:

> 31d. Looking tired and disgusted, the teacher, a normally calm and collected man, walked over to the desk and picked up a book.

■ *Day 5—Near Clause (Nominative Absolute)*: Ask students to replace the participle phrase with an introductory near clause and spot-check the results. Example:

> 31e. His head bent at an odd angle, the teacher, a normally calm and collected man, walked over to the desk and picked up a book.

You could continue with other tools: some adjectives out of order, an infinitive phrase, or a parallel structure of some sort. (A gerund does not easily fit into this particular sentence pattern.) If you want to take another step closer to reality, have the students write a beginning—an event or series of events that leads up to the newly created sentence. This beginning may have to change as you incorporate various structures.

Literary Goldmines The literature that you assign as a class can be mined for authentic examples of how successful professional authors use these tools. I mentioned using literary examples as a means of elaboration for each of the tools that were covered in this chapter. This presentation is a more holistic approach:

1. Select a passage that contains several examples of the various tools that you have placed in your students' grammar toolbox. Usually, such a passage can be found readily in something that the class has read. Number each line or sentence of the passage.

2. Divide students into groups, pass out the passage to each group, and establish a time limit.

3. Ask each group to go through the passage, underline and number every example of the tools that they can find, and write what tool each one is.

4. After the time has expired, ask each group to report its findings to the class. The group that finds and correctly labels the greatest number of examples wins the contest.

Students love competition, so this activity is invariably a lot of fun for them. Be sure to require that they name the structures—remember the Joshua Tree Syndrome.

Discussion Questions

1. Review your answers to the true–false questions at the beginning of this chapter. Have you changed any of your answers?

2. Explain the difference between *receptive* and *productive* language skills and why this distinction is important for composition teachers to keep in mind.

3. Why is it important for students to learn the names of various grammatical constructions?

4. How can you determine whether or not a given structure is a participle phrase?

5. What is the primary function of participle phrases?

6. In class, you introduce a grammatical structure (via an inquiry-based approach of course!) and follow it up with a sentence-combining exercise. A week later, you bring in another sentence-combining exercise. Why isn't the second sentence-combining exercise the best way to reintroduce the target structure and what could you do to improve on it?

7. In this chapter, two sentences were provided in which the identical phrase functioned as a participle in one and a gerund in the other. Come up with your own contrasting pair and show how you could verify which one was a gerund using only your Grammar Wizard.

8. What construction can sometimes be used to get rid of sentences that have a form of *to be* as the main verb? Provide an example to support your answer.

9. What is *parallelism* and why, from the reader's perspective, is it such a great tool for writers to use?

10. What is a *near clause (nominative absolute)* and on what does it focus the reader's attention?

## chapter 8

Brain-Based Punctuation

True or False?

1. Students' misuse of commas is, in part, due to the fact that students have not formed an internal set of rules to go by.

2. Students have trouble mastering punctuation in large part due to the complexities of traditional grammar pedagogy.

3. The primary function of a comma is to show readers where to chunk.

4. Speakers "punctuate" their speech with the vocal equivalent of commas and periods.

5. If students read their comma splices out loud, they will usually be able to hear where the comma splice occurs.

6. Items in a series are always separated by commas.

7. In formal written English, a colon can be used only after a complete sentence.

8. Hyphens, like apostrophes, are logically unnecessary; readers will always know what the writer means— with or without them.

Punctuation Whimsy

We explain. We practice. We drill. We correct essays. We drill some more. *And they still don't get it.* Commas seem to be placed according to whim. Sentence boundary errors (comma splices, run-ons, and fragments) abound. Apostrophes, hyphens, semi-colons, colons, dashes, parentheses— these marks are virtual no-shows!

What's going on here? Why is punctuation such a difficult skill to master for most student writers?

Let's start by putting one myth to rest. I have heard many teachers proclaim that their students seem to punctuate at random. If we took the time to analyze their writing carefully (and what English teacher has time?), we would probably find underlying patterns based on erroneous theories of how things work—pseudo-concepts, as Lev Vygotsky (1986) called them. So the real question is this: Why or how did students come up with these pseudo-concepts? Let me count the ways:

- *Inadequate Reading*: As previously noted, students today do not read as much professionally prepared material as students did years ago. Reading well-written, properly punctuated material helps students absorb good punctuation techniques through an osmosis-like process.

- *Inaccessible Explanations*: The arcane concepts and explanations that traditional grammar pedagogy (TGP) provides shed little light on how punctuation functions in writing.

- *Illogical Analyses*: Many more times than not, punctuation is *logical*. Often, however, TGP ignores the underlying logic, emphasizing instead a set of semi-fathomable rules to memorize.

- *Inadequate Connection with Speaking*: Traditional grammar pedagogy makes virtually no attempt to link punctuation conventions with spoken conventions—features that native speakers and advanced non-native speakers have already mastered.

In this chapter, we will examine punctuation from two nontraditional, but very effective, brain-based perspectives:

1. As in previous chapters, we will tap into what students already know, examining how speakers send processing signals to listeners. This information will help students make many punctuation decisions.

2. We will also examine the reader's brain as a *receiver*, a *processor* of information. Understanding what the brain needs in order to rapidly yet properly process writing will expose the logical underpinnings on which so much of punctuation is based.

Let's start with the most troublesome area first—the comma.[1]

Traditional Comma Explanations

One fundamental reason that punctuation is so hard for students to master involves how punctuation has been presented. Look, for example, at the following list. It contains a collection of the terminology that I compiled from one popular handbook (*The Little, Brown Handbook,* Fowler, Aaron, and Okoomian, 2001, pp. 467–490) in the section that purports to explain comma usage:

Absolute phrase	Introductory element
Adjective	Main clause
Adverb	Modifier
Appositives	Nonessential vs. essential
Clause	Parenthetical expression
Compound elements	Participle
Conjunctive adverb	Phrase
Contraction	Possessive case
Coordinate adjective	Predicate
Coordinating conjunction	Prepositional phrase
Cumulative adjective	Signal phrase
Direct address	Subject
Ellipsis	Subordinate clause
Indefinite pronoun	Tag question
Indirect quotation	Transitional expression
Interjections	Verbal (phrase)

There are 32 terms in this list. Your students do not know the vast majority of them when they first come to your classroom; they will not know the vast majority of them when they leave. In fact, most *English teachers* would be hard-pressed to define many of these terms, as would many professional authors. So how in the world can we expect students to internalize comma usage when concepts are explained in such a bewildering morass of terminology that professionals in the field can't make sense of it?

Proficient writers do not decide comma usage by consciously analyzing sentences into constituents, labeling them, and then using the results to make comma decisions. "Let's see—this sentence begins with a subordinate clause that also contains a conjunctive adverb. Furthermore, the main clause contains a nonessential appositive and some coordinate adjectives.

---

[1]Again, space constraints prevent me from presenting everything in an inquiry-based manner; however, I do so whenever possible in the classroom. And it is almost always possible.

Since the sentence begins with a subordinate clause, I need to put a comma at the boundary of the subordinate and main clause. . . ." No, proficient writers *feel* where most of the commas go. It's *procedural* knowledge, not *declarative*.

Unfortunately, we teachers do not have a direct pipeline into students' procedural memory; we can only feed the declarative side. Information then has to move itself from declarative to procedural, a process that is facilitated not by memorization and meaningless drill but by connecting new concepts to existing ones, by exposing the underlying logic, and by providing meaningful elaboration. Let's get started.

Omitting Commas

Did you ever try typing a paper or exercise, intentionally trying to omit commas? Then, when you go back to proof the paper, you find that you have stuck in a couple of commas that you intended to leave out? This auto-pilot mode, a hallmark of procedural knowledge, is the ultimate goal for our students in most punctuation situations.

Voice Commas and Voice Periods

The primary purpose of punctuation in general, and commas in specific, is to help readers know how to process the language—in other words, where to chunk. (See Chapter 2.) Read the following sentence:

1a. Whenever John eats food gets wasted.

You probably had to read this sentence at least two times before you could figure it out. The problem is that *Whenever John eats food* chunks very nicely, so that's exactly what your Grammar Wizard did. But then, when you hit *gets*, your Wizard realized that something was wrong: the chunking process broke down after *food*. So you started over. If the comma had been properly placed, you would not have had this problem:

1b. Whenever John eats, food gets wasted.

The comma provides a clear signal to the reader to chunk after *eats*, so the sentence is processed smoothly.

Okay, so readers need assistance in knowing where to chunk. The next logical question to ask, then, is this: Do listeners need similar assistance? And the answer is *yes*, they most certainly do. Speakers send signals to listeners all the time to help them make processing decisions—signals that your students have mastered completely. Look at the following example:

2a. After he ate my dog Sam took a nap.

As it is written, there are two possible interpretations for this sentence. The first (and the one your first reading undoubtedly gave it) involves weird Sam; evil, nefarious Sam; from a very different culture, if not planet

Sam. If that is the interpretation that the writer intends, then the sentence would be written as follows:

Chunk

2b. After he ate my dog, Sam took a nap.

If, however, the writer means my best friend Sam, it would be written differently:

Chunk

2c. After he ate, my dog Sam took a nap.

Now let's examine this same sentence as it would be spoken. If the speaker is talking about weird Sam, she would say the sentence one way. If the speaker is talking about her best friend Sam, then she would say it another way. I will use lines to represent intonation—how the voice rises and falls during speech—smoothing out the uninteresting parts with straight lines. Here's the weird Sam version. Read it out loud to follow the intonation changes as shown.

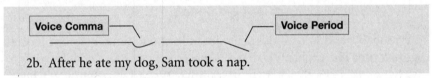

Voice Comma **Voice Period**

2b. After he ate my dog, Sam took a nap.

Here's the best friend Sam version:

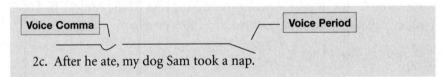

Voice Comma **Voice Period**

2c. After he ate, my dog Sam took a nap.

Let's define our terms:

- **Voice Comma:** A dip + rise in intonation (with an optional pause). Say 2b and 2c out loud, as if you were making a speech, and listen for the location of the dip in intonation.

- **Voice Period:** A drop in intonation. Say 2b and 2c out loud, noticing how your voice trails downward at the end of both versions.

As shown here, voice commas and voice periods are very clear signals that speakers send to listeners, telling them *where* and *how* to chunk.

- A voice comma means "Chunk here, but more follows."

- A voice period means, "Chunk here—it's over."

Keep in mind that we are dealing with intonation here; speakers can play games with it. However, when I tell students to say it as if they were making a formal speech, the standard intonation patterns—voice commas and voice periods—return almost without fail. The notions of voice commas and voice periods are deeply ingrained and are, therefore, very useful teaching tools.

Voice Commas and Introductory Elements

In 1988, Connors and Lundsford published an oft-cited analysis of errors on compositions as marked by English teachers. The most frequently occurring error in their study was the absence of an introductory element comma. Obviously, teachers were not too successful back then at getting rid of this problem; I doubt that the situation has changed much in the interim.

Definition What is an *introductory element*? I have good news and bad news.

Bad News Introductory elements are not easy to define. They can be one of several structures. To make matters worse, the same structure can be classified as an introductory element in one sentence and not in another. Example:

> 3a. *Down the road* we ran. (No introductory element)
> 3b. *Down the road*, a new school was being built. (Introductory element)

Good News *You don't have to define the concept*—your students will use a voice comma after an introductory element *every time they say a sentence that contains one.* Your job, then, is to help students tune in to the spoken signal and connect it to the written one. Try it yourself. Read Sentences 3a and 3b, above, out loud (as if you were making a speech) and then read the following sentences:

Pauses

In TGP, commas are often tied to pauses. That union doesn't work very well. Although it is true that we tend to pause at the end of a phrase or clause, we also pause for other reasons:

- We run out of breath.
- We can't find the exact word we want.
- We need time to find our next thought.
- We pause for dramatic effect.

In contrast, the voice comma is a pretty reliable indicator that a written comma is needed.

5. However, the game was cancelled.

6. Although I was very tired, I decided to study for a couple more hours.

7. In the first place, that's rude.

8. To ensure a smooth mixture, add the eggs slowly as you whisk.

Sentence 3 does not have a voice comma; all the rest of them do. Also notice that sentences 4 through 8 begin with a variety of structures. Again, there is no need to analyze, label, or list them—they all take voice commas. Pretty amazing, isn't it, that a native (or advanced non-native) speaker's Grammar Wizard is in total control of this rather complex feature of English?

Classroom Presentation Use the weird Sam/best friend Sam sentences (2a, 2b, and 2c) to introduce the voice comma concept—similar to the way it was introduced earlier:

1. Begin the lesson without saying a word. Simply display the entire sentence without commas (2a) and wait for student reaction as they read it.[2]

2. Inform the class that there are two possible interpretations for this sentence. Show them each one (2b and 2c), asking them to read silently and emphasizing that the commas are signals to the reader, showing them where to chunk.

3. After a brief discussion of the importance of commas, tell your students that they make commas with their voices when they talk. Then put the intonation lines above 2b (weird Sam) and say it out loud, tracing the intonation patterns in the air with your hand as you show them the voice comma and voice period. Repeat the process with 2c (best friend Sam), and then contrast it with 2b.

4. Finally, hand out a short passage that has several introductory elements, but is missing all of the commas. I have used the following sample passage with high school and college students. I read the passage out loud, asking students to raise their hands whenever they hear a voice comma and to place each comma on the handout:

> [1]If you ask people why humans yawn most of them will have an answer. [2]In fact scientists have yet to solve this puzzle completely. [3]They agree on a definition: a yawn is a voluntary activity that regulates carbon dioxide and oxygen levels in the body. [4]However they do not understand every aspect of this phenomenon.

---

[2]If you write the sentence on the board, ask the students not to watch as you write so that they can process it in its entirety when they read it.

[5]Although they don't know everything about yawning most scientists agree on the following: [6]When a person is tired or bored breathing is shallow. [7]As a result a decreased amount of oxygen enters the body. [8]Scientists think that this state of oxygen deprivation initiates a yawn reflex.

In sentence 3, above, a few students invariably raise their hands when I pause for the colon, despite the fact that I make a clear and natural voice period there. This little "oops" moment provides an excellent opportunity to contrast voice commas with voice periods and to remind students to concentrate on the *intonation*, not the *pauses*. Sentence 3 is also an excellent example of a sentence where student writers often feel the need to stick in a comma simply because it is so long and complex sounding.

I worked with and marked missing introductory element commas on student papers over and over and over again *for years*; nothing seemed to help. When I switched over to voice commas, however, when I helped students connect this new concept with existing knowledge, things changed dramatically. Students still omitted them from their writing for a while—it takes time and meaningful exposure for new concepts to become automatic:

- I would collect sample sentences (anonymously, of course), show them to the class in a quick 5-minute mini-session, and ask various students to read them out loud, pointing out the obvious voice commas that resulted.
- During individual conferences with students who still didn't get it, I would spend a couple of minutes asking each one to read his or her problem sentences out loud, pointing out the voice commas as I heard them.

By the end of one semester, every student was able to edit a piece of writing that had several problem areas and insert every missing introductory element comma.

Voice commas serve as Grammar Wizard Tests in other areas involving comma usage, areas that we will cover later in this chapter. However, before going further with commas, let's take a quick look at a very beneficial application of the voice period concept.

Voice Periods: Recognizing Comma Splices and Run-Ons

In the 1988 Connors and Lundsford study of the most commonly marked errors by English teachers, comma splices ranked eighth and run-ons ranked twelfth. In the ensuing decades, I suspect the situation has only gotten worse. Why? What is so difficult about recognizing sentence boundaries? In most cases there is nothing difficult about it at all. In fact, your students do it all the time when they talk—they use voice periods to help their listeners know how to process the language that they are producing. The primary value of voice periods in the composition classroom, then, is to help students recognize comma splices and run-ons—mistakes caused by the failure to mark the end of a sentence properly.

Definition Exactly what is a sentence? Again, I have good news and bad news:

Bad News Traditionally, a sentence has been defined as a "complete thought." This fuzzy, ill-defined notion of a sentence only confuses the issue. Look at the following examples:

> 9a. Sheila wanted pizza, but Bob got nachos. (1 sentence)
> 9b. Sheila wanted pizza, although Bob got nachos. (1 sentence)
> 9c. Sheila wanted pizza. However, Bob got nachos. (2 sentences)
> 9d. Sheila wanted pizza. *Although Bob got nachos. (1½ sentences)

You would have a *very* difficult time convincing your students (or anyone else, for that matter) that Sentences 9a and 9b represent one complete thought, whereas Sentence 9c represents two complete thoughts and Sentence 9d represents one and a half! What makes a sentence a sentence, it turns out, is very difficult to pin down.

Good News *You don't have to define it.* Sentence Wizards (Chapters 9 and 10) already know what a sentence is—once again, students just don't know that they know. If they can learn to get in touch with their Sentence Wizards, they can much more easily learn to recognize most sentence boundaries. Let me give you an example from my classroom: I had a student write the following on his essay:

> 10a. The car was a total wreck, it had to be towed away.

As far as the student was concerned, the first part wasn't a "complete thought" until he wrote the second part—a very common and logical source of comma splices in student writing. I asked the student to read the sentence out loud. Here is what he said:

> 10b. The car was a total wreck, it had to be towed away.

I asked him if he heard a voice comma when he said it out loud. He admitted that he didn't—he heard voice periods. So I told him to fix it. And he did.

Classroom Presentation In the voice comma presentation, voice periods were introduced at the same time, so all you have to do is briefly demonstrate them again. Then give the class a couple of paragraphs without capital letters and without periods—replace some of the periods with spaces and others with commas. Read the passage out loud, instructing students to raise their hands every time they hear a voice period and to fix the passage accordingly.

Now it's just a matter of time and meaningful elaboration: Ask students to read their comma splice or run-on structures out loud (as if they were giving a speech); they will almost always put a voice period at the sentence boundary. Your job is to *patiently reinforce the concept*. As I have said repeatedly, it takes time for a new concept (declarative) to become automatic (to transfer to procedural). Building on already established concepts, however, is an enormous shortcut.

I do not mean to imply that voice commas and voice periods are bulletproof. There are times when we use a voice period orally, but a comma is required in writing. (We will deal with a perfect example of this phenomenon, called *sentence expanders*, in Chapter 10.) There are also some occasions where written commas and voice commas do not match up. However, the correspondence between voice commas/voice periods and written commas/written periods is spot-on most of the time, making the concept a very powerful place to begin.

Now let's return to our analysis of commas.

Other Commas

Series Commas

Teaching students to put commas between items in a series does not present much of a challenge. Simply let them try to read a few sentences with series that do not have the commas to see how difficult it is to process. Here is one example:

> 11a. I like ham and eggs cereal biscuits and gravy pancakes with syrup
> or omelets for breakfast.

Now show them how properly placed commas greatly reduce the processing load:

> 11b. I like ham and eggs, cereal, biscuits and gravy, pancakes with
> syrup, or omelets for breakfast.

You might point out that speakers put voice commas between each element of a series and something similar to a voice period after the final one. (If the sentence continues, then speakers put another voice period at the end of it, of course.)

Adjective Commas

This one can be a real challenge. Sometimes, multiple adjectives before a noun require commas; sometimes they don't. And voice commas are not much help. Examples:

> 12a. I bought a *magnificent vintage* car. (No comma required)
>
> 13a. She was a *lovely, intelligent young* lady. (Comma required)

Explaining when to insert the adjective comma is a daunting task—unless you teach students how to tap into their Grammar Wizards to make the decision. Two Grammar Wizard Tests can be used:

> **Grammar Wizard Test—The Reversible Test:** If you can reverse the two adjectives, put a comma between them.

> 12b. *I bought a *vintage magnificent* car. (Sounds funny—no comma)
>
> 13b. She was an *intelligent, lovely young* lady. (Sounds fine—comma)

Notice that, in Sentence 13b, *young* cannot be easily reversed—no comma. If the writer were to decide to do so for rhetorical effect, then a comma would be obligatory:

> 13c. She was a *lovely, young, intelligent* lady.

> **Grammar Wizard Test—The *And* Test:** If you can put *and* between the adjectives, put a comma between them.

> 12c. *I bought a *magnificent and vintage* car. (Sounds funny—no comma)
>
> 13d. She was a *lovely and intelligent young* lady. (Sounds fine—comma)

Essential–Nonessential Commas

This concept is, once again, rather difficult to define. Commas become an issue with appositives[3] and relative clauses (clauses that usually begin with *who, which,* or *that*).

---

[3]As was mentioned in Chapter 7, the essential–nonessential concept is a good way to spiral appositives back into your lesson plans.

Whether or not to use commas hinges on whether or not the reader needs the information to better identify the primary noun. Example:

14a. My brother Tom lives in New York. (The appositive "Tom" is essential.)

14b. My brother, Tom, lives in New York. (The appositive "Tom" is nonessential.)

Essential When you do *not* surround the appositive with commas, you are telling the reader that the appositive information is necessary in order to better identify the person or thing that you are writing about. In Sentence 14a, the author has more than one brother, so "Tom" is essential in order to know which brother he is referring to.

Nonessential When you surround the appositive with commas, you are telling the reader that the appositive information is *not* necessary in order to better identify the person or thing that you are writing about. In Sentence 14b, the author has only one brother, so "Tom" is not essential in order to know which brother he is referring to—it's extra information.

Two Grammar Wizard Tests will make this knotty problem much easier for students to master.

Grammar Wizard Test—The *By the Way* Test: If you can put *by the way* in the appositive or relative clause and it makes sense, then use commas.

In Sentence 14b, you could put *by the way* after Tom and it would make sense; in Sentence 14a, you couldn't. The distinction is easier to see, however, if we work with a more developed structure:

15a. Eminem, who grew up in Detroit, was one of the highest-selling rap artists of all time.

15b. A performer who grew up in Detroit was one of the highest-selling rap artists of all time.

Nonessential In Sentence 15a, "who grew up in Detroit" is not essential in order for the reader to further identify Eminem—Eminem is Eminem. So you could very easily write "who, *by the way*, grew up in Detroit."

Essential In Sentence 15b, however, "who grew up in Detroit" is essential in order for the reader to narrow down or better define which performer you are writing about. Inserting *by the way* into this clause would not be logical. No *by the way*? No commas.

Grammar Wizard Test—Voice Comma: If you hear a voice comma at the *beginning* of the phrase or clause, you need commas.

This Grammar Wizard Test comes with a caveat: Only listen for a voice comma at the *beginning* of the phrase or clause; there will almost always be one at the end whether or not one is needed, so it can be misleading. Try it for yourself: When you say Sentence 15a out loud, you will hear a clear voice comma between *Eminem* and *who*. In 15b, you will *not* hear one between *performer* and *who*. However, you will hear a voice comma after *Detroit* in both versions. This is the only place that I have found where voice commas routinely do not match up with written commas.

Contrary Commas

Commas act as speed bumps for readers. So far, we have seen commas whose primary purpose is to signal readers to chunk. The contrary comma is different: This one signals a change in direction. Thus, it may sound more like a voice period than a voice comma. Example:

16. It is the war on people, not on drugs, that we are losing.

The first comma signals the change in direction (from positive to negative); the second one signals the return back to the original direction. If the contrary phrase comes at the end of a sentence, then a period is used instead of a second comma:

17. Look at life through the windshield, not through the rear view mirror.

Commas between Clauses

The next chapter deals with joining coordinate and subordinate clauses, but in terms that students and their Grammar Wizards can understand. I'll save the discussion about comma usage between clauses for that chapter.

Other Commas

The remaining commas—such as commas in dates, commas between city and state, and commas between name and title—just have to be learned as rules. From a processing perspective, many of them are unnecessary. For example, does the absence of the comma in either example below cause you to misread the phrase?

18. *December 16 2020
19. *Denver Colorado

Because they are not logically necessary, there is no correlate when speaking; therefore, Grammar Wizards aren't much help here. The commas are required by widely accepted convention, so we certainly must teach them to our students. However, I have found no way to tie them back to oral language.

Note: There are two kinds of commas: those that are required by rule, and those that the reader wants to insert to affect how the reader interacts with the sentence. This chapter has covered the former; Chapter 11 will deal with the latter.

Serial Semi-Colons

The primary purpose of a semi-colon is to join two clauses together in one sentence. The next chapter deals with that usage in great detail, so I won't go into it here. However, there is one other usage of the semi-colon that requires further discussion: the *serial semi-colon*. So that we don't lose sight of good brain-based technique, let's explore this usage in an inquiry-based format. Read the example sentences in Table 8.1 and answer the questions before reading the discussion:

Table 8.2 Serial Semi-Colon Data

#	Sentence
1A	We visited Texas, New Mexico, and California.
1B	We visited Dallas, Texas; Santa Fe, New Mexico; and San Diego, California.
1C	We visited Texas; New Mexico; and San Diego, California.
2A	We met three important people: Jose, Juan, and Carlos.
2B	We met some important people: Jose, the president; Juan, the vice-president; and Carlos, the secretary-treasurer.
2C	We met three important people: Jose; Juan; and Carlos, my brother.

Questions for Table 8.2

1. Why are commas used in 1A and 2A?
2. Why do you think that semi-colons are used in 1B and 2B?
3. What would be the problem if commas were used instead of semi-colons in 1B and 2B?
4. Versions 1C and 2C provide the final piece of evidence to help you answer the crucial question: When should you use semi-colons instead of commas in a series?

Discussion   When writing a series, if *any* of the items in the series contains a comma, then a comma can no longer be used to mark the boundary between series items—it would get too confusing. Look at item 2B in Table 8.2, for example, with nothing but commas:

> * We met some important people: Jose, the president, Juan, the vice-president, and Carlos, the secretary-treasurer.

How many people are we introducing? Clearly, Carlos is the secretary-treasurer. The rest of the series is unclear: Jose could be the president or they could be two separate people. The same could be said for Juan. Note that the requirement isn't that every item in a series must have a comma before switching to semi-colon separators. Sentences 1C and 2C in Table 8.1 demonstrate that as soon as *one item* in a series has a comma, we must switch to semi-colons.

Colons

I have found that the easiest way for students to understand the colon is to show them the effect it has on the information processing of readers. Show them the following sentence:

20a. The student made several mistakes.

Ask them to *guess* what might come next, writing down their suggestions on the board. With some prompting, they generate a list of possible continuations:

- A list of mistakes (The mistakes included . . .)
- The causes of the mistakes (These mistakes happened because . . .)
- The effects of the mistakes (As a result, . . .)
- How the student overcame the mistakes (However, the student . . .)

- How the student could have avoided the mistakes (If the student had only . . .)
- Nothing—the end.
- Etc.

Repeat the process, but make one change to the sentence—change the period to a colon:

> 20b. The student made several mistakes:

Ask the students to *guess* what comes next. Several possible directions become reduced to one: a list of the mistakes. Understanding the colon from the perspective of its effect on the reader makes its usage more tangible, more real.

The next step is to have your students put the effect of the colon on the reader into words. Two of my favorite outcomes from in-class discussions are as follows:

1. The colon says to the reader, "Here's what I'm talking about."
2. To the left of a colon is general information; to the right is specific information. We display it as follows:

General Information: Specific Detail(s)

Notice the optional plural for "Detail(s)." A colon does not have to be followed by a list; it is often used to introduce a single specific detail. Example:

> 21. Jerry wanted one thing for his birthday: a new guitar.
>   General   Specific

There is one more piece of information to add: In formal writing situations, colons may be used only after complete sentences. You can let your students uncover this rule via an inquiry-based presentation. Be sure to include at least one pair where "as follows" or "the following" completes the sentence. Here are some examples:

> 22a. *The three cost categories are: X, Y, and Z.
> 22b. The three cost categories are as follows: X, Y, and Z.
> 23a. *Several different brands went on sale, such as: X, Y, and Z.
> 23b. Several different brands went on sale, such as the following: X, Y, and Z.

Periods
There are five punctuation marks that contain a period: the period, the semi-colon, the colon, the question mark, and the exclamation mark. All five of them have one characteristic in common in SWAE: They all require a complete sentence to their left.

Hyphens

Hyphenating words to divide them at the end of a line of print is a dying art due to word processing, so I am not going to discuss it here. However, the need to hyphenate *compound modifiers* still exists, and for good reason: Hyphens help readers know how to process the material. Fortunately, once again, the Grammar Wizard comes to the rescue.

> **Grammar Wizard Test for Hyphens:** Try each modifier separately with the noun it modifies. If the modifiers need a hyphen between them, then at least one will not fit.

Look at the following examples:

> 24. She is a well-known doctor.

One could say that she is a *known doctor*, but not a *well doctor*. Therefore, a hyphen is required in order to let the reader know to chunk *well* and *known* together as a phrase.

> 25. She is a brown-eyed girl.

She may or may not be a *brown girl*, but she most certainly is not an *eyed girl*. A hyphen is required.

Occasionally, hyphens can change the meaning:

> 26a. That is a picture of a man-eating fish. (The fish is doing the eating.)
> 26b. That is a picture of a man eating fish. (The man is doing the eating.)

Two exceptions exist; however, they are logical exceptions because they are easily processed by readers. The first exception is as follows: If the first modifier is clearly an adverb, no hyphen is required. Example:

> 27a. That is a beautifully written book.

Grammar Wizards have an intuitive feeling for adverbs. There is no possibility of misinterpretation here: Readers *know* that *beautifully* cannot go with *book*, a fact that was developed in Chapter 5. In contrast, look at this sentence:

> 27b. That is a well-written book.

The word *well* can be an adjective or an adverb, so, although it is functioning here as an adverb, the hyphen is commonly used to help the reader make a rapid determination.

The second exception to the rule is this: If the modifiers come *after* the noun, hyphens are normally not required. Example:

> 27c. The book is well written.

No Grammar Wizard is going to err in processing *well* here—it clearly modifies *written*.

Apostrophes

As was stated in Chapter 5, people in all walks of life misuse this little stroke, and for good reason: apostrophe usage requires writers to attend to details that are not attended to when speaking—a scenario that is always a source of trouble. To make matters worse, most apostrophes, from a position of pure logic, are not required. Context allows the *listener* to figure out what the meaning is; context would allow the *reader* to do the same. In fact, I had to think long and hard before coming up with two sentences whose general meaning changed by the presence or absence of an apostrophe:[4]

> 27a. Those toy animals are my dogs. (I think of them as pets.)
> 27b. Those toy animals are my dog's. (They belong to my dog.)

Possession with Nouns and Pronouns

This usage of the apostrophe was covered in Chapter 5.

Contractions

The other primary usage of an apostrophe is to show that one or more letters is/are missing. Students have little trouble grasping this concept; by the time they get to high school, they have, for the most part, mastered this convention. Therefore, other than mentioning its existence, I will not go into this rather simple usage.

---

[4] The position of the apostrophe can indicate whether the noun is singular or plural, but that relatively minor point is usually made clear by context.

Dashes and Parentheses

Dashes can be used instead of a colon or a pair of commas. Parentheses can often be substituted for a pair of commas or dashes. Since the decision about which piece of punctuation to use is rhetorical rather than grammatical, I will cover these punctuation marks in Chapter 11.

Discussion Questions

1. Review your answers to the true–false questions at the beginning of this chapter. Have you changed any of your answers?

2. What factors combine to confuse students about proper punctuation usage?

3. Discuss how the concept of *voice commas* and *voice periods* can be used in the following situations:
   a. Introductory element commas
   b. Comma splices or run-ons

4. How can you decide whether or not to put a comma between multiple adjectives that occur before the noun that they modify?

5. Show how *voice commas* can be both a help and a hindrance when deciding whether a phrase or clause is *essential* or *nonessential*.

6. When should you use commas to separate items of a series and when should you use semi-colons?

7. When reading a sentence out loud that contains a colon, the speaker uses a *voice period* to mark where the colon occurs. But how can writers decide whether to use a colon or a period?

8. How can you determine whether to use a hyphen between compound modifiers in a noun phrase?

## chapter 9

Bridges

True or False?

1. Comma splices, run-ons, and fragments are three different versions of the same underlying error.

2. By the time students reach high school, most of them know that they cannot join two sentences with just a comma.

3. Grammar Wizards are capable of recognizing fragments as long as students ask it the right question.

4. Any time you join two sentences together, the relationship between them must be expressed.

5. It is grammatically correct to join two sentences with the word *then*.

6. Students can learn which words can and cannot be used to join two sentences together grammatically without memorizing lists.

7. Deciding to use a comma when joining two sentences together is not logical.

8. Omitting a required comma when joining two sentences will not interfere with the reading process.

Sentence Boundaries

An unfortunate co-occurrence haunts English teachers. One of the most highly stigmatized errors a writer can make, especially in the academic world, is failing to mark sentence boundaries successfully. (You probably know this error by its end-product names: comma splice, fragment, or run-on.) It is also, seemingly, one of the most difficult problem areas to get rid of.

Sentence boundary errors send the wrong chunking signals to readers, thereby slowing down the reading process. However, they do not usually interfere with the delivery of the message: Readers can, often with minimal effort, figure out what the writer intended. Yet these errors are considered to be mortal sins, not venal—felonies, not misdemeanors. As a result, English teachers spend a great deal of time and energy trying to exorcise them from student writing—often with minimal success.

Why are these errors so difficult to remove? A large part of the problem is the traditional approach that we take when we try to explain things in the classroom. To illustrate, I present the following imaginary—but, for the most part, not very imaginative—conversation between a student and a teacher. The student has written the following in his composition:

I went to town. Because I was hungry.

The teacher sits down to discuss the problem with the student:

Teacher: This last sentence is a fragment. The word *because* is a subordinating conjunction. When it is added to an independent clause, that clause becomes dependent.

(*Obviously, this "explanation" does nothing to help the student understand the situation, but he really wants to get it, so he perseveres.*)

Student: What'sa dependent clause?

Teacher: A dependent clause is an independent clause to which a subordinating conjunction has been added.

Student: What's a subordinating conjunction?

Teacher: Something that you add to an independent clause to make it dependent.

(*This bit of circularity only clouds the issue. But the student perseveres. Now, I am getting truly imaginative.*)

Student: Right. So, for example, if I add *however* to an independent clause, it becomes a dependent clause?

Teacher: No. *However* is a conjunctive adverb. *Although* is the subordinating conjunction for contrast, and *but* is the coordinating conjunction.

Student: How can I know whether a word is a coordinating thing, a sub thing, or that other thing?

Teacher: You just have to remember which is which.

Student: Right.

No wonder students don't get it! The traditional terminology and the associated concepts are unfathomable to the average student. A few students manage to figure things out—not *because* of the traditional explanation, but almost *in spite* of it. But most are more confused after the "explanations" than they were before. Not only are the definitions circular but they are also far removed from any knowledge that our students already have about English. Rather than tying into and building on what's already there, this approach attempts to establish new models and theories in the hopes, I suppose, that everything will transfer to existing language skills. It doesn't. As a result, sentence boundary errors appear to be intractable. They aren't. There has to be a better way to attack the problem. There is.

I will take you step-by-step through a classroom-tested approach that helps students get in touch with their *Sentence and Grammar Wizards*. It allows them to leverage what they already know about English in order to resolve sentence boundary issues. Three separate, but interrelated areas await our analysis:

1. Failure to recognize the end of a sentence
2. Marking a group of words as a sentence when it isn't
3. Failure to join sentences together "legally"

Recognizing Sentence Boundaries

Student writers sometimes blow right past the end of a sentence without marking it as such. This oversight results in either a comma splice or a run-on sentence. For years, I used to harp on the fact that sentences cannot be joined by a comma nor can they be joined by nothing. Then one day, it dawned on me that I was not attacking the problem. Students already *knew* what I was telling them—they grasped this concept fairly quickly, just like the "person, place, or thing" noun definition that we examined in Chapter 1. The problem was that they did not always *recognize* the end of a sentence as they were writing. Once I managed to see the obvious, the solution became equally obvious: *voice periods.* (Voice periods are explained in Chapter 8. If you haven't read that section, please go back and do so before continuing.)

I still show the students, as you will see later on, that sentences must be joined by something other than a comma or a blank space. However, I very quickly start helping them see where one sentence ends and another begins by demonstrating how to tap into the **Sentence Wizards** that constantly guide them as they speak. Once they understand voice periods, then the following activities help them begin to build end-of-sentence recognition skills:

- I read problem sentences out loud, tracing the intonation in the air with my hand and emphasizing the voice period.
- In one-on-one conferences, I have them read their own sentences and self-report.
- I ask other students to read some of the ill-formed sentences, asking the rest of the students (including the anonymous author) to raise their hands when they hear the voice period.

An interesting progression takes place as students become consciously aware of their Sentence Wizards. At first, students literally have to say their sentences out loud. However, with a bit of practice, they develop the ability to "say" the sentences in their heads, listening to the intonation patterns silently—a sure sign of Sentence Wizard growth!

Here are some student examples from years gone by. Say each of them, either out loud or in your head, listening for the voice periods. And remember: Pauses are not reliable indicators; you have to listen for voice periods:

1. Every time you sit down to eat, the phone rings.
2. There is no way to describe it all you can do is feel it.
3. I have lost many points due to poor handwriting, I hate losing points for something so basic.
4. John had always dreamed of becoming a doctor, he would spend hours reading medical books and watching medical shows.

The first sentence allows a very clear voice comma—not the end of a sentence. The remainder have voice periods in the middle, but there is no corresponding end-of-sentence marker.

Sentence Wizards (a part of procedural memory) take time to develop. The magic, of course, is that once they are fully developed, students are able to cruise on auto pilot. Their brains will send up a flare when they encounter a problem. Even the most seasoned professional authors can generate sentence boundary errors in the heat of creation; however, when they reread their work, they spot the problems intuitively. This ability is the ultimate goal for our students.

Recognizing Incomplete Sentences

A less common but equally serious error involves creating a structure that, for whatever reason, is not a complete sentence—a fragment. Complicated analyses—dividing sentences into and labeling constituents in order to spot the cause of the problem—can eventually, I suppose, pay dividends. However, such analyses, not for the grammatically faint of heart, are not a very efficient way to build skills. A kinder, gentler way is to show students how to tap into their existing Sentence Wizards and Grammar Wizards. (These two Wizards, as with most things in the brain, are intertwined.) Once they can do that, meaningful exposure across time will hone Sentence Wizard skills.

Two possible Sentence Wizard Tests are available, one of which we saw in Chapter 5:

Two possible Sentence Wizard Tests are available, one of which we saw in Chapter 5:

> **Sentence Wizard Test for Fragments—The *It Is True That* Test**: Begin a suspect sentence with *It is true that . . . .*

Place the phrase *It is true that . . .* in front of any structure that is suspect. If that structure is not a complete sentence, your Sentence/Grammar Wizard will reject the result. Example:

Because I was hungry. → *It is true that because I was hungry.

I went to town because I was hungry. → It is true that I went to town because I was hungry.

> **Sentence Wizard Test for Fragments—Yes–No Questions:** Try to make a question that can be answered by a simple *yes* or *no* out of the suspect sentence.

Try to create a yes–no question out of a sentence that is suspect. (See Chapter 6 for details on yes–no question formation.) If that structure is not a complete sentence, you will be unable to do so. Example:

The person who was sitting in the corner. → [Cannot make a yes–no question]

The person who was sitting in the corner is my cousin. → Is the person who was sitting in the corner your cousin? [No problem]

I tell my students to make whichever test works better for them their primary test and to use the other as a backup if uncertainties persist.

Here, once again, are some student examples from years gone by. Try both tests on them to see how they feel:

1. Who you are and what you are.
2. After the jetpack and the lower arms are welded on the robot.
3. Trying to be gentle and not hurt the animal.
4. That one pitch being a fastball.

I let my students know that professional authors use sentence fragments for rhetorical effect when they write—examples pop up regularly in both literary and expository writing. (I have used them occasionally in this text.) However, I caution my students that these writers have considerably more experience than they do and that they should probably wait until they have more exposure before trying it. (I will cover using fragments for rhetorical effect in Chapter 12.)

Joining Sentences "Legally": Bridges

How to join sentences in Standard Written American English is the green-eyed monster that has been historically so difficult to slay. The concept is not new for your students—they have been doing so in an oral environment for many years. The problem, of course, is that in a writing environment, the rules change. I always tell my students that they have to learn to play by the rules if they want to do well in the game of writing. I didn't make up the rules, but I do know them, and I do enforce them.

I will take you through a seven-step, inquiry-based approach to the problem, "penciling in" suggested answers. This approach isn't a magic bullet. It does not work overnight to rid student writing of sentence boundary errors. Again, we are trying to build Sentence Wizards—procedural knowledge that can only be created across time with meaningful exposure. However, the approach *does work*: I have had student after student tell me throughout the years that, for the first time, they truly understand. Some of them get it quickly; others take about a semester. Their writing and their ability to repair problems bear evidence that they have truly internalized the concepts.

Expect to spend 5 to 10 minutes to complete each of the following steps; follow-up and homework take an additional 10 to 20 minutes. I prefer to work through each of the data sets in class. Sometimes I lead the analysis, soliciting answers to the questions from the whole class. Other times I have them work in small groups to come up with consensus answers, usually allotting 3 to 5 minutes to complete the task. You can, of course, assign the questions as homework or use them as class work. Once the questions have been answered, I lead a discussion that explains the issue(s).

As you read through the seven steps, keep the following in mind: You are receiving all of this information in a condensed manner. You probably will not reflect on the new concepts across several days, manipulate the data very much, or do the recommended exercises and activities so as to strengthen the new relationships. When you present this approach to your students across time (usually 2 to 3 weeks), however, they will do all of the above. They like playing language detectives as they solve the problems that are presented, and *they will get it*, many of them for the first time.

Step 1: Connectors[1]

Explain the following concept to your students: In any language, sentences are not joined together randomly; they are joined together because a relationship exists between them. An absolutely inviolable rule (a rarity in language) is as follows:

> **RULE:** When two sentences are combined, the relationship between the two sentences *must be* expressed.

For example, here are two sentences:

> I had an accident. I bought a new car.

I want to join them into one sentence in my essay. Answer the following questions by examining the sentences that are contained in the data set in Table 9.1. The answers are "penciled" in for your benefit—they are not given to the students.

1. Fill in the relationship that is expressed by each of the five sentences. *See Table 9.1.*

2. Two of the five sentences violate our new rule. Which sentences are they? *4 & 5*

3. Three of the five sentences follow the new rule. Underline the words that were added in order to make them conform. *so, after, then*

4. The main purpose of this exercise is to introduce you to a new term: *connector*. Based on your analysis of the data, how would you define this term? *Words that show the relationship between sentences.*

Table 9.1 Bridge Data: Step 1

#	New Sentence	Relationship
1	I had an accident, so I bought a new car.	*Cause/effect or result*
2	After I had an accident, I bought a new car.	*Time—accident first*
3	I bought a new car, and then I had an accident.	*Time—accident second*
4	I had an accident I bought a new car.	*None*
5	I had an accident, I bought a new car.	*None*

---

[1] I have created PowerPoints in support of each of the seven steps in this chapter. They are available at http://BrainBasedWriting.com/6.html.

Discussion Here are the main points to hit when you discuss this concept:

- You cannot join two sentences with nothing. Doing so violates the basic rule—no relationship is expressed.
- You cannot join two sentences with a comma. Doing so violates the basic rule—no relationship is expressed.
- Certain words are used when you join sentences. These words show the reader what the relationship is between the two sentences.
- Words that show the relationship between sentences are called *connectors*.

Follow-Up/Homework Prepare 10 to 15 sentences, many of which are well-formed, but include some that have comma splices and run-ons in the mix. The students' job is to underline the connectors in each sentence or to note those sentences that have no connectors. Do not ask them to repair the bad ones yet.

Step 2: Bridges and Nonbridges

Examine the data in Table 9.2 and answer the questions that follow:

1. In Table 9.2, sentences 1 and 2 are good sentences. What happened in sentence 3 to make it bad? *Two sentences were joined with nothing.*
2. Whatever was added in sentence 4 didn't help very much. What was added? *A comma.*
3. In terms of joining two sentences together, what conclusions can you draw from sentence 3? From sentence 4? *Can't join sentences without a connector. Can't join sentences with a comma.*
4. What happened in sentence 5 to make it good? *Added "but"*

Table 9.2 Bridge Data: Step 2

#	Sentence	Analysis
1	John likes Mary.	Good
2	Mary doesn't like John.	Good
3	John likes Mary Mary doesn't like John.	Bad
4	John likes Mary, Mary doesn't like John.	Bad
5	John likes Mary, but Mary doesn't like John.	Good
6	John likes Mary, however, Mary doesn't like John.	Bad

5. *Extra Credit:* Why do you think sentence 6 is bad?[2] (See footnote.)

6. What conclusions can you draw about joining sentences from the above evidence? (See Discussion.)

Discussion Here are the main points to hit:

- You cannot simply stick two sentences together (sentence 3). (Doing so creates a run-on sentence.)
- You cannot join two sentences with just a comma (sentence 4). (Doing so creates a comma splice.)
- In order to join two sentences together, you have to add a connector (sentences 5 and 6).
- However, you cannot simply pick any connector that you want. Some connectors work (*but* in sentence 5); others don't (*however* in sentence 6).

Definition of Terms

Connector: a device that shows the relationship between two clauses

Bridge: any *connector* that allows you to join two clauses "legally"

In the data set in Table 9.2, we see that both *but* and *however* are connectors; however, only *but* is a bridge. The following statements are true:

- All bridges are connectors. (Example: *but*)
- Not all connectors are bridges. (Example: *however*)

We now come to the most important rule of all:

> **RULE:** When two sentences are combined, a bridge is *always* required.

Why isn't *however* a bridge? Or better yet, how can you tell whether or not a word is a bridge? Stay tuned for further details.[3]

Follow-Up/Homework There is no homework yet. Just be sure to hammer home the following:

---

[2]This is a hard question. I am trying to get the students to say something like, "For whatever reason, you can't use *however* to join two sentences together." Sometimes they do; sometimes they don't. Either way, I'm happy.

[3]I have had participants in workshops who were very disturbed at the prospect of leaving questions unanswered in a lesson. I am not the least bit unhappy: As stated earlier, curiosity is the brain's aphrodisiac. Curiosity that is later resolved leaves much deeper memory traces than a mere recitation of reasons or facts.

In the next few steps, we will accomplish the following, with the aid of your Sentence/Grammar Wizards:

1. Develop two different categories of bridges.
2. Discover a way to test whether or not a word or phrase is a bridge.

If you can grasp these two concepts, you will begin to see comma splices, run-ons, and fragments disappear from your writing!

Step 3: Center Bridges (Coordinating Conjunctions)

Ask your students to answer the following questions:

1. John likes Mary, but Mary doesn't like John. (Good)
   a. Is *but* a bridge? Yes. How do you know? Two clauses are joined and the result is marked "Good." Or You told us that it was a bridge in the previous step.
   b. Is it OK to switch the clauses around? No.

   John likes Mary, but Mary doesn't like John.

   But Mary doesn't like John, John likes Mary.

   c. Is it OK to move *but* someplace else within its own sentence (that is, to the right)? No.

   John likes Mary, Mary but doesn't like John.
   John likes Mary, Mary doesn't but like John.

2. John likes Mary, and Mary likes John. (Good)
   a. Answer the same questions (a, b, and c above) about *and* in sentence 2. (All of the answers are the same.)
   b. Based on the above data, what conclusion can you draw about the *position* of bridges like *and* and *but* whenever they join clauses? They must be in between the two clauses.

Discussion *But* and *and* are bridges—they can join two sentences together "legally." They can be placed in only one position: exactly between the two clauses. Because these connectors are bridges, and because they must be placed between the two clauses, let's call them **center bridges**. (Traditional grammar calls them *coordinating conjunctions*.)[4] The pattern is as follows:

---

[4]It is important to reinforce the connection between the new name and the traditional one. Students will understand and relate to *center bridge*, but most of their future English teachers and books will use the traditional name (coordinating conjunction).

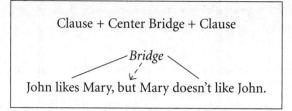

Clause + Center Bridge + Clause

John likes Mary, but Mary doesn't like John.

Summary

- Bridges contain the grammatical "cement" to allow you to combine two sentences (or clauses) into one sentence.
- Both *and* and *but* are center bridges (coordinating conjunctions).
- Center bridges *cannot* be moved. They must be at the boundary between the two clauses.

Step 4: Center Bridges (Continued)

Explain to your students that each of the following sentences is good because it contains a center bridge (coordinating conjunction). Instruct them to write the center bridge for each sentence in the blank. When they finish, they will have a list of all the center bridge words in English.

1. John went to town, for he had forgotten his medicine. <u>for</u>
2. John went to town, and Mary stayed home. <u>and</u>
3. John didn't go to town, nor did Mary. <u>nor</u>
4. John went to town, but Mary stayed home. <u>but</u>
5. John had to take his medicine, or he would get sick. <u>or</u>
6. John went to town, yet Mary stayed home. <u>yet</u>
7. John went to town, so Mary stayed home. <u>so</u>

Now, ask your students to answer these questions about center bridges (coordinating conjunctions):

1. If you take the first letter of each of these center bridges and put them together, they sort of spell a word. What is it? FANBOYS
2. What is the maximum number of letters in a FANBOYS bridge? Three.
3. If you see a connector that has more than three letters, what can you say about it? It isn't a center bridge.

Note: From this point forward, the class and I refer to center bridges as FANBOYS bridges or simply **FANBOYS**.

Follow-Up/Homework Let students practice deciding whether sentences are good or bad by locating clauses and center bridges (coordinating conjunctions):

- Be sure to include a couple of simple sentences to reinforce the concept that a bridge is required only to join multiple clauses.
- Since all coordinating conjunctions function in English in other roles, include a sentence or two that use FANBOYS in a nonbridge capacity. (See Table 9.8 near the end of this chapter for examples.) Reinforce: *It isn't a bridge unless it joins two clauses.*
- Let students repair the bad sentences by adding a FANBOYS.

Our question remains: Why isn't *however* a bridge? Keep going—we will answer that question soon.

Step 5: Swinging Bridges (Subordinating Conjunctions)

Ask your students to answer the following questions:

1. John stopped eating because he was full. (Good)
   a. Is *because* a bridge? Why or why not? Yes, because two clauses are joined and the result is marked "Good."
   b. Is it OK to switch the clauses? Yes.

      John stopped eating <u>because he was full</u>.

      <u>Because he was full</u>, John stopped eating.

   c. How is this bridge different from a center bridge? A center bridge cannot be moved to the front of the sentence—it must be between the clauses.
   d. Is it possible to move *because* to any other position within its own clause? For example, is the following acceptable? No.

      John stopped eating *because* he was full. →
      *John stopped eating he was *because* full.

2. Answer questions 1a, b, c (above) about the connector *whenever* in the following sentence:

   John takes a nap whenever he is tired. (Good)

   All of the answers are the same.

3. Based on the above data, what conclusion can you draw about the position of bridges like *because* and *whenever* in a sentence? They can be in two positions: between the clauses or at the front of the sentence.

Discussion This type of bridge can be moved *as long as the clause to which it is attached moves with it.* However, this type of bridge must always be at the beginning of its clause—*it cannot move within its own clause (i.e., to the right).* We will see why this fact is important later.

Since this type of connector can "swing" from the beginning of a sentence

Whenever he is tired, John takes a nap.

to the middle of a sentence

John takes a nap *whenever* he is tired.

we call these **swinging bridges**. (Traditional grammar calls them *subordinating conjunctions*.) The patterns are as follows:

Clause + Swinging Bridge + Clause

John takes a nap *whenever* he is tired.

OR

Swinging Bridge + Clause, Clause

Whenever he is tired, John takes a nap.

Note: Students do not need to memorize a list of swinging bridges. In the final two steps, we will develop two very reliable Grammar Wizard Tests, either of which will allow students to identify swinging bridges on the fly.

Follow-Up/Homework Students now need two activities to reinforce this concept:

1. Create a short essay that contains several different swinging bridges. Require students to find them—not to memorize them, just to find them. Be sure to include swinging bridges in both positions in the short essay.

2. Give students sentences, a couple of which are well-formed, but most of which have missing swinging bridges (i.e., comma splices or run-ons). Be careful to avoid conjunctive adverbs (*however, nevertheless,* etc.)—they are covered next. Ask them to use swinging bridges to fix the improperly formed sentences.

So . . . why isn't *however* a bridge? We answer that question in the next two steps—keep reading!

Table 9.3 Bridge Data: Step 6

#	Sentence	Analysis
1A	John likes Mary, *however,* Mary doesn't like John.	Bad
1B	John likes Mary; *however,* Mary doesn't like John.	Good
1C	John likes Mary. *However,* Mary doesn't like John.	Good

Step 6: Floating Connectors (Conjunctive Adverbs)

Ask your students to look at Table 9.3 and then answer these questions:

1. Why is sentence 1A "Bad"? In other words, what grammatical ingredient is it missing? There is no bridge.
2. What is added in sentence 1B to make it change from "Bad" to "Good"? A semi-colon.
3. Is a semi-colon (;) a bridge? How do you know? Yes. 1B contains two clauses that are joined together and the result is "Good."
4. Is a semi-colon a center bridge or a swinging bridge? Center bridge—it must be placed between the two clauses.
5. The data set shows that there are two ways to make a nonbridge connector work grammatically. What are they? Use a semi-colon or don't join the two sentences—use a period.

Discussion There exists a rather large category of connectors that cannot be used as bridges. If you want to join two clauses using one of these nonbridge connectors, then you must either make a new sentence or provide a bridge—usually a semi-colon, which is a center bridge.[5]

I still haven't answered the million-dollar question: Why isn't *however* a bridge? Let's examine the non-bridge connector to see what makes it different from a center or swinging bridge.

Step 7: Floating Connectors (Conjunctive Adverbs, Continued)

Ask your students to examine Table 9.4 and then answer these questions:

1. What does the evidence show you insofar as the mobility of connectors (bridge vs. nonbridge) is concerned? Nonbridge connectors are movable; bridges are not movable.

---

[5]Both dashes and colons can also function as bridges.

Table 9.4 Bridge Data: Step 7

#	Nonbridge Connector	Analysis
1A	John likes Mary; *however,* Mary doesn't like John.	Good
1B	John likes Mary; Mary, *however,* doesn't like John.	Good
1C	John likes Mary; Mary doesn't like John, *however.*	Good
	Center Bridge	
2A	John likes Mary, *but* Mary doesn't like John.	Good
2B	John likes Mary, Mary *but* doesn't like John.	Impossible
2C	John likes Mary, Mary doesn't like John *but.*	Impossible
	Swinging Bridge	
3A	John likes Mary, *although* Mary doesn't like John.	Good
3B	John likes Mary, Mary *although* doesn't like John.	Impossible
3C	John likes Mary, Mary doesn't like John *although.*	Impossible

2. Based on the evidence, in which direction can a nonbridge connector move? To the right.

3. So . . . why isn't *however* a bridge? It can move to the right.

4. Based on the above evidence, what rule can you come up with that would allow you to determine whether or not a connector is a bridge? If a connector can move to the right, it isn't a bridge.

Discussion There are three types of connectors in English: center (*FANBOYS* + semi-colon), swinging (*although, because,* etc.), and nonbridge connectors, as shown above. Nonbridge connectors differ from center and swinging bridge connectors in one important way:

■ This type of connector can be moved to different locations *within its own clause*—that is, to the right. *Only nonbridge connectors have this ability.*

Because it can move, this type of connector can *never* be a bridge. It makes sense when you think about it: How can something that isn't connected serve as a bridge? It might not be there when you need it!

Let's call this third type of connector a **floating connector**—it can float to one or more positions to the right. (Traditional grammar calls them *conjunctive adverbs.*)

We can express this concept as a rule:

> **RULE:** A floating connector is *never* a bridge.

If you can "teach" your Grammar Wizard this single fact, you will remove forever a primary source of comma splices and run-ons.

We now have two new Grammar Wizard Tests:

> **Sentence Wizard Test for a Swinging Bridge—the Floating Test:** If a word or phrase can float to a different position within its clause (to the right), it is *not* a bridge.

> **Sentence Wizard Test for a Swinging Bridge—the Movement Test:** If you can move the word or phrase + its clause from the middle of the sentence to the front (and vice versa), it *is* a bridge.

Let's try all of this out on a few sentences:

- The word *then* is often the cause of problems for student writers. Is it a bridge? Let's find out by examining Table 9.5.
- The word *therefore* is also a frequent flyer over these troubled waters. Look at Table 9.6.
- Now let's try it with *although*. (See Table 9.7.)

Table 9.5 Bridge Test with "Then"

GW Test	Evidence	Result	Bridge?
Test Sentence: I got out of bed, **then** I discovered the problem.			
Does it float?	I got out of bed, I **then** discovered the problem. OR I got out of bed, I discovered the problem **then**.	Yes—it floats.	NO!
Does it move with its clause?	*****Then** I discovered the problem, I got out of bed.	No—it cannot move with its clause.	NO!
Solutions: I got out of bed, **and then** I discovered the problem. (Add FANBOYS *and*) OR I got out of bed; **then** I discovered the problem. (Add semi-colon)			

Table 9.6 Bridge Test with "Therefore"

GW Test	Evidence	Result	Bridge?
Test Sentence: The battery was dead, **therefore,** the car would not start.			
Does it float?	The battery was dead, the car, **therefore**, would not start. OR The battery was dead, the car would not start, **therefore**.	Yes—it floats.	NO!
Does it move with its clause?	*__Therefore__, the car would not start, the battery was dead.	No—it cannot move with its clause.	NO!
Solutions: The battery was dead, **so** the car would not start. (Replace *therefore* with *so*) The battery was dead**; therefore**, the car would not start. (Add semi-colon)			

Table 9.7 Bridge Test with "Although"

GW Test	Evidence	Result	Bridge?
Test Sentence: He drowned **although** the water was shallow.			
Does it float?	*He drowned the water **although** was shallow. OR *He drowned the water was shallow **although**.	No—it does not float to the right.	YES!
Does it move with its clause?	**Although** the water was shallow, he drowned.	Yes—it moves with its clause.	YES!
Solutions: None needed—the two clauses are joined by a bridge.			

There are two notes to make about the "floatability" of a connector:

1. Both of the negative examples, *then* and *therefore*, have connectors that can float to two or more locations. Floating to two or more locations is not a requirement. If the connector can float to *any other single position to the right*, that connector is not a bridge.

2. A connector may *sound better* in one position over the other, but that's not the issue. The issue is whether it is *possible* for it to float to any other position to the right. As illustrated with *although*, your Grammar Wizard will quickly reject any attempt to float a bridge to the right. There will be no doubt.

Figure 9.1 Connectors

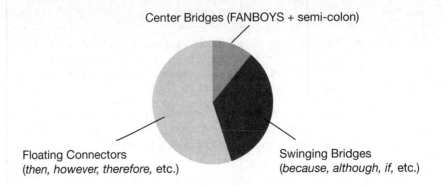

Summary

Connectors show how one clause relates to the next. There are three types (see Figure 9.1):

1. *Center Bridges (Coordinating Conjunctions + semi-colons):*
   - These connectors are FANBOYS (*for, and, nor, but, or, yet, so*) and semi-colons.
   - They must be placed precisely where one clause ends and the next one begins.
   - They are attached to both clauses: *They cannot be moved at all.*

2. *Swinging Bridges (Subordinating Conjunctions):*
   - These connectors are attached only to the clause that follows them.
   - They can move *with the clause to which they are attached*, but they cannot otherwise be moved.

3. *Floating Connectors (Conjunctive Adverbs):*
   - These connectors are *never* bridges.
   - They are *contained* by a clause, but they are not *attached* to a single position within it.
   - They can, therefore, float within their own clauses (i.e., to the right).

Terminology

When I do workshops that incorporate the Bridge Approach, I occasionally encounter people who understand the traditional approach perfectly well and are resistant to change, especially any change in terminology. Why did I opt to change the traditional terminology, knowing full well that other texts and teachers would not be using it?

1. Traditional terminology does nothing to communicate how things work.
2. The traditional approach contains breakdowns that only confuse the issue:

- *Comma Splices, Run-Ons, and Fragments*: These three errors are nothing more than surface manifestations of a single underlying error: a *subject-verb (S-V) bridge error*:

   Comma Splice: The sentence is missing a bridge.

   Run-On: The sentence is missing a bridge.

   Fragment: The sentence has one bridge too many (connects to nothing) OR the sentence is missing a subject and/or verb.

   So, when I mark student compositions, the notation that I use for any of the three traditional errors is *S-V Bridge*. With the Bridge Approach, any exercise that requires students to identify which of the three surface manifestations is present in a given sentence is a waste of time.

- *Simple, Compound, Complex, and Compound/Complex*: If the objective is to provide a method for students to classify sentences, then fine—this is one way. If, however, the intent is to improve student writing, these efforts are misguided. This classification system is so far removed from how we actually *think* about language that it is rendered virtually useless as an aid to composition. How often do *you* analyze your writing according to this breakdown?

- *Independent versus Dependent Clause*: This issue has plagued students for decades, if not centuries. As was shown at the beginning of this chapter, the definitions are circular. There are important rhetorical issues inherent in this distinction (see Kolln [2007]), but the two concepts do not make a very significant contribution to the understanding of sentence boundaries.

- *Coordination vs. Subordination*: Again, this distinction has rhetorical implications (see Kolln [2007]); otherwise, it is an unnecessary complication. When working on sentence boundaries in writing, there is no reason to introduce this breakdown—save it for later.

Recursiveness and Elaboration

As is true of any new area of knowledge, repeated exposure across time is a key component.

Exercises

Provide a variety of exercises that attack the issue from different perspectives:

- Give students pairs of sentences and three or four different connectors for each. Have them join the sentences using each of the connectors, adding punctuation as required. Example:

The axe has a short memory. The tree never forgets. (*however, but, although, on the other hand*)

Include a variety of relationships (time, contrast, conditional [if–then], addition). Occasionally ask students to *prove* to you that a certain connector is or is not a bridge—even if the answer they give is perfectly well formed.

- Give students pairs of sentences and have them join the sentences with connectors that they come up with—either chosen from a table of options or, later on, from their heads.

- Have students edit short essays that you have salted with several bridge errors.

- Here is an exercise that I have used with great success:

  1. Ask students to copy and paste 10 sentences from the Internet that contain bridges. Warn them to watch out for nonbridge FANBOYS—they don't count. (See Table 9.8 for examples.)

  2. Ask them to number the sentences, and print out the result.

  3. Then ask them to replace most (but not all) of the bridges in their sentences with a combination of commas, spaces, and floating connectors and print out the resulting "exercise."

  4. Working in pairs, have students exchange the erroneous papers so that they can repair each other's sentences. The original versions serve as answer keys.

Table 9.8 FANBOYS in Nonbridge Usages

Word	Nonbridge Usage	Example
for	Can be a preposition	■ He bought it *for* me.
and	Can join all sorts of nonbridge elements	■ John *and* I ■ eat *and* drink
nor	Can join nonbridge elements	■ Neither John *nor* I wanted to go.
but	Can mark excluded elements	■ nothing *but* the best
or	Can join non-bridge elements	■ John *or* I will be there.
yet	Can be an adverb	■ He hasn't gone *yet*.
so	Can be an adverb, adjective, or substitute	■ I think *so*. ■ He said things that were not *so*. ■ I told you *so*.

Graphic Representations

As was previously discussed, representing newly learned information visually brings in additional sensory channels and aids in long-term retention. Here are some suggested possibilities:

- Have students make graphic representations of a center bridge, a swinging bridge, and a floating connector in action.
- Have students do a Venn diagram contrasting bridges with floating connectors (nonbridges). See Figure 9.2 for one possible example.
- Have students do a Venn diagram contrasting center bridges with swinging bridges. See Figure 9.3 for one possible example.

Figure 9.2 Venn Diagram: Bridges versus Floating Connectors

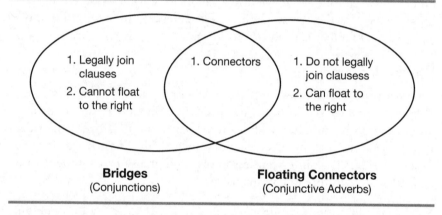

Figure 9.3 Venn Diagram: FANBOYS versus Swinging Bridges

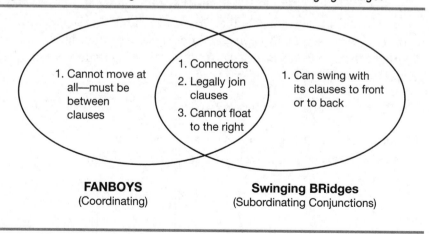

Literature

Occasionally, out of the blue, ask the class questions about specific sentences in whatever the class is reading. Here are some example areas:

- Prove via a Grammar Wizard Test whether a specific sentence containing a bridge is written correctly.
- Ask the students why they think the author put a swinging bridge clause at the beginning of a sentence and what would be the effect of moving it to the end.
- Point out a FANBOYS word and ask whether or not that word is being used as a bridge.

Student Writing

Students will continue to make bridge errors for a while—sometimes quite a while—as they write. Gather their sentences (anonymously) into an exercise of authentic problems to solve.

Bridge Commas

Comma usage with clauses is often a troublesome area for students. However, when viewed from the perspective of what the *reader* needs in order to smoothly process the data on the page, comma usage with bridges is *very logical*. Explaining this logic not only provides another way for you to spiral bridges back into your lesson plans but it also helps students truly *understand* this feature of comma usage:

Center Bridges (FANBOYS)

The words that comprise the FANBOYS group are used all over the place in nonbridge capacities. See Table 9.8 for examples. When a FANBOYS word is used as a bridge, wouldn't it be nice if writers could signal readers so that they could chunk the data accordingly? Well, writers can and *should* send this signal—by putting a comma in front of the FANBOYS bridge. Look at the following examples from the perspective of a proficient reader:

1a. I bought flowers for Mary and [GUESS].

- *Another Person*: I bought flowers for Mary and Martha.
- *Another Verb*: I bought flowers for Mary and gave them to her yesterday.

■ *Another Item*: I bought flowers for Mary and candy for Martha.

> 1b. I bought flowers for Mary, and [GUESS].

■ *Another Clause*: I bought flowers for Mary, and I gave them to her yesterday. OR
I bought flowers for Mary, and Jerry bought her some candy.

Because of the comma, only one GUESS is possible. Thus is born a simple, logical rule:

> **RULE:** Always put a comma in front of a FANBOYS bridge.

Whenever readers come across a comma + a FANBOYS, their Grammar Wizards will know that they are at the end of a clause. They need to chunk the information accordingly and set up for a new clause. There are two exceptions to this rule:

1. If the two clauses are short and balanced (of fairly equal length), the comma is optional because the reader can pick up the clausal structure easily. Example:

   I told her and she listened.

2. A comma may, optionally, be placed in front of *and* in a series. However, Grammar Wizards will have already recognized the fact that a series is being processed, so they will not misinterpret the signal: This comma marks the end of the series.

Swinging Bridges Sending the proper signals to readers is once again the issue.

■ If the swinging bridge clause comes first, then a comma is always needed. Readers need to be able to see where the swinging bridge clause ends and the main clause begins so that they can chunk appropriately. (Remember evil Sam versus best friend Sam in Chapter 8?) Speakers will always put a voice comma here for their listeners; readers need similar assistance.

■ If the swinging bridge clause comes last, no comma is needed normally. Look at the following example:

> 2. He went to town because [GUESS].

There is only one possibility: a new clause. In sharp contrast to FANBOYS words, swinging bridge words are used almost exclusively as bridges. Therefore, they, *by themselves*, serve as excellent signals to chunk the previous information as complete clauses.

The swinging bridge comma rule, therefore, is also borne of logic:

> **RULE:** If a swinging bridge clause is first, put a comma between the clauses.
> If it isn't, don't.

The exception to this rule is usually rhetorical in nature, driven by the desire to force a different reading on the sentence. Look at the following examples:

> 3a. John bought a new car even though he couldn't afford one.
> 3b. John bought a new car, even though he couldn't afford one.

The first sentence, without the comma, invites a straight-through, matter-of-fact reading. The second sentence, with the comma, forces the reader to pause, thereby emphasizing the swinging bridge clause. I'll go into more detail about this comma usage in Chapter 11.

Discussion Questions

1. Review your answers to the true–false questions at the beginning of this chapter. Have you changed any of your answers?

2. Create a graphic that demonstrates how the circular definitions inherent in TGP explanations of how to join sentences are a source of confusion.

3. How would you explain the difference between a *center bridge* (*FANBOYS*) and a *swinging bridge* to a friend who was having difficulties in this area?

4. Explain how the concept of *voice period* is better than the TGP definition of a sentence when helping students know where one sentence ends and the next one begins.

5. Two Sentence Wizard Tests were given for helping students spot fragments. Which one do you prefer and why?

6. Support the following statement with some examples: All *bridges* are *connectors*, but not all *connectors* are *bridges*.

7. Why should teachers treat the semi-colon as a *FANBOYS*?

8. Two Sentence Wizard Tests were given for helping students know whether a word or phrase was a *swinging bridge* or a *floating connector*. Which one do you prefer and why?

9. When are commas required for *swinging bridge clauses*?

10. From the reader's perspective, why is it important to provide a comma before a *FANBOYS*? After a *swinging bridge clause*?

## chapter 10

Sentence Fluency

True or False?

1. Most of your students already have a well-developed sense of good written style.

2. The main clause of a sentence makes the greatest contribution to the reader's perception of good style.

3. Structures that begin or end with voice commas make the greatest contribution to the reader's perception of good style.

4. If a passage is grammatically correct, but lacks good style, it will sound childish.

5. Students are in receptive control of the vast majority of the structures that professional writers use to create a sophisticated writing style.

6. Deciding where a movable structure best fits cannot normally be made out of context.

7. It is possible for a well-written sentence to have two voice periods.

8. Readers will be impressed by the writer's style if all of the sentences are long and complex.

Sentence Fluency Definition

Sentence fluency contributes to a piece of writing in these ways:

1. Words and phrases combine to make easily processed sentences.
2. These sentences then flow smoothly from one to the next.
3. Sentence structures and sentence lengths vary across the writing to keep it interesting.

These factors combine to make a passage that is both engaging and easy to process. Writing something that is effortless for proficient readers to process is critical: This kind of writing allows the writer to sneak in beneath the readers' radar and take control of their brains. If readers become overly aware of the writer's presence while reading (except, perhaps, to admire her style), the writer has failed. Sentence fluency plays a major role in making the writer "invisible."

In this chapter, we will primarily look at ways to create sentence structures that add elegance and sophistication to one's writing. Doing so often helps with tying sentences together, thereby making a piece more cohesive and coherent.

Sentence Wizards Revisited

By the time students reach middle school or, at the latest, high school, most of them have read sentences numbering well into the hundreds of thousands, both in literature and in texts from a variety of content areas. Most of the academic material to which they have been exposed has been written by professional authors and/or edited by professional editors. The net result is that they have had considerable exposure to well-written material. This type of varied, meaningful exposure practically guarantees that they have developed a sense of, or a feel for, good style. In other words, students have, as a part of their Sentence Wizards, some intuitive judgment about sentence structures that sound mature.

The following classroom activity—an activity that I have done many times with middle school, high school, and college students—supports this assertion. One at a time, I unveil the following four versions of the same text, asking the students the same question after each:

Version 1: I ate my lunch. I went to the park. I played with my friends. We had a great time.

What grade would you guess the writer is in? Consensus: 2nd or 3rd grade

Version 2: I ate my lunch and I went to the park. I played with my friends and we had a great time.

What grade would you guess the writer is in? Consensus: 4th or 5th grade

Version 3: After I ate my lunch, I went to the park. I played with my friends and had a great time.

What grade would you guess the writer is in? Consensus: middle school

Version 4: After eating lunch, I went to the park and played with my friends; we had a great time.

What grade would you guess the writer is in? Consensus: high school or college

I then engage students in a conversation that goes something like this:

Me: I wrote all four of these versions. What did I do to cause this writer to mature before your very eyes? How did I create the impression of an increase in sophistication?

Students: [Confused silence]

Me: Did I change the vocabulary?

Students: No.

Me: What did I change?

Students: The sentences—you joined them together differently.

Me: What you are referring to is called *sentence structure*, a feature that plays a very important role in how readers judge a writer's style and maturity. In fact, it is one of the most important factors that readers use to make such judgments. Vocabulary certainly contributes, but it is not as critical as sentence structure. I'm going to show you a few basic things that you can do to help create this same impression on *your* readers.

Classroom Activity Ask the class to help you create a short passage in simple sentences like Version 1. Then work as a class or in small groups to make the writer appear to be more and more mature as you create three or four additional versions of the same story, retaining most of the vocabulary of the original, but varying the sentence structure and punctuation.

So, you ask yourself, if our students have fairly well-developed Sentence Wizards by the time they are in middle or high school, if they can distinguish between well-written and poorly written material, why don't they, themselves, produce more sophisticated writing? The answer is that most students have a well-developed *receptive* sense of stylistic maturity: They know it when they see it—they just don't know how to *produce* it yet. (See Chapter 7 for a more detailed examination.) Just as their Grammar Wizards do not provide conscious awareness of the inner workings of the grammar system that they know so well (as we saw in Chapter 2), their Sentence Wizards do not provide conscious awareness of the components that comprise a sophisticated style. The situation is somewhat analogous to the art world: I am able to distinguish between a professional painting and an amateurish one, but that ability most certainly does not mean that I am capable of producing the former.

Once they learn to read well, most students only occasionally struggle with a sentence or reading passage due to *structural* complexities; if they struggle with a reading passage, it is usually due to vocabulary deficits and/or content complexity. So it is safe to conclude that most students are in receptive control of the *structures* that comprise a mature style. We should take full advantage of this valuable resource in the composition classroom. We should

1. Make students consciously aware of the structures that good writers use.
2. Help students recognize these structures when they read them.
3. Guide students as they attempt to gain productive control over them.

In Chapters 7 and 9, we examined the principal structures that professional authors use, showing how the structures are formed, how to present them, and how to reinforce them. These structures are as follows:

- Participle Phrases
- Gerund Phrases
- Appositive Phrases
- Infinitive Phrases
- Parallelism
- Near Clauses (Nominative Absolutes)
- Adjectives Out of Order
- Swinging Bridge (Subordinate) Clauses
- Floating Connectors (Conjunctive Adverbs)

Additional grammatical structures certainly exist in English, but they do not normally make as great a contribution to the impression of stylistic maturity—a position that I will support below.

The Christensen Perspective

Francis Christensen, an English professor at the University of Southern California in the mid-1900s, was a true pioneer in the field of composition analysis. His methods were primitive by today's standards, but the results that they produced were spot on. He maintained, "If [English teachers] are not to inflict on our students our subjective impressions, we must look outside ourselves for standards—to authority or to the practice of professional writers" (Christensen and Christensen, 2007, p. 52). So he placed jars on his desk, each one labeled with the name of a grammatical construction. He then spent hour after untold hour reading a fairly wide variety of literary and expository material. Every time he would come across one of the named structures, he would drop a bean in the proper jar. When a jar filled up, he would dump out the beans, count them, and enter the total in a spreadsheet (manually, of course—desktop computers were decades away). After several years of data collection, he had a good handle on the structural components of good writing.

His conclusion was very clear and straightforward: The main clause (i.e., the subject and predicate) serves as the foundation for good sentences; however, the hallmark of good writing comes from things that are *added to the main clause*—**free modifiers**, as he called them.

In one of his essays, Christensen provided a crystal-clear example to support his position: "What I have seen of attempts to bring structural grammar to bear on composition usually boils down to the injunction to 'load the patterns.' Thus 'pattern practice' sets students to accreting sentences like this: 'The small boy on the red bicycle who lives with his happy parents on our shady street often coasts down the steep street until he comes to the city park.'" Such a sentence "has no rhythm and hence no life; it is tone-deaf" (Christensen and Christensen, 2007, p. 22).

Christensen later quotes a sentence from Hemingway, whom he calls "the master of the simple sentence" (Christensen and Christensen, 2007, p. 24):

> George was coming down in the telemark position,[1] kneeling, one leg forward and bent, the other trailing, his sticks hanging like some insect's thin legs, kicking up puffs of snow, and finally the whole kneeling, trailing figure coming around in a beautiful right curve, crouching, the legs shot forward and back, the body leaning out against the swing, the sticks accenting the curve like points of light, all in a wild cloud of snow.

Christensen then rightfully observes that "only from the standpoint of school grammar is this a simple sentence" (p. 24).[2]

Anybody could write the main clause of this sentence ("George was coming down in the telemark position")—assuming one knew the meaning of "telemark." The additional modifiers are what give the sentence its flair, its grace, its elegance. Obviously, we do not expect our students to rise to Hemingway's level of writing, nor would such a beautifully descriptive sentence fit comfortably in most nonfiction writing genres. Christensen's point is well taken, however: The entire sentence contains 74 words. The main clause takes up 8 of them; the remaining 66 are in free modifiers. Contrast those numbers with the breakdown of his counterexample, the "small boy" sentence: That sentence is 30 words long, without a

---

[1]Telemark is a body position while snow skiing.
[2]A simple sentence in grammar means that there is only one clause—the main one.

single free modifier. If we can teach our students to use free modifiers, we have taken a huge step in the right direction.

How can we instruct our students on the ins and outs of incorporating these structures without overwhelming them with complex grammatical details? Start off by appealing to their Grammar Wizards and Sentence Wizards, by tapping into what they already know. Two fairly simple generalizations provide a good starting point:

1. Structures that directly contribute to the overall impression of maturity and sophistication (free modifiers) usually require *voice commas* (see Chapter 8).

2. These free modifiers are *not* part of the main clause (thus the commas). They appear in one of three positions:

   a. *Sentence Beginners*: Structures that appear *before* the main clause.

   b. *Sentence Interrupters*: Structures that are inserted *into* the main clause.

   c. *Sentence Expanders*: Structures that are tacked on *after* the main clause.

Sentence Beginners

The most commonly employed technique for achieving sentence variety and sophistication is by occasionally beginning a sentence with a device that requires a voice comma, structures often referred to generically as *introductory elements* (see Chapter 8). Professional writers use them in 25 to 33 percent of their sentences (Christensen and Christensen, 2007, p. 58; Schuster, 2003, p. 121).

Researchers long ago discovered the value of teaching composition students to vary sentence beginnings. For example, in an article about sentence variety written over 50 years ago, Don Wolfe (1950) made the following observation: "When a student opens a sentence with an infinitive phrase or a past participle, we immediately stamp him as more mature in the sense of style than the average student" (p. 396).

Another interesting, albeit small and informal study was conducted by Amy Benjamin ("Syntactical," n.d., p. 1). She analyzed six fifth-grade essays sentence by sentence. She randomly chose three essays that were judged to be well above average and three that were judged to be well below average. Her first research questions was, "What strengths in sentence-writing skills do we find in the writing of students with above average ability?" All three papers in the top set contained some sentences that utilized Sentence Beginners. In sharp contrast, none of the papers in the lower half had even one of them. I am not trying to claim (nor was Amy) that the presence of Sentence Beginners is all that is required in order to make a composition smooth and polished. But they do make a significant contribution to that impression.

The following inquiry-based exercise is an excellent way to begin the instructional process for Sentence Beginners (assuming that you have already covered the material in Chapter 7, Grammar Wizard Toolbox). Tell your students that you are going to show them two versions of the same story. They are to read each and then answer the questions that follow:

Version 1: [1]I went to a garage sale with my friends. [2]I saw an ugly, sun-bleached picture of a horse in a rather neat-looking frame. [3]I took it to pay for it. [4]My friends made fun of me. [5]I wasn't interested in the picture; I was interested only in the frame. [6]I happily paid five dollars for it. [7]My friends thought I had lost my mind. [8]I took my new possession home and removed the picture. [9]I discovered another picture underneath it. [10]My eyes widened in disbelief—it was an original by Norman Rockwell. [11]He is a very famous American artist who is very popular with collectors. [12]I sold the painting at auction for a lot of money. [13]My friends never made fun of me at garage sales again.

Version 2: [1]At a garage sale with my friends, I saw an ugly, sun-bleached picture of a horse in a rather neat-looking frame. [2]When I took it to pay for it, my friends made fun of me. [3]However, I wasn't interested in the picture; I was interested only in the frame. [4]Because I happily paid five dollars for it, my friends thought I had lost my mind. [5]Happy with my purchase, I took my new possession home. [6]To see what was underneath, I removed the old picture. [7]My eyes widening in disbelief, I discovered another picture underneath it—an original by Norman Rockwell. [8]A famous American artist, Rockwell is very popular with collectors. [9]I sold it at auction for a lot of money. [10]Subdued by my success, my friends never made fun of me again at garage sales.

Questions

1. Which passage sounds better? Why?

2. Comment on the style of Version 1:

    a. Does it sound childish? Why or why not?

    b. Does it sound like a professional author wrote it? Why or why not?

    c. Is there anything about the writing that makes it sound repetitive?

3. Answer the same three questions (a. through c.) about Version 2.

4. What is the primary difference between the two versions?

5. Contrast the comma usage in both versions.

The preceding questions will provide some interesting and insightful answers that can give you a good idea about what you need to emphasize in the classroom. Follow the Q&A session with your own observations. Below are the typical points I try to make.

Discussion on Version 1 This version (on page 163) is certainly not childish. In fact, it contains some rather sophisticated features (a semicolon in #5, a compound verb in #8, a dash in #10, and a relative clause in #11). This version quickly becomes repetitive, however, because every sentence begins in a similar manner—with the subject phrase of the sentence. Furthermore, every sentence is approximately the same length. Readers get bored with writing that contains the same sentence pattern and length over and over—the writing begins to sound sing-songy.

Discussion on Version 2 This version (on page 163) isn't God's gift to good writing, but it is certainly better than Version 1. The primary difference is Sentence Beginners: Version 2 contains several sentences that begin with introductory elements; Version 1 has none. (In fact, Version 2 is intentionally overloaded with introductory elements so that it can be used in an exercise that we will go over in a few minutes.) Not only do these Sentence Beginners add variety to the paragraph, but they also help tie the thoughts together so that one flows more readily into the next. They also make the sentences different lengths (e.g., notice how #5 and #9 are much shorter than the others).

Next, hand out Table 10.1 to your students. Go over each Sentence Beginner, reading the examples out loud to demonstrate the voice comma. Ask students to check the Yes box in the final column if they can *easily read and understand* the example(s) or the No box if they cannot. (Only rarely do you have a student who checks any of the No boxes.) The reason you ask them to check the appropriate box is so you can impress on the students that these structures are really nothing new to them—they have been reading them for years. You are just trying to make them aware of the devices and to encourage them to use the devices in their writing.

Classroom Activity Tell your class that Version 2 is intentionally overloaded with Sentence Beginners. It contains at least one example of each of the eight types. Their task is to name each of the Sentence Beginners in Version 2, using Table 10.1 as a resource.

Because it is always important that students understand *why* we teachers want them to do something, explain to your class that there are two very important reasons for them to learn the names of the structures:

1. *The Joshua Tree Syndrome:* Once you learn the name of something, you have power over it. If your class has not read the Joshua tree passage (Chapter 7), I suggest that you do so now.

Table 10.1 Sentence Beginners

#	Device	Definition	Example	Under-standable?
1	Adverb (Word or Phrase)	A word that ends in *–ly*, or words/phrases like *however, therefore, as a result*, etc.	1. *Incidentally,* you need to be careful . . . 2. *In addition,* the survey indicated . . .	☐ Yes ☐ No
2	Swinging Bridge (Subordinate) Clause	A clause that begins with words like *because, if, although*—swinging bridges	*Because Jo had grown up in the mountains,* she knew how to . . .	☐ Yes ☐ No
3	Prepositional Phrase	A phrase that begins with a preposition (*at, of, in, from*, etc.)	*In the back of the room,* I saw an old woman.	☐ Yes ☐ No
4	Participle Phrase	A phrase that begins with an *–ing* or *–ed* form of a verb	1. *Wiggling with impatience,* the child wanted . . . 2. *Filled with fear,* the people ran . . .	☐ Yes ☐ No
5	Infinitive Phrase	A phrase that begins with *to* + a verb. Often, the words *in order* are understood	*To demonstrate the effect of the treatment,* half of the subjects were given . . .	☐ Yes ☐ No
6	Near Clause (Noun Absolute)	A clause with a form of the helping verb *to be* omitted	*Engines roaring loudly,* the cars leapt off of the finish line.	☐ Yes ☐ No
7	Appositive	A noun phrase that further develops another noun phrase	*A very popular band from the 1960s,* the Beatles were pioneers . . .	☐ Yes ☐ No
8	Adjectives Out of Order	One or more adjectives or adjective phrases	*Happy that the ordeal was over,* the victim breathed a sigh of relief.	☐ Yes ☐ No

2. *Reusability:* Most of these same eight structures are also used as Sentence Interrupters and Sentence Expanders. Learning them well now will serve as a good foundation.

Table 10.2 contains the answers to the Classroom Activity exercise.

Recursiveness and Elaboration   Students are now ready to experiment with Sentence Beginners; gradual release of control is critical now.

Voice Commas

■ Review voice commas by providing a passage that omits most (not all) of the Sentence Beginner commas. (Version 2, on page 163 serves nicely as the passage.) Have students put them back in.

Table 10.2 Sentence Beginner Exercise with Answers

#	Sentence Beginner	Device
1	At a garage sale with my friends,	#3: Prep. phrase (two, actually)
2	When I took it to pay for it,	#2: Swinging Bridge Clause
3	However,	#1: Adverb Phrase
4	Because I happily paid five dollars for it,	#2: Swinging Bridge Clause
5	Happy with my purchase,	#8: Adjectives Out of Order
6	To see what was underneath,	#5: Infinitive Phrase
7	My eyes widening in disbelief,	#6: Near Clause
8	A famous American artist,	#7: Appositive
9	N/A	
10	Subdued by my success,	#4: Participle

Sentence Level[3]

- *Separate*: Practice using the various Sentence Beginner devices by giving students sentences to combine or rearrange. Make each Sentence Beginner device a separate exercise. Table 10.3 provides an example for each of the devices.

- *Cumulative Controlled*: Give students sentences to combine or rearrange using all of the devices. Each sentence is marked with the number of the device that you want them to use, keyed to Table 10.1.

- *Cumulative Free*: Give students sentences to combine or rearrange, allowing the students to choose one of the eight devices themselves. Discuss the results.

- *Movable Elements*: Give students sentences, most of which contain at least one element that could be moved to the front to serve as a Sentence Beginner. Have them identify the possibilities, choose one, and move it.

Literature

- Work together as a class, going through passages that the class has read and identifying Sentence Beginners.

- Divide students into teams. Point out Sentence Beginners that appear in a piece of literature that the class has read and have the teams take turns

---

[3]In real life, the decision to combine or rearrange is driven by the rhetorical effect the writer wants to create, which is, in turn, driven by context. Sentence-level exercises are devoid of context by definition, so the manipulation is purely mechanical. Nevertheless, these types of exercises are excellent practice for building basic Sentence Wizard skills.

Table 10.3 Sample Sentence Beginner Exercises

#	Device	Original	Possible Answer
1	Adverb (Word or Phrase)	The Earth revolves around the sun. The Earth also revolves around its axis.	The Earth revolves around the sun. In addition, it revolves around its axis.
2	Swinging Bridge (Subordinate) Clause	Jeremy finished his homework. He then played video games until midnight.	After he finished his homework, Jeremy played video games until midnight.
3	Prepositional Phrase	The reader knows from the beginning of the story that the main character is going to die.	From the beginning of the story, the reader knows that the main character is going to die.
4	Participle Phrase	Many people made the trek to California during the mid-1800s. They hoped to find gold.	Hoping to find gold, many people made the trek to California during the mid-1800s.
5	Infinitive Phrase	The scientists wanted to see if the new medicine was effective. They first tested it on laboratory rats.	To see if the new medicine was effective, the scientists first tested it on laboratory rats.
6	Near Clause (Noun Absolute)	The prisoner decided to make his break. His heart was pounding furiously.	His heart pounding furiously, the prisoner decided to make his break.
7	Appositive	Harry Truman was an unpopular president while in office. He went down in history as one of the best.	An unpopular president while in office, Harry Truman went down in history as one of the best.
8	Adjectives Out of Order	The policeman entered the house. He was brave, but he was cautious.	Brave but cautious, the policeman entered the house.

naming the device that was used. A team gets a point for each correct identification. If one team misidentifies the structure, the other team can "steal" the point with a correct answer.

- Let students find and identify Sentence Beginners individually, as small groups, or as teams in a competition.

- Find effective sentences or short passages that contain Sentence Beginners. Ask students to create their own sentences using the same *structure* as the ones you have targeted, but substituting their own ideas and words.

Student Writing

- Tell students not to worry about Sentence Beginners while writing their first drafts. During revision, ask them to model professional authors. Have them go through their essays and be sure that approximately one out of every three or four sentences has a Sentence Beginner.

There is another very powerful category of beginning structures that I mention only in passing right now. These are sentences that have some element of the main clause moved to the front for emphasis. However, the moved element is usually not separated from the main clause by a written comma and is normally not spoken with a voice comma. Here are three examples taken from the first chapter of *Call of the Wild* by Jack London. Contrast London's original sentences with their nonfronted versions:

1a. *Original:* Here he was born, and here he had lived the four years of his life.

1b. *Nonfronted:* He was born here, and he had lived here the four years of his life.

2a. *Original:* Judge Miller's place, it was called.

2b. *Nonfronted:* It was called Judge Miller's place.

3a. *Original:* So changed was he that the Judge himself would not have recognized him . . .

3b. *Nonfronted:* He was so changed that the Judge himself would not have recognized him . . .

We will discuss this type of pseudo-Sentence Beginner in Chapter 12.

Sentence Interrupters

A Sentence Interrupter is defined as a structure that is inserted into the main clause. Sentence Interrupters are not nearly as common as Sentence Beginners or Sentence Expanders (discussed later in this chapter), but they are most certainly used by the finest of professional authors. In order to qualify as a Sentence Interrupter, the device must require commas to mark where it begins and ends. These written commas normally correspond to voice commas.

As was stated earlier, most of the same eight devices that can be used as Sentence Beginners can also be used as Sentence Interrupters. Table 10.4 provides examples. For consistency, I retain the device number from the original eight.

Follow the same procedure as you did with Sentence Beginners: Read the examples out loud to demonstrate the voice comma and ask students to check the Yes box in the final column if they can *easily read and understand* the example(s) or the No box if they cannot.

Note that Item 3 (Prepositional Phrases) and Item 5 (Infinitive Phrases) have been omitted from the list in Table 10.4 each for its own reason(s).

Table 10.4 Sentence Interrupters

#	Device	Definition	Example	Under-standable?
1	Adverb (Word or Phrase)	A word that ends in *–ly*, or words/phrases like *however, therefore, as a result*, etc.	1. You need to be careful, *incidentally*, about your ID number. 2. The survey indicated, *in addition*, that customer service was poor.	☐ Yes ☐ No
2	Swinging Bridge (Subordinate) Clause	A clause that begins with words like *because, if, although*—swinging bridges	Jo, *because she had grown up in the mountains*, knew how to . . .	☐ Yes ☐ No
4	Participle Phrase	A phrase that begins with an *–ing* or *–ed* form of a verb	1. The child, *wiggling with impatience*, wanted . . . 2. The people, *filled with fear*, ran . . .	☐ Yes ☐ No
6	Near Clause (Noun Absolute)	A clause with a form of the helping verb *to be* omitted.	The cars, *engines roaring loudly*, leapt off of the finish line.	☐ Yes ☐ No
7	Appositive	A noun phrase that further develops another noun phrase	The Beatles, *a very popular band from the 1960s*, were pioneers . . .	☐ Yes ☐ No
8	Adjectives Out of Order	One or more adjectives or adjective phrases	The victim, *happy that the ordeal was over*, breathed a sigh of relief.	☐ Yes ☐ No

■ *Prepositional Phrases:* These structures very commonly occur in the middle of main clauses. However, they do so most often without requiring commas, so they fail to meet our basic requirement. Prepositional phrases will certainly add more detail, but they make little contribution to a reader's impression of stylistic maturity. Let's look again at Christensen's example of a lifeless sentence to demonstrate (cited on page 161 of this book). I have underlined the prepositional phrases that are contained within the main clause:

The small boy on the red bicycle who lives with his happy parents on our shady street often coasts down the steep street until he comes to the city park.

There is nothing *wrong* with the prepositional phrases here; they simply do not have much stylistic pop. Readers see them so often that they will not be impressed by them.

■ *Infinitive Phrases:* There are two problems here. The first is, like prepositional phrases, infinitive phrases are very commonly used inside main clauses without commas and fail, therefore, to meet the basic requirement of a Sentence Interrupter. Look at the following examples:

> 4a. I started *to go to town.*
>
> 4b. I decided *to go to town.*
>
> 4c. I wanted *to go to town.*
>
> 4d. I like *to go to town.*

The second problem is that a true infinitive phrase Sentence Interrupter that requires commas, while possible in English, often feels awkward and, as a result, is rarely used. Note how the example of an infinitive phrase that we used in the Sentence Beginners table feels strange when moved ("legally") inside the main clause:

> 5a. *Original: To demonstrate the effect of the treatment,* half of the subjects were given . . .
>
> 5b. *Moved:* Half of the subjects, *to demonstrate the effect of the treatment,* were given . . .

Two of the Sentence Interrupter structures require further comment:

■ *Swinging Bridge (Subordinate) Clauses:* As we saw in Chapter 7, swinging bridge clauses often come after the main clause, with no intervening comma. This usage is common and certainly valid; however, it does not count as a Sentence Interrupter.

■ *Appositives:* In Sentence Interrupter position, appositives bring up the issue of essential–nonessential once again. (See Chapter 8 for details.) Therefore, you have another opportunity to revisit this concept with your students. Essential appositives fail to satisfy the comma requirement and are, therefore, not considered to be Sentence Interrupters.

Students may very well ask, if the same phrase can be used as a Sentence Beginner or Sentence Interrupter in a sentence (as the Examples columns of Tables 10.1 and 10.4 demonstrate), how can you know where to use it? The answer is very simple: You can't. There are rules that govern whether a structure can move—your Grammar Wizard and Sentence Wizard know them well. But if a structure is movable, there is no hard and fast rule to determine where it best fits. That decision is made based on what *feels* right, what the writer wants the reader to experience or emphasize—a facility that I call one's Rhetorical Wizard. I will return to this movability decision in Chapter 12. For now, let's just acknowledge that the writer has choices with movable structures and concentrate, instead, on getting students to think about them and to manipulate them.

Recursiveness and Elaboration All of the suggestions that applied to skill building with Sentence Beginners also apply to Sentence Interrupters. The only additional practice that students need is working with sentences where the same device could be used as either a Sentence Beginner or a Sentence Interrupter:

- *Decontextualized*: Take sentence-level exercises that the class did for Sentence Beginners and see which ones contain Sentence Beginners that could be Sentence Interrupters. Discuss which position sounds better without discussing context. Next, discuss various contexts that might favor one position over the other.

- *Contextualized*: Gather examples of sentences that contain Sentence Beginners and Sentence Interrupters from the literature that the class is reading. Make the Sentence Beginners and Sentence Interrupters into stand-alone sentences. Give the class enough context to make an informed decision and ask them to recombine the sentences. Then compare the students' versions with the original. (You can, optionally, tell them which device(s) to use with each sentence.) This exercise leads to very rich discussions, putting into words some of the thought processes that a writer goes through during revision. Here are a couple of example sentences, taken from Chapter 1 of Jack London's *Call of the Wild*:

Appositive	Appositive

Original: His father, Elmo, a huge St. Bernard, had been the Judge's inseparable companion.

Separated: [1]His father's name was Elmo. [2]Elmo was a huge St. Bernard. Elmo had been the Judge's inseparable companion.

Context: The author is describing Buck's parents so that the reader could have some general background information about his upbringing.

You could instruct the students to use appositives to combine the sentences or you could let them chose their own devices.

Participle	Participle	Prep. Phrase

Original: Dazed, suffering intolerable pain from throat and tongue, with the life half throttled out of him, Buck attempted to face his tormentors.

Separated: Buck was dazed. He was suffering intolerable pain from throat and tongue. He had had half the life throttled out of him. He attempted to face his tormentors.

Context: Buck had been roped, defeated, tied up, and transported to another place by his kidnappers. The author was trying to show that Buck still had some fight in him, however.

Be sure to include activities for Literature and Student Writing that were suggested earlier under Sentence Beginners. As was stated, sentence-level exercises are good starting points, but the real work is done with fully contextualized, real language—whether it be analyzing professional writing or revising one's own.

Sentence Expanders

Sentence Expanders are devices that professional writers use fairly frequently. This frequency of usage, as you probably know by now, is good news for us writing teachers. Students have been exposed to these structures over and over as they read literature and content area texts. They know what the structures mean and, in an exercise environment, they can quickly learn how to construct them; unfortunately, students rarely think to use them in a free-form writing environment. The very same devices that are used as Sentence Interrupters are also used as Sentence Expanders, a fact that lightens the teaching load considerably. (In the previous sentence, the part after the comma is a Sentence Expander.)

Before a sentence can be classified as having a Sentence Expander in this system, it must satisfy two requirements:

1. When read out loud, the sentence can easily have *two voice periods*.
2. The first voice period is the one that marks the end of the main clause. It is punctuated by a comma (or, less frequently, by a dash).

Look at the following:

The thieves were hiding in the alley, waiting for their next victim.
         Sentence   Sentence Expander

Two facts about Sentence Expanders need amplification: First, as noted previously, intonation is a bit of a slippery animal. I use it, nevertheless, because students have complete mastery over it. Note that the first voice period (after *alley*) could be rendered as a voice comma in speech. That's why requirement 1, above, states that the sentence *can easily have* two voice periods. Your students may prefer one over the other when they read it out loud, but they will quickly admit that either is possible.

Second, this Sentence Expander (a participle phrase), like many of them, is movable. In this example, it can also be used as a Sentence Beginner (before *The thieves*) or as a Sentence Interrupter (after *thieves*). The preferred placement is determined by feel—by one's Rhetorical Wizard, which is explored in Chapter 12. In this example, most people prefer the Sentence Expander position because the sequence of the verbs matches reality: The thieves *hide* before they *wait*.

Table 10.5 Sentence Expanders

#	Device	Definition	Example	Under-standable?
1	Adverb (Word or Phrase)	A word that ends in *–ly*, or words/phrases like *however, therefore, as a result*, etc.	The crowd refused to disperse, *however*.	☐ Yes ☐ No
2	Swinging Bridge (Subordinate) Clause	A clause that begins with words like *because, if, although*—swinging bridges	The child went walking alone in the woods, *even though her parents had told her not to do so*.	☐ Yes ☐ No
4	Participle Phrase	A phrase that begins with an *–ing* or *–ed* form of a verb	The snake coiled in strike position, *rattling its tail in warning*.	☐ Yes ☐ No
6	Near Clause (Noun Absolute)	A clause with a form of the helping verb *to be* omitted	The snake coiled in strike position, *its tail rattling menacingly*.	☐ Yes ☐ No
7	Appositive	A noun phrase that further develops another noun phrase	The fastest land animal is the cheetah, *a creature that can run as fast as 70 mph*.	☐ Yes ☐ No
8	Adjectives out of order	An adjective phrase or multiple adjectives	The victim breathed a sigh of relief, *happy that the ordeal was over*.	☐ Yes ☐ No

Table 10.5 provides examples of the various devices that can be used as Sentence Expanders. For consistency, I retain the device number from the original eight. Items 1 and 2 (Adverb and Swinging Bridge [Subordinate] Clauses) are minor players; participles, near clauses (Noun Absolutes), and appositives are the stars in the Sentence Expander show. Let's look at each device separately.

Adverb These devices are used so commonly that readers will not be very impressed by a writer who uses them.

Swinging Bridge (Subordinate) Clause These structures are in common usage after the main clause, a position that makes them look like Sentence Expanders—but they most often aren't. Look at the following examples:

> 6. I wouldn't do that *if I were you*.
> 7. I went to town *because I was hungry*.

Why aren't these Sentence Expanders? They do not meet either of the requirements: They have only one voice period, and they are not separated from the main clause by a comma. Swinging bridge clauses in this position that require commas are relatively rare. The comma is often used for rhetorical effect—that is, to force the reader to pause and regather momentum. In example sentences 6 and 7 there is absolutely no reason to force such a pause—you certainly wouldn't do so in speech. In example sentences 8 and 9, below, the contrast is made all the more extreme by the commas:

8. Boys and girls grow up in different worlds, even if they live next door to each other.
9. The man was furious at the police, even though they caught him red-handed.

Participle Phrase Participle phrases make powerful Sentence Expanders. Examples of this usage abound in literature. The Hemingway sentence that was quoted by Christensen, for example (page 161), uses three of them, mixed in with other structures. Showing participles in Sentence Expander position also provides an excellent opportunity to revisit troublesome aspects of their usage:

- *Present or Past Participle:* Whether to use a present participle (ending in *–ing*) or a past participle (ending in *–en*) is an issue that will rarely trouble a native speaker, but can be problematic for even advanced non-natives. (See Chapter 7 for details.)

- *Dangling or Misplaced Participle*: As was stated in Chapter 7, the subject of a participle is not stated, so the reader must figure it out. Punctuation (as well as common sense) comes to the rescue here: If there is a comma before the Sentence Expander, the subject of the participle is the subject of the sentence. Otherwise, the subject is the closest noun to the left. Look at the following examples:

10a. The poodle stood behind the tree, shivering in the cold wind. (Clearly the poodle is doing the shivering—trees can't perform that action.)
10b. The poodle stood behind its master, shivering in the cold wind. (Again, the poodle is doing the shivering, even though its master is capable of doing so. Why? The comma very clearly denotes that assignment.)
10c. *The poodle stood behind its master, reading a book. (Common sense tells us that the master is doing the reading, but the comma usage makes the author sound like he is running a deficit in the common sense department.)
10d. I really liked the blue sports car sitting on the showroom floor. (Even though I *could* be doing the sitting, the lack of a comma marks the car as the actor. Note that this usage is *not* an example of a Sentence Expander—no comma.)

Near Clause (Noun Absolute) Near clauses are commonly used as Sentence Expanders, especially in literary genres. Unlike participles, the subject of a near clause is always specified, so "dangling" problems disappear. Here are two examples from Jack London's *Call of the Wild*, along with some review that I would provide for my students:

> 12. "Then the rope tightened mercilessly, while Buck struggled in a fury, [a]*his tongue lolling out of his mouth* and [b]*his great chest panting futilely.*"

Review Remember that near clauses are usually formed by dropping some form of the verb *to be*. The above example has two near clauses. What would you have to add to each to make it into a complete sentence?

> 12a. His tongue _was_ lolling out of his mouth.
> 12b. His great chest _was_ panting futilely.

I omitted one of the Sentence Expanders from our analysis because it is not a near clause: *while Buck struggled in a fury*. What is this an example of? A swinging bridge (subordinate) clause.

> 13. "And Buck was truly a red-eyed devil, as he drew himself together for the spring, [a]*hair bristling,* [b]*mouth foaming,* [c]*a mad glitter in his bloodshot eyes.*"

Review This sentence has three Sentence Expanders formed by near clauses. What would you have to add to each to make it into a complete sentence?

> 13a. (His) hair _was_ bristling.
> 13b. (His) mouth _was_ foaming.
> 13c. A mad glitter _was_ in his bloodshot eyes.

Write your own sentence, using the same pattern, but describe a different scene in your own words.

Appositive This type of Sentence Expander is used in all genres, but seems to be especially prevalent in expository writing. I divide this type of Sentence Expander into three categories:

Type I—Repetition In the appositive phrase, the noun is repeated, with extra detail(s) added in:

1. The music belonged to another era, *an era of carefree innocence.*

2. The mistake went unnoticed, *a mistake in judgment that had devastating consequences.*

Type II—Synonymy Rather than repeating the original noun, a synonym is used in the appositive phrase:

1. Everybody seems to hate snakes, *unappreciated creatures that play an important role in the food chain.*

2. The addiction ruined his life, *an unbreakable, all-consuming urge to get high.*

Type III—Summation Two or more items in a series are compressed into one noun in the appositive phrase:

1. The beachcomber collected cowries, scallops, tritons, helmets, and conch—*shells that were frequently washed up on shore.*

2. Guitar, piano, and trumpet were his specialty, *very dissimilar instruments to learn how to play.*

Adjectives Out of Order

Placing adjectives or an adjective phrase in the Sentence Expander position is done for rhetorical effect—usually emphasis. There is another, more subtle effect that also takes place: The reader will be impressed (albeit subliminally, perhaps) by the writer's facility with language.

Adjective phrases in Sentence Expander positions are usually movable. Look at the following examples:

14a. The small, deadly tornado dipped out of the sky. (Normal placement)

14b. Small, but deadly, the tornado dipped out of the sky. (Sentence Beginner)

14c. The tornado, small, but deadly, dipped out of the sky. (Sentence Interrupter)

14d. The tornado dipped out of the sky, small, but deadly. (Sentence Expander)

Sentence 1d clearly is the most dramatic. One can almost feel the sense of fear and impending doom that such a placement creates.

Recursiveness and Elaboration

Once you have covered the types of free modifiers and the three possible positions that they can occupy, the world is yours. Start out with sentence-combining practice to familiarize your students with the process of creating Sentence Expanders, just like we did with Sentence Beginners and Interrupters. Then analyze literature as follows:

1. *Teacher*: Point out free modifiers, asking students to tell you whether each is a Sentence Beginner, Sentence Interrupter, or Sentence Expander and asking them to name the device that was used.
2. *Student*: Have students, as a class or in small groups, locate and identify free modifiers.
3. *Competition*: Divide students into teams and have them scour a passage, looking for and naming free modifiers.

Since much of this may be new to you, I invite you to try your hand at this type of task yourself.

Classroom Activity The following is a paragraph from Chapter 1 of *Call of the Wild*. Fill in Table 10.6 with the free modifiers that it contains. A completed analysis is given in Table 10.7.

> [1]Buck had accepted the rope with quiet dignity. [2]To be sure, it was an unwonted performance but he had learned to trust in men he knew, and to give them credit for a wisdom that outreached his own. [3]But when the ends of the rope were placed in the stranger's hands, he growled menacingly. [4]He had merely intimated his displeasure, in his pride believing that to intimate was to command. [5]But to his surprise the rope tightened around his neck, shutting off his breath. [6]In a quick rage he sprang at the man, who met him halfway, grappled him close by the throat, and with a deft twist threw him over on his back. [7]Then the rope tightened mercilessly, while Buck struggled in a fury, his tongue lolling out of his mouth and his great chest panting futilely.

Table 10.6 Free Modifiers

Sent. #	Phrase	Type	Device
2			
3			
4			
5			
5			
6			
7			
7			
7			
7			

Table 10.7 Free Modifiers—Completed

Sent. #	Phrase	Type	Device
2	To be sure	Beginner	Infinitive Phrase
3	when the ends of the rope were placed in the stranger's hands	Beginner	Swinging Bridge Clause
4	in his pride believing that to intimate was to command	Expander	Participle Phrase
5	to his surprise	Beginner	Prepositional Phrase
5	shutting off his breath	Expander	Participle Phrase
6	In a quick rage	Beginner	Prepositional Phrase
7	Then	Beginner	Adverb
7	while Buck struggled in a fury	Expander	Swinging Bridge Clause
7	his tongue lolling out of his mouth	Expander	Near Clause
7	his great chest panting futilely	Expander	Near Clause

Language is a notoriously squishy thing to categorize. Whenever you work with actual literature, you will see things that don't quite fit the mold that you are trying to create for your students. This *Call of the Wild* passage is no exception. You need to be prepared for these things. I'm going to discuss this paragraph, sentence by sentence, showing things that I would anticipate.

#1: The structure of this sentence is very straightforward.

#2: Students might want to call the following phrase a Sentence Expander: "and to give them credit for a wisdom that outreached his own" and identify it as an infinitive phrase. I would be delighted with such an interpretation. (It's actually two infinitives joined by "and" ("to trust" and "to give.")

#3: This sentence begins with "But." Some books and teachers tell you never to begin a sentence with "but" or "and." This advice flies in the face of current practice. The finest of professional authors in all genres do so for rhetorical effect.

#4: The Sentence Expander begins with "in his pride," so students may want to call this a prepositional phrase device instead of a participle phrase. Once again, I would be delighted to hear such an analysis. If, however, the author had chosen to write "believing, in his pride, that . . .", then everyone would agree that "in his pride" is part of a participle phrase.

#5: Again, this sentence begins with "But." See #3, above.

#6: The author chooses not to put a comma after "In a quick rage." I would point out that a voice comma very clearly belongs here, but that authors can, with short Sentence Beginners, opt to not use one.

#7: "Then" is a Sentence Beginner that takes neither comma nor voice comma. It is an exception to the rule. Students may want to know if it is acceptable to put a comma before the "and" that joins the two near clauses. This is a great opportunity to explain that some commas come from the head (by rule) while others come from the heart. Using a comma forces a break in the action that is not warranted: Those two actions are closely tied to each other. So my heart (the feeling of the passage) tells me that we should not put a comma there. I will deal with this concept in the next chapter.

Sentence Length

Tufte (2006) states, "Variation in sentence types as well as sentence lengths is the mark of the professional" (p. 141). Structural variation has been the topic of this entire chapter; however, no discussion of sentence fluency would be complete without saying a few words about sentence length.

There are two extremes to examine: too many short sentences and too many long ones.

Too Short I began this chapter with a simple narrative:

> I ate my lunch. I went to the park. I played with my friends. We had a great time.

I noted that sentence structure is the primary marker of immaturity in this piece of writing. Another factor, however, is sentence length. When all of the sentences in a piece are similar in length, not only does the author run the risk of boring the reader but he also misses opportunities to drive his point home occasionally with the short sentence (i.e., using short sentences for rhetorical effect).

Too Long The other extreme is writing that consists of nothing but long, complex sentences, best represented by "legalese." Examples of legalese abound in our society. One easy source is the End User License Agreement (EULA) for software or websites. Look at the following excerpt from worldofwarcraft.com, a website for gamers:

> This software program, and any files that are delivered to you by Blizzard Entertainment, Inc. (via on-line transmission or otherwise) to "patch," update, or otherwise modify the software program, as well as any printed materials and any on-line or electronic documentation

(the "Manual"), and any and all copies and derivative works of such software program and Manual (collectively, with the "Game Client" defined below, the "Game") is the copyrighted work of Blizzard Entertainment, Inc. or its licensors (collectively referred to herein as "Blizzard").

This excerpt consists of a single sentence that contains 84 words! The vocabulary in this passage is not very difficult; the structure, however, is horrific.

I present these examples merely to show the double-edged sword that sentence length can be. Students beyond the third grade generally do not produce text that falls into either extreme. Their writing is often dull and lifeless in part due to three factors:

1. Most of their sentences begin with the subject.
2. Most of them do not contain free modifiers.
3. Most of them are approximately the same length.

Working with Sentence Beginners, Interrupters, and Expanders will help students resolve the first two issues. However, if they take the lessons too much to heart, if they add free modifiers all over the place, their writing will become stilted and, once again, boring. As with all things in life, moderation is the key. Mix and match sentence lengths and types across a piece of writing, a task best left for the revision phase of the writing process.

Finally, throwing a short sentence, or even a one-sentence paragraph, at your readers is an excellent way to really drive home a point. I have an example of this device in Chapter 9:

> Rather than tying into and building on what's already there, this approach attempts to establish new models and theories in the hopes, I suppose, that everything will transfer to existing language skills. It doesn't. As a result, sentence boundary errors appear to be intractable. They aren't. There has to be a better way to attack the problem. There is.

Notice how the short sentences drive my points home. I could have easily avoided the short sentences by expanding them or incorporating them into surrounding sentences. However, I wanted to really grab the reader's attention here, so I chose to slap him or her in the face with a series of very short sentences.

I will return to the short sentence for rhetorical effect in Chapter 12.

Discussion Questions

1. Review your answers to the true–false questions at the beginning of this chapter. Have you changed any of your answers?

2. Discuss the following statement and what it means for English teachers: *If your students are good readers, they are already in control of the vast majority of structures that professional authors use to create a sophisticated writing style.*

3. Christensen asserts that the main clause of a sentence is not a major contributor to good style in the eyes of readers. Do you agree with his position? Why or why not?

4. Why are voice commas so important when determining what structures are major contributors?

5. This chapter discusses free modifiers: Sentence Beginners, Sentence Interrupters, and Sentence Expanders. Discuss how the same grammatical structure can play all three roles in a given sentence.

6. If we follow the example of professional authors, what percentage of sentences in a passage should contain Sentence Beginners? What happens if a writer doesn't use any Sentence Beginners? What if a writer uses too many?

7. Can the same structure be a free modifier in one sentence but not be one in another? Discuss.

8. In Chapter 9, we stated that a swinging bridge clause could be in two positions: before or after the main clause.

   a. Discuss whether or not the clause would be a free modifier in both positions.

   b. In this chapter, we saw that such a clause could be a Sentence Interrupter. Provide your own example of this phenomenon.

9. What is meant by a Sentence Expander? Provide your own example of one and show why it fits the definition.

10. Discuss the impact that a very short sentence that is nestled among long sentences can have. Provide your own example in support.

## chapter 11

Rhetorical Choices: Mechanics and Word Choice

True or False?

1. Students in your classroom already know that they need to change their language to fit the audience and situation when they speak.

2. Standard Written American English is the most efficient, logical way to express one's thoughts.

3. Before students can learn to write correctly, they must learn to speak correctly.

4. Virtually every comma in every piece of writing represents the application of a rule.

5. The usage of dashes and parentheses is governed by rules of SWAE.

6. The fancier the words that your students use, the more favorable the impression will be on their readers.

7. If a student misuses some new words on a composition, her or his grade should suffer.

8. Students will learn to differentiate between confusing word pairs (e.g., *affect* vs. *effect*) by carefully studying their definitions before practicing.

Rhetorical Choices: Divide and Conquer

I am going to divide coverage of rhetorical choices into two complementary areas: mechanics and word choice (this chapter) and structural choices (Chapter 12). Please keep in mind that complete coverage of this very complex subject is beyond the scope of this text. For a much more in-depth analysis of rhetorical choices in writing, please see Martha Kolln's (2007) excellent text, *Rhetorical Grammar: Grammatical Choices, Rhetorical Effects*.

Rhetorical Choices: Exploring the Term

Before we explore rhetorical choices, let's be sure that we understand what is meant by the phrase. When writers write (or speakers speak), they have a wide variety of choices to make about how to express a given thought. Authors can vary the words, the structures, and/or the punctuation (to include fonts such as italics) to express a variety of emotions, emphasize specific features, hide certain facts, create different impressions, and so on.

Words

One of the first rhetorical choices a writer makes is which words to use to express a given thought, an act referred to as *diction*. If, for example, an author wanted one character to tell another to be quiet, he could have her say things like the following:

> "Would you please hold it down?"
> "Please be quiet."
> "Be quiet!"
> "Shhh!"
> "Shut up!"

The list of options could, of course, go on and on. How would this author decide which words to use in his story? By making **rhetorical choices**—by carefully choosing those words that best fit the situation, the relationship between characters, and the emotional state of the speaker.[1]

Structures

Let's imagine that a reporter wants to state that the president made several errors in judgment. That reporter could write things like the following:

---

[1] I made a different type of rhetorical choice (a structural one) in this sentence: I intentionally used a fragment to maintain a friendlier, more relaxed tone.

The president made several mistakes. (A simple statement of fact)

Several mistakes were made. (Hiding who made the mistakes)

Several mistakes were made by the president. (Gently emphasizing that the president, himself, made the mistakes)

Punctuation

When we speak, we are able to express characteristics such as emotion or emphasis by using the tone, pitch, and loudness of our voices. Writers try to capture that channel of expression by punctuation. Imagine that a writer knows that John ate a cricket. She could express that thought using different punctuation tools. Note how each of the following versions would differ when stated orally:

John ate a cricket.

John ate a cricket!

John ate a cricket. (Not Bob)

John *ate* a cricket. (Not captured)

John ate a *cricket*. (Not a hamburger)

Registers

Do your students have Rhetorical Wizards tucked away in their brains? Absolutely. When they speak, they manipulate rhetorical choices—and have been doing so for years. When children first learn to speak, they are notoriously frank and straightforward—if it hits their brains, it hits their mouths. By the time they reach grade school, they have developed much greater control over the choices they make as they speak (a skill that, normally, only improves with age). They have already mastered several **registers**—patterns of communication that change according to audience and purpose. They switch registers, an act known as **code switching**, with ease: They speak one way to their friends, another way to their teachers, another way to their parents, and so on. They know when to try to sound cool, knowledgeable, polite, respectful, or whatever other characteristic they think the situation requires. Within these broad registers, your students can make further refinements in order to express degrees of sincerity, honesty, emotional involvement, confidence, sympathy, sorrow, and the like.

Selecting a register is analogous to choosing the right clothing: If you show up at a formal wedding in cut-offs, a tee shirt, and flip-flops, people will judge you harshly. Your apparel has certainly satisfied the most basic function of clothing—everything that needs to be covered is covered. However, your poor choice of clothing would make you stand out like a sore thumb. Speaking or writing in the wrong register has a similar effect.

By way of illustration, let's imagine that I am hanging out with my friends watching a football game. One of them says something. I respond by saying, "To whom were you speaking?" Imagine their reaction! Everybody would understand what I was trying to communicate, but they would mark that utterance as weird—and me with it. Why? Because I made a bad rhetorical choice; that is, I was in an informal situation, but I chose to express myself in a formal register. The question itself was certainly well formed, but the *way* I decided to phrase it was definitely off target.

As a composition teacher, you should engrave this fact in your brain: *Standard Written American English (SWAE) is a register*. It is a way of expressing oneself in order to meet the social expectations of a particular audience—the educated reader. As stated in Chapter 4, from a communication perspective, SWAE is neither more logical nor more capable of expressing one's thoughts than any other register, to include the so-called nonstandard dialects. However, SWAE is expected in academic and business/professional circles; failure to produce it is stigmatized. As composition teachers, therefore, we have an absolute obligation to help our students master SWAE.

Here is part of the beauty of language: Registers, like clothing, are *additive*. I don't have to throw away my cut-offs, tee shirt, and flip-flops in order to dress properly for a wedding. Likewise, students do not have to "unlearn" one register in order to acquire another. In fact, as you have already seen, your students have already mastered several registers. When you teach composition, you are *helping them acquire another one*.

One of the mistakes that we have made all too often in the English classroom is to tell students that the language they speak is *wrong*, and that our job is to *correct* it. The language isn't wrong; the *register*, however, may very well be. This point is crucial to keep in mind, especially when working with standard English learners.

Wheeler and Swords (2006) demonstrate an approach that respects the home language of students while instilling a register better suited for an SWAE environment. Here is a conversation from one of their classes:

> **Student:** Mrs. Swords, Sydni want to know if she can work in my group.
>
> **Mrs. Swords:** Jawan, right now we're practicing talking formally, like we would with the principal or the mayor. Can you code switch to standard English?
>
> **Student:** OK, Sydni wants to know if she can work in my group. (p. 8)

In this example, the teacher was working on developing a spoken register—standard English instead of SWAE. Also, obviously, some groundwork had been established prior to this snippet. The approach, however, is spot on: Rather than overtly or covertly telling the student that his language is *wrong*, the teacher encourages him to switch to another *register*.

In the composition classroom, I often cringe when my students ask me if a certain word choice or construction is correct. As a self-standing entity, the structure is *correct* if it communicates properly. It may not be acceptable in an SWAE register, however; it may not meet the social expectations of the audience for whom the student is writing. I tell my classes over and over that the language they hear and use in the home or on the street is *perfect* for that environment. It may not be a very good choice, however, in an environment where SWAE is expected.

Classroom Activity Early in the school year or semester, have your students relate an event in writing, but ask them to imagine that they are telling the story to their best friend. Ask them to do whatever they can to make their writing capture exactly how they would *tell* the story to this person. Then ask them to rewrite the same story as if they were going to hand it in to you for a grade. Take up the papers and, anonymously, read both versions of a few stories out loud, complimenting the students on their excellent ability to code switch. Two caveats:

1. Students often use words with their friends that are unacceptable in many areas of society. When I do this activity at the college freshman level, I tell them to use absolutely natural language—bad words and all. If I am working with younger students, I ask them to keep the language clean. Use your own good judgment.

2. The versions they are pretending to write for a grade may not, in fact, be very good. Ignore all of the problems that you may see as you read the more formal version, praising, instead, their ability to switch between the two registers.

In the brain-based composition classroom, then, you are not working with a *right versus wrong* distinction; you are working with a *formal versus informal* distinction (or whatever you want to name it). Take full advantage of your students' Rhetorical Wizards and recognize those areas of students' spoken language that are congruent with SWAE (and there will be many) while helping them to acquire the full spectrum of this new register.

Punctuation

An important role of punctuation is to impose certain rhetorical effects upon sentences. The following example of the power of punctuation has been around for a long time, but it is still a very useful demonstration in the classroom. Write the first version and then change the punctuation:

Version 1: A woman without her man is useless. (Boys cheer and girls boo.)

Version 2: A woman: without her, man is useless. (Girls cheer and boys boo.)

Which one is correct? The one that more accurately reflects the *rhetorical intent of the writer.*

Let's examine some punctuation marks that can be used for rhetorical effect.

The Rhetorical Comma

There are two kinds of commas in English: I call one of them *head commas* (those required by rule) and the other *heart commas* (those used to impose a specific way of interpretation). The basic functioning of commas, as outlined in Chapter 8, remains unchanged: they are used to separate things, and they are signals to readers to chunk. However, they can also have more subtle effects. As readers process sentences, they gather a certain momentum. Commas can act as speed bumps, slowing the readers down a bit and adding some drama. Deciding when and where to insert heart commas is part of the art of good writing. Consider the following two sentences:

> 1a. John bought a new car even though he couldn't afford one.
> 1b. John bought a new car, even though he couldn't afford one.

The first sentence is a simple, straightforward statement of fact. The second is more dramatic, placing greater emphasis on John's financial situation. If students write sentences such as these, they may very well ask you about this type of comma. Here is a typical exchange that might occur in my classroom:

> **Student:** Do I need a comma after *car* in this sentence?
>
> **Me:** That depends on how you want the reader to interpret what you are saying.

I then read each version out loud, showing how the comma forces a pause and a more dramatic reading of the second clause. This comma is not required by rule, but is certainly acceptable—a classic example of a heart comma.

Here are two more examples of heart commas, this time taken from Chapter 1 of Jack London's *Call of the Wild.* Imagine how you would say each sentence with and without the comma, noting how each comma acts as a speed bump to add a dramatic flair:

> There were great stables, where a dozen grooms and boys held forth . . .
> Then the rope tightened mercilessly, while Buck struggled in a fury . . .

Classroom Activity Divide your class into small groups and have them go on a heart comma scavenger hunt. Tell them to scour the literature that

Heart
Commas
I have spent most of the day putting in a comma and the rest of the day taking it out.

—Oscar Wilde

you are reading for instances of heart commas. They will undoubtedly mark some head commas (required by rule) as they attempt this activity, providing an excellent opportunity for you to briefly review comma requirements (e.g., "No, this is a head comma. It is required because . . . .").

Semi-Colons

As we saw in Chapter 9, semi-colons between sentences signal to readers that the preceding one is finished (chunk accordingly) and that the next one is closely related. When to use semi-colons between sentences is a purely rhetorical decision. Semi-colons can always be replaced by periods, but the opposite is not true, of course: Periods cannot always be replaced by semi-colons.

While revising the previous chapter, for example, I originally wrote the following as two sentences, separated by a period. During revision, however, I decided that I wanted to emphasize for the reader that the two thoughts were closely interrelated, so I changed the period to a semi-colon:

> Once they learn to read well, most students only occasionally struggle with a sentence or reading passage due to *structural* complexities; if they struggle with a reading passage, it is usually due to vocabulary deficits and/or content complexity.

Dashes and Parentheses

Dashes and parentheses are rarely, if ever, required by rule; instead, their usage is a rhetorical choice that writers make. (Incidentally, the previous sentence happens to be another example of two closely related thoughts joined by a semi-colon. And these two sentences, obviously, happen to be an illustration of the usage of parentheses.) The primary reason for using dashes or parentheses is to signal to readers that you are adding extra information or taking a side trip—like this one—from the main thrust of a sentence. Dashes add drama or flair to the contained info; parentheses mark the information as relatively unimportant or tangential. Let's look at some examples:

> 1c. John bought a new car, even though he couldn't afford one. (Heart comma)
>
> 1d. John bought a new car—even though he couldn't afford one. (More dramatic than the previous version)
>
> 1e. John bought a new car (even though he couldn't afford one). (Relatively trivial, extra information)

In the above set, the dash represents a more striking break. When spoken, the pause between clauses would be more pronounced, and changes in nonverbal language would accompany it. I cannot readily imagine a context where the information in the second clause is so unimportant that the writer would choose to put it in parentheses; however, I suppose one could contrive such a context.

Here's another set to examine:

> 2a. Common garden herbs, basil, oregano, parsley, and thyme, grow easily in most locations.
>
> 2b. Common garden herbs—basil, oregano, parsley, and thyme—grow easily in most locations.
>
> 2c. Common garden (herbs, basil, oregano, parsley, and thyme) grow easily in most locations.

Sentence 2a, although "legal," is difficult to read. The dashes in Sentence 2b could be interpreted as adding more flair, but the primary reason for using them is to clearly mark the boundaries between the series and the rest of the sentence, making it easier to process.[2] In the last sentence, however, parentheses are use for a more specific effect: The writer is either signaling to the reader that the contained information is not very important or indicating that the reader probably knows this information already.

Here is a final example of this distinction: During the revision process in this chapter, I made a rhetorical change to one of my sentences. I originally wrote the sentence with a comma after *speak*:

> By the time they reach grade school, they have developed much greater control over the choices they make as they speak, a skill that, normally, only improves with age.

When I reread the sentence, I decided that the information after the second comma is probably well known to you, my reader, so I made it parenthetical:

> By the time they reach grade school, they have developed much greater control over the choices they make as they speak (a skill that, normally, only improves with age).

And so it goes with dashes and parentheses: The decision to use one or the other is a rhetorical choice, one that is made depending on how you want the reader to interact with or respond to the content. Your students' Rhetorical Wizards probably do not encompass the usage of dashes and parentheses. Furthermore, these types of rhetorical choices cannot be practiced in decontextualized, drill-and-kill exercises. Instead, students need to examine well-written material, consciously analyzing why the author made the choices she or he did and then try it themselves in their own writing.

---

[2]Note that a colon cannot be used here. In formal writing, a colon cannot be used unless it marks the end of a complete sentence.

Classroom Activity Again, divide your class into groups and send them on a scavenger hunt for these two punctuation marks. Let them search through something you are reading in class or articles from the web. Tell the groups to be prepared to explain to the class why the author decided to use the dashes or parentheses—and how the text would change if one were substituted for the other or they were deleted.

Student Writing Encourage students to look for places in their writing to incorporate dashes and/or parentheses during revision. As you go over their papers, suggest areas where these punctuation marks might be effective.

Word Choice

A very powerful, yet often overlooked, function of language is that it serves as an efficient way to organize experience. For example, you have almost certainly had some exposure to dogs. This experience has left traces—memories—in your brain. The mere mention of the word *dog* allows you to access that experience: to know what they look like, know what it feels like to pet them, know how they smell when wet, know what they sound like, recall specific pleasant or unpleasant interactions with them, remember dogs that you have known—the list could go on and on. Richard Anderson (1977) referred to these collections of knowledge as *schemata*. (The singular is *schema*—we have just examined one's dog schema, for example.) Every human builds and maintains schemata about a wide range of phenomena. Language provides an entry point into schemata.

What if we didn't have language, didn't have a way to symbolically refer to that entity that we English speakers know as "dog"? Your brain would still *contain* all of the knowledge that you had learned naturally from experience (your *dog* schema), but you would not have any way to *organize* this information for quick and easy access.

Words, therefore, are labels for experience, gateways to our knowledge. When we speak or write, we try to find the best labels for the experiences that we are trying to relate. If words and experiences existed in a one-to-one relationship, a writer's task would be much simpler. But such is not the case: The same experience can have several labels, each with its own set of characteristics. What, for example, is the difference between *kill, murder, butcher, massacre,* and *assassinate*? They all refer to the same action, but they have very different connotations, or different shades of meaning. To illustrate, fill in the following blanks with *kill, murder, butcher, massacre,* or *assassinate* (more than one might fit), and then imagine the reaction of a reader if one of the other words were used:

The farmer _____ one of his hogs in order to feed his family.

The group wanted to _____ the president.

The army's goal was to _____ thousands of the territory's residents.

In a fit of anger, the husband _____ his wife.

One word is generic, capable of fitting in all four blanks (*kill*). The other four words have much more specific connotations and are, as a result, much more limited. How strange it would sound, for instance, if someone said that the husband *assassinated* his wife!

Knowing a vocabulary item, therefore, is not a simple matter of equating the word with its base meaning. Instead, words are acquired along a continuum: One end indicates some vague sense of what it means; the other end shows total control of the word's environment and connotations. No wonder, then, that choosing the right word or combination of words is a skill that takes so many years to master.

Because of the complexities involved, diction does not lend itself to neat categorization or analysis. Problems in word choice range from choosing the correct word to match the situation, to confusing word pairs, to clichés, to strong versus weak verbs, to slang/regionalisms, to misused words, to overly fancy words, to . . . you get the picture. A complete analysis of this very complex area lies well outside the scope of this text. Let's limit ourselves to four of these areas, chosen because they occur frequently in student writing and have a decidedly negative effect on readers.

Confusing Word Pairs

Using *there* instead of *their*, *brake* instead of *break*, *loose* instead of *lose*, and so on, places the writer on the fast track to disaster. Readers see mistakes like these and immediately begin to doubt the author's abilities: "Is that person uneducated, careless, not thorough, incapable, or what?" The content of the piece may be excellent, but it will suddenly be viewed with skepticism.

The Traditional Approach
Traditional treatment of confusing word pairs is, from a brain-based perspective, *way* off target. Let's look at a traditional treatment of one such pair, *loose* versus *lose*, to see what is wrong. Students are given definitions of each word:

Loose means not rigidly fashioned.

Lose means to miss from one's possession or customary place.

Students are asked to memorize these definitions and then are given fill-in-the-blank exercises and test items. This approach fails for two reasons:

1. It doesn't address the problem. Students already know the meaning of the two words. They never mispronounce them while speaking—a clear indicator that they have acquired the differences in meaning. Definitions aren't the problem; the problem is spelling. Students do not know which spelling to associate with which pronunciation; definitions make absolutely no contribution to the real problem.

2. It relies on rote memorization. Students can, indeed, memorize the definitions, associate them with the correct spellings, do the exercises, and pass the test. However, because the information is not interrelated with what they already know, students quickly forget the definitions or their associations with the correct spelling, winding up where they started—clueless.

A Brain-Based Approach One of the basic tenets of brain-based writing is to take advantage of what students already know, helping them relate the teaching point to existing networks of information. A brain-based approach for problem word pairs requires two pieces:

1. A clue (a statement that connects the spelling to something students already know)

2. An application (a guideline for applying the clue)

Here is how it might look for our example word pair:

■ *Clue*: *Loose* is "loose as a goose" or "loosey-goosey."

■ *Application*: If you cannot substitute one of these phrases (more or less) for the target word, do not use the one spelled like *goose*.

Provide a couple of examples of the application:

His pants were too *loose/lose*—they kept falling down. (Here, "loose as a goose" or "loosey-goosey" sort of fits, so use the one spelled like *goose*.)

I don't want to *loose/lose* my keys. (Here, "loose as a goose" or "loosey-goosey" most certainly does *not* fit , so do *not* use the one spelled like *goose*.)

Now practice and test as usual. Your students will have a much better chance of remembering how to differentiate between these two words weeks, months, or years down the line.

Virtually any pair (or, occasionally, trio) of confusing words lend themselves to a clue/application approach—all it takes is a little creative thinking on your part (or, better yet, the students'). Students who have problems with a specific word pair will have to train themselves to consciously examine each usage, applying the clue to ensure that they have the right form in place. Some word pair usages will become part of their procedural memory and will cease to be a problem; others will not. I, for example, still have to stop and think whenever I use *affect* or *effect*. (*Affect* means something similar to *alter*. If I can substitute the "a-word" (*alter*) for the target word, I must use the a-word (*affect*); otherwise, don't.)

Classroom Application Divide your students into small groups and let them devise their own clues and applications for problem word pairs. Then reconvene the class and compare the results. Have the students decide which one they like the best and make it the official approach for that word pair. This activity is certainly brain-based—more closely in tune with natural learning requirements. Students work together, think about the problem, and attempt to solve it in a nonthreatening environment. And, as a bonus, you will be surprised at how often their solutions are better than the ones you thought of!

Slang or Regionalisms

Every student in your classroom has been hearing and using slang or regionalisms for years. I, for example, grew up in the rural south. I still remember my amazement when I found out that *fixin' to* (*I'm fixin' to go*) was not used by all English speakers to signify the future, that *directly* (*I'll do it directly*) did not mean *later on* to most of the country, and that *irregardless* and *seldomly* were not words!

If students understand the concept of *register*, then explaining why slang or regional expressions don't work very well is simple—analogous to choosing the wrong outfit for the occasion. (Imagine a tennis player showing up to play football in tennis attire.) Again, don't treat the language as *wrong*; it's just not the right choice for the situation and audience.

Instant messaging or texting language is also its own register. The abbreviations that are so logical in that environment (*OMG! R U serious? LOL!*) are not inherently wrong, nor do they signal the demise of good English. They simply do not belong in the SWAE register.

I have my students individually keep a Slang List. Every time they use a word that I mark as slang (or a regionalism, although I do not differentiate), I ask them to add it to the list. Then, before they begin to write or edit a composition, I ask them to reread the list to refresh their memories.

Misused Words

As was stated earlier, words that are fully acquired are connected to all kinds of information and experiences that are stored in the brain. Acquiring new words usually takes multiple exposures in a variety of contexts. As students take on these new words and try to use them, they will, of course, make some mistakes. (One of my favorites involves a middle school teacher who once told me that one of her students wrote something like "He ensued the girl all the way home.") Although you will need to gently help students understand what is wrong with the misused words, you should recognize and celebrate the fact that they are trying to spread their wings. Errors are a normal part of natural learning. One of the quickest ways to discourage students from trying out new things is to penalize them or belittle them for doing so. Let them know that you are very pleased that they are attempting to use new vocabulary items and that you will certainly not deduct from their grades for trying. Then help them understand the problem.

Overly Fancy Words

Students often think that the sophistication of a piece of writing will increase by using fancy words, resulting in what is sometimes referred to as *thesaurus writing* (look up a word in the thesaurus and choose the one that looks to be the fanciest). I could provide thousands of examples from past compositions, but I'll settle for one from a student's narrative:

> After ingesting the evening repast, I settled in for some serene time.

None of the words are exactly *misused*, but readers most certainly will not be impressed with this student's erudition. Quite the opposite: Readers will be put off by this writer's obvious attempt to put on airs, to overreach.

Classroom Application
Your students' Rhetorical Wizards are usually very capable of spotting mixed vocabulary registers—occasional bursts of unnecessarily high-flung words in an otherwise routine piece of writing. Show them some writing samples, contrived by you or submitted by past students (anonymously, of course) and ask them to tell you where the writer goes astray.

This activity, by the way, is an excellent way to begin a discussion about plagiarism. Take a piece of student writing and insert some professionally written sentences in three or four places, making sure that they tie in logically. (See Spatt [2003], pp. 97–98, for excellent examples.) Then ask students to identify the plagiarisms. They will do so with deadly accuracy. After we complete the exercise, I tell my students, "If *you* can spot plagiarisms with zero years of teaching experience, I would have to be an eggplant not to be able to do it after X number of years. So don't even *think* about trying it!"

Word choice helps establish a tone, a voice to the writing. I will deal briefly with this complex issue in the next chapter.

Discussion Questions

1. Review your answers to the true-false questions at the beginning of this chapter. Have you changed any of your answers?

2. Provide an original example of possible rhetorical choices that one could make for each of the following areas:

   a. Diction

   b. Structure

   c. Punctuation

3. Discuss how the fact that your students can already code switch between several registers should impact the way you teach composition.

4. Provide an original example of a situation where you or a friend made a very poor rhetorical choice.

5. What is the difference between a head comma and a heart comma? Provide an original example of each.

6. What is meant by the statement that the decision about when to use a semi-colon between clauses is always a rhetorical choice?

7. When might a writer decide to use each of the following:

   a. Dashes instead of commas?

   b. Dashes instead of a colon?

   c. Parentheses instead of dashes?

8. What is meant by the statement that words serve as an efficient way to organize experience? Use an example other than the one used in this chapter to support your answer.

9. Explain how a student might misuse a word if he or she did not know the word's connotation.

10. Contrast the traditional approach to problem word pairs with the brain-based one given in this chapter, explaining why one works better than the other.

11. What is the difference between a student misusing a word and a student throwing in a bunch of fancy words?

12. How can you take advantage of your students' Rhetorical Wizards in the prevention of plagiarism?

## chapter 12

Rhetorical Choices: Structure

True or False?

1. There are rules to describe when a structure can be moved from one place in a sentence to another.

2. Elements at the end of a sentence usually have sharper focus than elements at the beginning.

3. Swinging bridge (subordinate) clauses can occur in only two places: before the main clause and after it.

4. Students should not be allowed to use passive voice in compositions.

5. Students already know how to *form* the passive when they speak; they just do not know how to *identify* passive voice when they see it.

6. Two- or three-word sentences are childish; they should be removed.

7. Professional authors never use fragments.

8. Students should not be expected to handle *voice* in their writing until they are taught to recognize it in the writing of others.

Given versus New Information

Before we can begin to explore some of the rhetorical choices in sentence structure, we need to establish an important baseline: the distinction between *given* information and *new* information.

Imagine that a friend of yours came up to you and, out of the blue, said, "Do you know where she is?" Your reaction would be immediate: "Who are you talking about?"[1] There is nothing wrong with the initial question: It is a properly structured, clearly expressed oral request for information. The breakdown occurs in the *given versus new* arena. In this imaginary setting, your friend posed such a question because she thought that you *knew* the person in question—that that information was a *given* between you.

Given information is shared information—an event that has occurred or information that has been exchanged prior to a sentence; **new information** consists of details that are added to the given information. In discourse, most sentences have at least one *given* element onto which one or more *new* elements are attached so as to maintain continuity. Your students are well aware of this distinction (albeit subconsciously) and how to maintain it. Young children quite often are not. They might very well just start talking about an event or person as if you had been there and knew all about the topic.

More often than not, the subject of a sentence contains the given information and the predicate contains the new. Here is a very simple example. The given information is typed in italics.

> Yesterday I bought a new (to me) car. *It was* a dark blue Ford pickup with well over 100,000 miles on it. *This high mileage* might have been a turn-off in most situations, *but it* wasn't in this case. *I* knew the owner very well; *he* had taken very good care of *the car*.

You can clearly see that, after the first sentence, which establishes context, the given information is, for the most part, in the subject position and the new information is attached as all or part of the predicate.

Since a lot of structural rhetorical choices are made to allow the writer to emphasize, downplay, or otherwise manipulate this given versus new equation, this issue will pop up as we explore rhetorical choices in sentence structure.

---

[1] I know, I know: If I am writing in SWAE, I should state the question as "About whom are you talking?" But I don't have any friends who speak that way, and my guess is that you don't either.

Movement

As we have discussed in past chapters, several structures can optionally be moved to various locations in a given sentence. The decision about where to put a movable structure is a rhetorical one, often related to the given versus new distinction.

Participle Phrases

Participle phrases can often be placed in one of three positions:

1. *Trying to appear brave*, the little boy fought back the tears.
2. The little boy, *trying to appear brave*, fought back the tears.
3. The little boy fought back the tears, *trying to appear brave*.

Which version is the best? That determination cannot be made out of context. It is primarily a question of focus:

- Since **n**ew information generally appears at the end of a sentence, sentence 3 emphasizes the "brave" component.

- In sentence 2, the "brave" component is the most out of focus. Because participle phrases are most often placed after the noun phrase that they modify, this position reduces the prominence of the participle phrase, so the emphasis here is on the "tears" component.

- In sentence 1, "trying to appear brave" is again brought into sharper focus, an example of a very basic concept of English rhetoric: Moving an element from its visual position usually causes that element to be in sharper focus.

So the question remains: If an author wants to move this phrase, how does that person decide among sentences 1, 2, and 3? By asking that question, we move, once again, from the realm of *head* to *heart*, much as we did with commas in the previous chapter. These types of decisions are made based on the overall flow of a paragraph, the rhythm of the sentence, and the given versus new information. No solid guidelines or rules exist; writers must depend on their Rhetorical Wizards.

Your students will already have fairly well-developed Rhetorical Wizards that will, in many cases, serve as a very good guide. Continued exposure to well-written literature, especially with you pointing out certain occurrences, will hone these Wizards without complicated explanations and lists of guidelines to memorize.

Appositives

Appositives generally appear after the noun phrase that they echo:

1a. Rosario, a straight-A student, failed his math test.

They can be fronted, however, for more dramatic effect:

> 1b. A straight-A student, Rosario failed his math test.

The decision about whether to front an appositive is, once again, a rhetorical one.

Generally, students have not had much exposure to appositives in sentence-initial position, so they tend to balk at them at first. Point them out when they appear in the literature and discuss why the author decided to place it there. Although this placement is not common, occasionally using such a structure heightens the drama a bit and leaves a subtle impression on the reader that this author writes well (assuming that everything else is properly handled, of course).

Floating Connectors (Conjunctive Adverbs)

In Chapter 9, I introduced floating connectors—conjunctive adverbs in traditional terminology. We established that they could be distinguished from bridges (coordinating and subordinating conjunctions) by the fact that they could move to different positions. The issue now before us is when and where to move them. Look at the following example:

> 2a. *However,* the bear decided to climb up the tree after the man.
>
> 2b. The bear, *however,* decided to climb up the tree after the man.
>
> 2c. The bear decided, *however,* to climb up the tree after the man.
>
> 2d. The bear decided to climb up the tree, *however,* after the man.
>
> 2e. The bear decided to climb up the tree after the man, *however.*

The assortment of possible placements for a floating connector, for the most part, does not need to be taught. Your students' Grammar Wizards and Rhetorical Wizards will have a very good feel for what is permissible. For example, all students, native or non-native, would reject the following:

> 2f. *The bear decided to climb up, however, the tree after the man.

They probably would not be very comfortable with the following placement either:

> 2g. ?The bear decided to climb, however, up the tree after the man.

Notice how a dash makes sentence 8 much less awkward:

> 2h. The bear decided to climb, however—up the tree after the man.

When to move this element and *where* to move it are, once again, determined by context. Since *however* shows contrast, you would tend to place the word near that element of the sentence that you want the contrast to focus on. In Sentence 2b, the contrastive focus is on *bear*; in Sentence 2c, it is on the decision itself, and so on. In the first sentence, the author wants the entire sentence to be in contrast with the previous one. Other floating connectors work similarly. Placing them in different locations does not change the relationship that the connector expresses; instead, it changes the focus of the relationship.

Swinging Bridge Clauses (Subordinate Clauses)

In Chapter 9, I stated that swinging bridge clauses could occupy one of two positions—before or after the main clause:

> 3a. *Because comic books have so many illustrations,* they are fun for children to read.
>
> 3b. Comic books are fun for children to read *because they have so many illustrations.*

When the swinging bridge clause comes first, it usually consists primarily of *given* information and serves more as a transition from the previous sentence. When it comes second, it contains *new* information (Kolln [2007], p. 158).

In Chapter 9, however, I didn't tell you the entire truth: Swinging bridge clauses are more flexible than that. Consider the following version:

> 3c . Comic books, *because they have so many illustrations,* are fun for children to read.

In reality, then, floating connectors and swinging bridge clauses are *both* movable. The true difference is that floating connectors move *by themselves,* whereas swinging bridges can only move with the clause to which they are attached.

Notice the required commas in Sentence 3c. In a position like this, the swinging bridge clause is a true Sentence Interrupter (Chapter 10) and must be punctuated accordingly. When read out loud, these commas are voice commas; therefore, they alter the focus, the rhythm, and the flow of the sentence.

When should a writer decide to place a swinging bridge clause in Sentence Interrupter position? You can probably predict the answer by now: There are no hard and fast rules. This decision is a rhetorical, heart-based one. It is safe to say, however, that making a swinging bridge clause into a Sentence Interrupter places much more emphasis on it than either of the other two positions.

Fronted Elements

English is a language that is very dependent on word order. In the vast majority of sentences, the subject is the first element of the main clause, followed by the predicate. (Don't get confused here: Sentence Beginners are normally not part of the main clause of a sentence.) Sometimes, however, authors choose to change things around. When some element of the main clause is moved to the beginning of a sentence, that element is said to be *fronted*. Table 12.1 has some examples.

Three points are of interest in this type of fronting:

1. Quite often, no comma (written or voice) is required.
2. The element that is fronted usually receives the emphasis.
3. The word order of the rest of the sentence is altered by the fronting. Native speakers have little problem with this reordering of the words, so, once again, there is no need for you to go into detail in the composition classroom. This is a definite problem area for non-native speakers, however—even very advanced ones.

Native speakers read sentences like these without a problem—they are in total receptive control of the structure. However, they may not think to include them at appropriate times when they write. As was noted, non-natives quite often have trouble with this construction, so plan to provide extra assistance for them if you decide to encourage students to incorporate an occasional fronted structure in their compositions.

Occasionally, every element in a sentence represents new information. When an element is fronted in this type of situation, things change just a bit. Imagine that you are reading a new paragraph in a narrative. The first sentence of the paragraph is as follows:

> One bright spring day, my mom and I were driving to school when we were startled by a very unusual sight.

Table 12.1 Fronted Structures

#	Regular	Fronted
1	I had never seen such a sight.	Never had I seen such a sight.
2	He had no sooner gotten in the door when it began to pour.	No sooner had he gotten in the door when it began to pour.
3	She was so happy to see her son that she screamed with delight.	So happy was she to see her son that she screamed with delight.

Here are two perfectly good versions of the next sentence in the paragraph:

> A huge coyote ran *across the road.*
>
> *Across the road* ran a huge coyote.

All of the information in this sentence is new. The only given information is that a surprising event took place; what took place and where it took place is new. In the second sentence, the author has fronted "across the road" and moved "a huge coyote" from the subject position, which typically contains given information, to the end position, which typically contains new information. This is a very special type of fronting—a fronting specifically designed to allow the writer to highlight the subject of the sentence as new information. In this situation, the fronted element ("across the road") does not receive the spotlight. Notice how much more prominent "a huge coyote" is in the second sentence than in the first sentence.

Active versus Passive Voice

Your students have been using passive structures orally for several years. However, the distinction between active and passive voice is buried deep inside their Grammar Wizards. In order to work with this structure in the composition classroom, students must first be taught to recognize the distinction—not an easy task.

Recognition

Having tried several different approaches, I have found the following to be the most successful:

1. Have the students name all the forms of the verb *to be*. Write the list on the board as they come up with them. They may need some hints along the way. Table 12.2 lists all of the forms.

2. Tell the class that if any form of *be* is followed by another verb, that verb usually ends in *–ing*. Examples:

   I *am* waiting, you *were* trying to sleep, they had *been* eating

3. Give the class the following guideline: If you see a form of *to be* followed by another verb, and that second verb does not end in *–ing*, the verb phrase is passive. Examples:

   The cake *was* eaten. The house *was* built in 1908.

We will look at some activities to help your students become consciously aware of passive constructions a bit later.

Table 12.2 Forms of *To Be*

Pronoun	Present	Past	Other Forms
I	*am*	*was*	▪ *been* (have/had been)
he/she/it	*is*	*was*	▪ *being* (is being, etc.)
you/we/they	*are*	*were*	▪ *will be*

Banning Passives?

Historically, some texts and many teachers have informed students that they should *never* use the passive voice. Such an instruction flies in the face of authentic writing: The finest of professional authors in all genres use passive constructions. The difference between them and your students is that they know *when* to use it, and your students often do not. What is the easiest solution to this dilemma? Ban passive voice! However, you do your students a disservice if you take this path of least resistance. If you truly want your students to master good writing, take the time to teach them *how* and *when* to use it.

I readily admit that active sentences are usually cleaner, easier to process, and more direct than passive ones. However, there are specific times when a passive structure is a better rhetorical choice than an active one. (If such were not the case, professional authors would never use it.) So we need to explore proper passive usage rather than ban it.

Primary Uses

The following is a list of the most common reasons for preferring passive voice:

1. The doer is unknown, unspecified, or unimportant. Consider the following examples:

   a. Yesterday we went to look at a house. It *was painted* a horrible shade of yellow. (I am not sure who did the painting—that piece of information is not relevant.)

   b. The terms of the agreement *were drawn* up after many hours of negations. (I don't know what people were involved in the negations, and I really don't care.)

   c. Rules *are made to be broken*. (This is a general statement with two passive structures (*are made* and *to be broken*). Who made the rules and who might break them are unimportant.)

2. The writer wants to hide the doer:

   a. Mistakes *were made*. (This is the political dodge that has become infamous today. The writer admits that errors occurred, but doesn't want to point a finger at anybody.)

   b. My instructions *were misinterpreted*. (The writer tactfully avoids naming the guilty party(ies).)

3. The doer of an action is *new* information. We established earlier that the subject of the sentence is usually the given information to which new information is attached. Sometimes, however, the subject of an active voice sentence is the new information. A writer may choose to use the passive voice in these instances to move the active subject into the new information position. Here is an example from a Pulitzer Prize–winning book by Lawrence Wright (2006; italics added):

   a. *Original:* "The city [Greeley, CO] *had not been settled* by minors or trappers or railroad workers who lived largely in a world without women; from the beginning, Greeley *had been populated* by well-educated families" (p. 23).

   b. *Nonpassive*: Minors or trappers or railroad workers who lived largely in a world without women did not settle the city [Greeley, CO]; from the beginning, well-educated families populated Greeley.

   Notice how the nonpassive version loses its pop: the fact that Greeley was the town being discussed had already been established in this context, yet it appears at the end of each clause in what is usually the new information position. The passive construction reverses the placement: The given is the subject and the new is in the predicate where it belongs.

4. The writer wants to appear to be neutral. This usage is common in scientific writing. For example, rather than describing an experiment in first person (I or we), the author uses the passive voice. Here are two sentences from a sample report provided by North Carolina State Department of Physics ("Department of Physics"):

   a. "Two photogates were set alongside the track about 0.5 m apart."

   b. "They were connected through an interface to a desktop computer."

Classroom Activities Try some of these activities to increase skills:

■ *Formation*: Native speakers need no instruction on how to form the passive in their natural speech—they do it without thinking about it. Show them a couple of examples of active sentences becoming passive so that they can see what you are talking about. With some practice, they learn to perform the transformation easily. Non-native speakers, however, will probably need special help with this construction.

- *Identification*: As was stated earlier, native and non-native speakers alike need practice at identifying passive voice. And it is important practice: You cannot expect students to clean up passive constructions in their writing until they can recognize it.

  1. Start out with short sentence-level exercises where students are simply required to identify active versus passive sentences.

  2. Point out passive voice usage in common readings, asking the class which of the four reasons given above explain why this author decided not to use an active sentence.

  3. Ask students, individually or in small groups, to examine a passage of text for passive constructions and report back to the class whether the rhetorical choice was good in each instance. If they think that the usage is good, ask them which of the four reasons, given above, supports their decision.

- *Student Writing*: During revision, set aside 5 minutes and ask students to locate all the passive constructions in a writing assignment and identify which of the four reasons (listed above) justifies its usage. If a student finds a passive structure but cannot find a good reason for it, he or she should probably change the sentence to active.

Sentence Length

Sentence length is an important dimension that is all too often overlooked in the composition classroom. In Chapter 10, we saw how short, choppy sentences sound childish. We also saw how nothing but long, complex sentences can either lose the reader or lull the reader to sleep. As with most things in life, variety is the key.

Professional writers know how to vary sentence length so as to keep readers interested. They also know how to throw in short sentences for rhetorical effect. A sudden short sentence can deliver a message with emphasis, with pop. It is somewhat analogous to a speaker who unexpectedly lowers her voice to make a point: The audience suddenly listens very carefully to what the speaker has to say. A very short sentence has a similar effect when writing, irrespective of the genre. Look at the following quote from an economics textbook, paying attention to how the author reaches out from the page and grabs you with the short sentence at the end:

> How an incredibly complex, high-tech economy can operate without any central direction is baffling to many. The last president of the Soviet Union, Mikhail Gorbachev, is said to have asked British Prime Minister Margaret Thatcher: How do you see to it that people get food? The answer was that she didn't. Prices did that. (Sowell, p. 7)

Here is another example, taken from this book. When writing Chapter 1, I used a very short sentence to drive home my point:

> I do not share this example because I believe that the ability to identify a noun from a list of decontextualized words is an important skill. It isn't. Instead, I present it as a microcosm of what's wrong with traditional grammar pedagogy (TGP).

Compare the above version with the following, where I expand the short sentence into a longer sentence that expresses the same thought:

> I do not share this example because I believe that the ability to identify a noun from a list of decontextualized words is an important skill. *In fact, I do not believe this ability is important at all.* Instead, I present it as a microcosm of what's wrong with traditional grammar pedagogy (TGP).

The longer sentence, although well-formed and clear, does not have the pop, does not drive home the point as emphatically. I wanted to make my point strongly, so I made the rhetorical choice of the very short sentence.

Again, I encourage you to point out effective uses of short sentences in common readings. Bringing this technique into sharp focus will help your students appreciate the power that it possesses and perhaps stimulate them to try it in their own writing.

Classroom Activity Martha Kolln (2007, p. 35) provides an excellent classroom activity for the upper grades or college classrooms, based on a study that was done by a college professor with his students:

1. Select four to eight paragraphs from something the class has read. Ask the students to make the following calculations in the selected passage:

   - The average number of words per sentence
   - The average number of sentences per paragraph
   - The number of sentences that were at least 10 words longer than average
   - The number of sentences that were at least five words shorter than average

2. Have students make the same calculations using one of their essays.

3. Compare the results

Typically, students will have fewer *short* sentences than the professional author. This analysis serves as an excellent springboard for discussions on the importance of sentence length variety.

A less time-consuming analysis can be conducted using a computer. Most word-processing programs have a way to check the readability of a document. (Search the Help function for "readability" to get specific instructions.) Included in the readability statistics is the average number of words per sentence. Have your students find out what the average is on their essays, pointing out the following:

- AskOxford.com recommends keeping the average sentence length between 15 and 20 words ("Plain English").

- If a student's writing falls very much above or below this range, she or he needs to do some revision.

- If a student's writing falls within this range, she or he needs to ensure that there are some sentences that are *above* and *below* this range so as to provide variety.

Intentional Fragments

In the composition classroom, fragments are anathema, and for good reason: Fragments are a part of the trinity of mortal sins that educated society abhors (the others being comma splices and run-ons). In real life, however, professional authors make surprisingly frequent use of fragments—for rhetorical effect. Whether or not you want to introduce this concept into your composition classroom is up to you. Doing so runs the risk of students abusing the usage; not doing so misrepresents reality. Sooner or later, a sharp-eyed student is going to spot a fragment used by Hemingway, Faulkner, Steinbeck, or some other highly respected author and ask you about it. Personally, I prefer a preemptive strike: I tell my students about intentional fragments but, since they lack the experience of professional writers, advise them to use them at their own risk—and to footnote them as intentional if they do.

Before we explore intentional fragments, let's remove from consideration one category: fragments within quotation marks. Fragments are quite common in speech. It would be unusual, for example, for a person to respond to a question by repeating the question so as to avoid a fragment:

Speaker A: What are you eating?

Speaker B: (I am eating) A burrito. Why?

Speaker A: (I am) Just curious.

So, if someone is writing dialog, anything that is included inside the quotation marks is exempt from the fragment ban.

Intentional fragments are almost always used either for emphasis or for establishing a less formal voice. Their usage is a way to replicate in writing what a speaker can do with his or her voice and nonverbal language to stress a certain phrase or establish a certain rapport.

Stress Notice how each of the following versions increases the prominence of the final thought. Imagine that you were an actor reading each line at a separate audition:

> Most of the students failed the test, but not all of them did so.
>
> Most of the students failed the test—but not all of them.
>
> Most of the students failed the test. But not all of them.

The second version certainly sharpens the focus on the final five words, necessitating a change in the way the sentence would be read. The third version, however, really turns up the heat, requiring a change in voice, and a pronounced combination of nonverbal gestures.

Informality Note how the level of formality decreases with each of the following versions:

> A few basic points need to be established before we begin our examination.
>
> Let's establish a few basic points first.
>
> First, the basics:

Again, common readings are an excellent source of examples in authentic literature. When you or your students spot a fragment in a professionally written piece, lead a brief discussion of why the author made the rhetorical choice of using one in this context. I repeat, however: Do not encourage students to try to incorporate this device into their own writing unless they feel very confident about their ability to discriminate between rhetorical effectiveness and pure error.

Voice

When we speak, we have what is often referred to as *voice* or *tone of voice*. Speech can be made to sound sincere, pitiful, confident, cool, calm, nervous, and so on. Speakers have a number of tools at their disposal to convey tone of voice: words, sentence structure, stress, cadence, pitch, rhythm, volume, and a vast array of nonverbal signals and gestures.

When we write, we also have a "tone of voice" (simply called *voice* in writing) that is no less important in a writing medium than it is in a speaking medium. The problem, of course, is that writers have only four tools at their disposal: words (diction), sentence structure (grammar), punctuation, and font (bold, all caps, and the like). Achieving and maintaining voice while writing, therefore, is a much more difficult task, but a very important one nevertheless.

Voice is established from the very beginning of a writing piece. Let's begin our examination by playing with the opening lines of T. S. Eliot's poem, "The Love Song of J. Alfred Prufrock" (adapted from an exercise by Castle, 2000). Here is the opening line:

"Let us go, then, you and I."

The voice is at once formal and somber, lilting and poetic, lofty yet down to earth (due in part to the intentional *I* instead of the grammatically correct *me*). A writer's tone can change in an instant. To illustrate, how would your expectations have changed if Eliot had decided to use one of these opening lines instead of the one he chose?

1. "Let us proceed."
2. "Let's you and me go."
3. "Let's git 'r done!"
4. "Let's haul ass."

Voice, then, is the essence of the writer–reader relationship. The reader "feels" the mood, the drama, the humor, the scholarship, or whatever, by the way the writer manipulates the language. All of the rhetorical choices, word choices, and structural choices that we have been describing throughout this book contribute to voice.

At the risk of being overly repetitious, I would point out that students in your classroom are the masters of establishing a variety of voices when they speak. The best way to teach them to recognize, manipulate, and control voice when writing, therefore, is to relate it to what they already know about speaking. Their ability to control voice while speaking is an unconscious act—a part of their Rhetorical Wizards. We need to spend some time, however, making them aware of voice in writing. Toward that end, I recommend the following four-step progression of activities:

1. *Analyze*: Select a passage from a common reading that exhibits a strong sense of voice.
   a. *Identification of Voice:* Prepare a list of questions for students to respond to regarding the voice of the passage. Include things such as level of education, personality, geography, emotional level, and so on.
   b. *Voice Analysis:* Prepare questions for students to answer that force them to explore how they derived their responses to the voice identification points. What features of word choice, grammar, punctuation, and font led students to make the decisions they made?
2. *Detect*: Have students find short passages from *any* written source that contains strong or distinctive elements of voice. These passages can be from outside reading, the Web, emails, wherever. Ask them to

a. Paste the passage into a word-processing document, showing the source, of course.

b. Analyze the voice that is established and the characteristics that contribute to it.

c. Write a passage that copies the voice, but on an entirely different topic (of their choosing).

Here is an example of the detection exercise:

Passage "Still photographers may wait by a water hole for animals to come in and drink; they may spread a little bait; they may lure in animals with decoys or with calls. All of these strategies cause problems" (McKibben, 1997, p. 51).

Analysis The author expresses the frustration of still photography in a calm, professional manner by using the same sentence structure (parallelism) to string together methods photographers employ. The first time, he gives the exact subject ("still photographers") + "may." After that, he just uses the word *they*. The reader can sense that these are just some of the many things photographers do because the author uses semi-colons without using *and* to mark the end of the series.

My Passage New bands may try to gain exposure by providing free downloads on the Internet; they may send demo tapes to record companies and music producers large and small; they may play free gigs. Most of their efforts are in vain.

3. *Imagine*: Have students choose two characters from a novel they are reading. Ask them to imagine that each character had to write the same letter. Have them write the two versions, each in the proper voice of the selected character. The further apart the voices of the two characters are, the better.

4. *Apply*: As was suggested in Chapter 11, have students write two versions of the same event: one as if they were writing for their best friends and one as if they were handing it in to you for a grade. Then have them analyze the differences in language that create the differences in voice.

Reading and Writing

The ability to write is enhanced through exposure to well-written material. Although students today are in control of many different kinds of literacies (the Internet, texting, instant messaging, etc.), they do not spend as much time reading professionally edited works as past generations did. In fact, the reading that you require in your classroom may well constitute a substantial majority of their exposure to professional writing. In order to improve writing skills, you have to take greater advantage of this limited exposure. You have to help students identify and discuss various tools and techniques that good writers use to establish voice and to communicate clearly and intelligently.

Many times throughout this text, I have suggested ways for you to elaborate on a given teaching point by working with examples from common readings. I have two more overarching activities to suggest:

1. Spend 5 minutes every day looking at rhetorical choices that writers have made in common readings. Let the students help you decide on a name for this activity so that you can announce it and everyone knows the drill. You can have them look for very specific devices that you name in advance, or you can simply examine a given passage to see what you can find. Vary the way you conduct this activity. Begin by simply pointing things out to your students. Then gradually release control to them: Have them name and/or analyze structures and devices that you or, later, they locate.

2. Toward the end of the semester or school year, assign passages to individuals or small groups, asking them to be prepared to show the class what they discovered about the rhetorical choices and/or the voice that the author established. If at all possible, project each passage so that the students can point to the relevant areas during the discussion. The adage that you really learn something well when you teach it comes into play here: Let the students "teach" the class about the rhetorical choices and resulting voice of their assigned passages.

Recognizing techniques employed by professional authors develops receptive skills; however, mere recognition is not sufficient to develop good writing skills. You have to push students out of their comfort zones. Encourage or require students to breathe new life into their own writing by incorporating new structures, making new rhetorical choices, experimenting with new techniques to establish and control voice. Reward them for trying, even if they do not get it right the first time. Then help them see what they need to do next time to move toward perfection.

As the old saying goes, you can't steal second with one foot on first.

Discussion Questions

1. Review your answers to the true–false questions at the beginning of this chapter. Have you changed any of your answers?

2. The following exchange is comical when you think about it, but it is also very logical:

   Speaker A: What is George's last name?

   Speaker B: George who?

   Explain why, from a *given versus new* perspective, Speaker B's response makes perfect sense.

3. Why do authors occasionally move a structure from its normal position in a sentence to another position? Support your answer with an original example.

4. How does the concept of *essential versus nonessential* interact with the movement of participle phrases and appositives?

5. How does a writer decide where to place a *floating connector (conjunctive adverb)* in a given clause?

6. This chapter showed that *swinging bridge (subordinate) clauses* can be placed in Sentence Interrupter position. Provide an original example of this phenomenon.

7. Teachers have, historically, banned the use of passive voice in student compositions.

   a. Explain why this ban is nonsensical.

   b. Explain how students can judge whether their passive sentences should be changed to active ones.

8. How does sentence length provide another way for a writer to grab a reader's attention?

9. Why do professional writers use intentional fragments in their writing?

10. In your opinion, should composition students be allowed to use intentional fragments? Defend your answer.

11. If students are, indeed, very capable of establishing and controlling *voice* when speaking, why aren't they equally adept at it when writing?

12. What can you do in your classroom to help students master *voice* in a writing environment?

Glossary

As with many fields of endeavor, the literature dealing with the teaching of English is an alphabet soup of acronyms, not all of which are universally agreed on. Moreover, although I generally use standard grammatical terminology, some of the terms in this book are not widely used in English pedagogical literature. This glossary spells out the acronyms used in this book and defines terms that are not in general use across the English teaching profession.

Bridge: Any word, phrase, or punctuation mark that allows a writer to join two sentences together "legally." There is no traditional grammar term for this concept.

Center bridge: Any **bridge** that must be placed exactly at the boundary between two sentences. The traditional grammar term is *coordinating conjunction*.

Chunking: Combining small units of information into larger meaningful units of information so as to conserve short-term memory (**STM**).

Close reading: Mining a reading passage for constructions and techniques that the author used in order to communicate effectively with readers.

Closure activity: "The covert process whereby the learner's working memory summarizes for itself its perception of what has been learned" (Sousa, 2001, p. 70).

Code switching: Changing **registers** as required by the social situation.

Connector: Any word, phrase, or punctuation mark that shows the relationship between two sentences. A **connector** may or may not be a **bridge**.

Content words: The words that carry most of the meaning of a sentence (e.g., nouns, verbs, adjectives, and adverbs).

Declarative knowledge: Facts stored in long-term memory.

Determiners: Any of a limited set of words that are usually required at the beginning of a noun phrase that is headed by a singular noun.

Elaboration: Exposing students to meaningful applications of concepts.

English language arts (ELA): That area of study, commonly referred to simply as English, that includes reading, writing, literature, and vocabulary acquisition.

English language learner (ELL): A non-native speaker of English.

English as a second language (ESL): The language of a non-native speaker of English.

FANBOYS: Another name for **center bridges** (*coordinating conjunctions*). The name comes from the first letters of those words that can function in that capacity.

Floating connector: A nonbridge connector—that is, a word or phrase that shows the relationship between two joined sentences, but one that does not fulfill the role of a **bridge**. The traditional grammar term is *conjunctive adverb*.

Free modifier: A phrase or clause that is added to the main clause, set off by comma(s).

Function words: The words that have relatively little meaning in a sentence, but that are required by the grammar of English.

Given information: Information that is assumed to be known to one's audience when speaking or writing. **New information** is normally attached to it in discourse.

Grammar Wizard: A metaphor for that subconscious body of knowledge that native speakers or advanced non-native speakers possess about English grammar.

Grammar Wizard Test: A way to query one's implicit knowledge of grammar in order to resolve writing issues.

Inquiry-based approach: A method for presenting new concepts to students. Students are given data to analyze and questions to guide the analysis. They try to figure out the concept by answering the questions. Afterwards, the teacher leads a discussion, answering the questions in the process.

Long-term memory (LTM): A metaphor for the capacity of the brain to store a seemingly infinite amount of information for long periods of time.

Manipulatives: Any items that students can handle and maneuver as they learn or practice a concept.

Near clause: A **free modifier** that is usually formed by removing some form of the verb *to be* from a fully specified clause. The traditional grammar term is *nominative* or *noun absolute*.

New information: That part of an utterance or written sentence that is unknown to one's audience. It is usually attached to **given information** in discourse.

Procedural knowledge: Skills, "how-to" knowledge stored in long-term memory.

Productive: Knowledge or skills that are necessary in order to *use* a word, phrase, or clause when speaking or writing. The opposite is **receptive**.

Receptive: Knowledge or skills that are necessary in order to *understand* a word, phrase, or clause when listening or reading. The opposite is **productive**.

Recursiveness: Repeatedly introducing concepts into one's lesson plans across time. This spiraling allows for a scaffolded presentation of concepts in ever-increasing detail.

Register: A style of language that meets the expectations of a particular social group or serves a special purpose.

Rhetorical choice: A careful choice of words that best fit the situation, the relationship between characters, and the emotional state of the speaker.

Rhetorical Wizard: A metaphor for a subconscious body of knowledge that native speakers or advanced non-native speakers possess about how to use language effectively.

Sentence Wizard: A metaphor for a subconscious body of knowledge that native speakers or advanced non-native speakers possess about properly formed sentences.

Short-term memory (STM): A metaphor for the capacity of the brain to store a finite amount of information for a short period of time so that the brain can carry out a complex cognitive task on it. Also known as *working memory*.

Standard English Learners (SEL): Native English speakers who were born into an environment where a nonstandard dialect is the primary means of communication.

Standard Written American English (SWAE): Written language that conforms to societal expectations in the United States, especially in the academic and business/professional worlds.

Swinging bridge: Any **bridge** that can move with its sentence to the front of the main sentence or to the back of it. The traditional grammar term is *subordinating conjunction*.

Tag question: A question or statement added to the end of a sentence either to indicate that it's the other speaker's turn to talk or to seek confirmation. Example: You are going to the meeting, *aren't you?*

Traditional grammar: A collection of concepts and terminology relating to the analysis of language. This collection, typically taught in schools, originated from ancient Greek and Latin analyses.

Traditional grammar pedagogy (TGP): The traditional way of teaching grammar in U.S. classrooms.

Voice comma: A dip + rise in intonation that a speaker uses to signal to the listener that a constituent (but not a sentence) is finished.

Voice period: A dip in intonation that a speaker uses to signal to the listener that a sentence is finished.

Yes–no question: Any question that can be answered by a simple "yes" or "no" Example: Are you going to the meeting?

Works Cited

Adelson, Edward H. http://web.mit.edu/persci/people/adelson/ checkershadow_downloads.html. Retrieved November 11, 2008.

Allen, Rick. "Q&A ... Making Lasting Memories: A Conversation with Marilee Sprenger." *Education Update, 50,* (5), May 2008. www.ascd.org/ portal/site/ascd/menuitem.ab1d8e6fc42e2ffcdeb3ffdb62108a0c/. Retrieved October 23, 2008. Path: Archived Issues; May 2008.

Anderson, Jeff. *Mechanically Inclined: Building Grammar, Usage, and Style into Writer's Workshop.* Portland, MA: Stenhouse, 2005.

Anderson, Richard C. "The Notion of Schemata and the Educational Enterprise: General Discussion of the Conference." In *Schooling and the Acquisition of Knowledge,* ed. Richard C. Anderson, Rand J. Spiro, and William E. Montague. Hillsdale, NJ: Erlbaum, 1977.

Benjamin, Amy. *Engaging Grammar: Practical Advice for Real Classrooms.* National Council of Teachers of English, 2007.

————. "Syntactical Analysis of 5th Grade Papers." Unpublished, no date.

"Beyond Grammar Drills: How Language Works in Learning to Write." *The Council Chronicle Online,* October 25, 2006. www.ncte.org/about/press/. Retrieved December 10, 2006.

Blaauw-Hara, Mark. "Why Our Students Need Instruction in Grammar, and How We Should Go about It." *Teaching English in the Two-Year College* 34.2, December 2006, pp. 165–178.

Blakemore, Sarah-Jayne, and Frith, Uta. *The Learning Brain: Lessons for Education.* Malden, MA: Blackwell, 2005.

Braddock, Richard, Lloyd-Jones, Richard, and Schoer, Lowell. *Research in Written Composition.* Champaign, IL: National Council of Teachers of English, 1963.

Caine, Renate N., and Caine, Geoffrey. *Education on the Edge of Possibility.* Alexandria, VA: Association for Supervision & Curriculum Development, 1997.

————. *Making Connections: Teaching and the Human Brain.* Menlo Park, CA: Innovative Learning Publications, 1994.

————. *Unleashing the Power of Perceptual Change: The Potential of Brain-Based Teaching.* Alexandria, VA: Association for Supervision & Curriculum Development, 1997.

Castle, Mort. "Tone: The Writer's Voice in the Reader's Mind." *The Internet Writing Journal: Writers Write,* September, 2000. www.writerswrite.com/ journal/sep00/castle2.htm. Retrieved September 21, 2008.

Chomsky, Noam. *Syntactic Structures*. The Hague: Mouton, 1957.

Christensen, Francis, and Christensen, Bonniejean. *Notes toward a New Rhetoric: 9 Essays for Teachers*. Ed. Don Stewart. Booklocker.com, Inc., November 14, 2007.

Connors, Robert J., and Lunsford, Andrea. "Frequency of Formal Errors in Current College Writing, or Ma and Pa Kettle Do Research," *College Composition and Communication*, 39, 1988, pp. 395–409.

Craik, Fergus I. M., & Tulving, Endel. "Depth of Processing and the Retention of Words in Episodic Memory." *Journal of Experimental Psychology, 104*, 1975, pp. 268–294.

"Create Your Own Adventure." PBS. www.pbs.org/kratts/crazy/madlibs/. Retrieved January 8, 2007.

de Zwann, Herman. *One-Liners and Proverbs*. A1: Oneliners and proverbs Aa–Af. 22 www.oneliners-and-proverbs.com/. Retrieved July 22, 2008.

"Department of Physics Laboratory Report Sample: PY 205, 208, 211, 212." North Carolina State University. www4.ncsu.edu/~mowat/ H&M_WebSite/SampleReport/report.html. Retrieved September 19, 2008.

"Determiner." Wikipedia. en.wikipedia.org/wiki/Determiner. Retrieved January 5, 2007.

Felder, Richard. "Reaching the Second Tier: Learning and Teaching Styles in College Science Education." *Journal of College Science Teaching, 23* (5), 1993, pp. 286–290.

Fowler, H. Ramsey, Aaron, Jane E., and Okoomian, Janice. *The Little, Brown Handbook*, 8th ed. New York: Longman, 2001.

"Funbrain Reading." Pearson Education, Inc. www.funbrain.com/brain/ ReadingBrain/ReadingBrain.html. Retrieved January 8, 2007.

Gallagher, Kelly. *Teaching Adolescent Writers*. Portland, MA: Stenhouse, 2006.

Graham, Steve, and Perin, Delores. *Writing Next: Effective Strategies to Improve Writing of Adolescents in Middle and High Schools*. New York: Carnegie Corporation, 2006.

Hancock, Craig. *Meaning-Centered Grammar: An Introductory Text*. London: Equinox, 2005.

Hillocks, George, Jr. *Research on Written Composition: New Directions for Teaching*. Champaign, IL: ERIC Clearinghouse on Reading and Communication Skills, National Institute for Education, 1986.

Hillocks, George Jr., and Smith, Michael W. "Grammars and Literacy Learning," in *Handbook of Research on Teaching the English Language Arts,* 2nd. ed. Mahwah, NJ: Erlbaum, 2003.

Huitt, William. "The Information Processing Approach to Cognition." *Educational Psychology Interactive*. Valdosta, GA: Valdosta State University, 2003. http://chiron.valdosta.edu/whuitt/col/cogsys/infoproc.html. Retrieved December 10, 2008.

Jensen, Eric. *Brain-Based Learning: The New Science of Teaching & Training*. rev. ed. San Diego: The Brain Store, 2000.

Klammer, Thomas P., Schulz, Muriel R., and Volpe, Angela Della. *Analyzing English Grammar*, 5th ed. New York: Pearson Longman, 2007.

Kolln, Martha. *Rhetorical Grammar: Grammatical Choices, Rhetorical Effects*, 5th ed. New York: Pearson Education, 2007.

Lai, Gerald, Nesbitt, Scott, Fong, Ed, and Ha, Phat. "Neural Pathways to Long Term Memory." http://ahsmail.uwaterloo.ca/kin356/ltm/procedural.htm. Retrieved December 1, 2006.

London, Jack. *Call of the Wild.* http://london.sonoma.edu/Writings/CallOfTheWild/chapter1.html. Retrieved June 1, 2008.

Marzano, Robert J., Pickering, Debra J., and Pullock, Jane E. *Classroom Instruction That Works: Research-Based Strategies for Increasing Student Achievement.* Upper Saddle River, NJ: Pearson Merrill Prentice Hall, 2005.

McKibben, Bill. "The Problem with Wildlife Photography," *Doubletake, 10,* Fall 1997, pp. 50–56.

Merriam-Webster Online. http://m-w.com/dictionary/preposition. Retrieved November 11, 2007.

Miller, George. "The Magical Number Seven, Plus or Minus Two: Some Limits on Our Capacity for Processing Information." *The Psychological Review, 63,* 1956, 81–97.

Mulroy, David. *The War Against Grammar.* Portsmouth, NH: Boynton/Cook, 2003.

National Commission on Writing in America's Schools and Colleges. *Writing: A Ticket to Work . . . Or a Ticket Out: A Survey of Business Leaders.* College Entrance Examination Board, 2004.

Noden, Harry. *Image Grammar: Using Grammatical Structures to Teach Writing.* Portsmouth, NH: Boynton/Cook, 1999.

Noguchi, Rei R. *Grammar and the Teaching of Writing: Limits and Possibilities.* Urbana, IL: NCTE, 1991.

NW Regional Educational Laboratory, "Assessment." August 11, 2007. www.nwrel.org/assessment/definitions.php?odelay=0&d=1. Retrieved February 2, 2008.

"Optical Illusions." Wikimedia Commons. July 12, 2008. http://commons.wikimedia.org/wiki/Optical_illusion?uselang=de. Retrieved November 11, 2008.

"Plain English Guidelines: Keep Sentences Short." *Better Writing.* Oxford Dictionaries. <http://www.askoxford.com/betterwriting/plainenglish/sentencelength/?view=uk>. Retrieved October 25, 2008.

Rawlinson, Graham E. *The Significance of Letter Position in Word Recognition.* Unpublished PhD Thesis, Psychology Department, University of Nottingham, Nottingham UK, 1976.

"Reading Rods Simple Sentences Kit." ETA Cuisenaire. January 5, 2007. www.etacuisenaire.com/readingrods/simple.jsp.

Rothenberg, Carol, and Fisher, Douglas. *Teaching English Language Learners: A Differentiated Approach.* Upper Saddle River, NJ: Pearson Education, 2007.

Schuster, Edgar. *Breaking the Rules: Liberating Writers through Innovative Grammar Instruction*. Portsmouth, NH: Heinemann, 2003.

Schwarzbaum, Lisa. Movie Review: *Enchanted (2007)*. November 21, 2007. www.ew.com/ew/article/0,,20161967,00.html. Retrieved November 25, 2007.

Sousa, David A. *How the Brain Learns,* 2nd ed. Thousand Oaks, CA: Corwin, 2001.

Sowell, Thomas, *Basic Economics: A Citizen's Guide to the Economy*, 2nd ed. New York: Basic Books, 2003.

Spatt, Brenda. *Writing from Sources*, 6th ed. Boston: Bedford/St. Martin's, 2003.

Tufte, Virginia. *Artful Sentences: Syntax as Style*. Chesire, CT: Graphics Press LLC, 2006.

Vygotsky, Lev. *Thought and Language*. Ed. and Trans. A. Kozulin. Cambridge, MA: MIT Press, 1986.

"Wacky Word Tales." Education Place, Houghton-Mifflin. January 6, 2007, www.eduplace.com/tales/.

Wallis, Claudia, and Dell, Kristina. "What Makes Teens Tick." *Time in Partnership with CNN*. May 10, 2004. www.time.com/time/magazine/article/0,9171,994126-2,00.html. Retrieved March 31, 2007.

Walsh, Brian E. *Unleashing Your Brilliance: Tools & Techniques to Achieve Personal, Professional & Academic Success*. Walsh Seminars, 2005.

Weaver, Constance. *Grammar to Enrich & Enhance Writing*. Portsmouth, NH: Heinemann, 2008.

———. *Teaching Grammar in Context*. Portsmouth, NH: Boynton/Cook, 1996.

"What Is Brain/Mind Learning?" Caine Learning Institute. www.cainelearning.com/principles.html. Retrieved November 25, 2006.

Wheeler, Rebecca S., and Swords, Rachel. *Code-Switching: Teaching Standard English in Urban Classrooms*. Urbana, IL: NCTE, 2006.

Williams, Robin. *The Non-Designer's Design Book: Design and Typographic Principles for the Visual Novice*, 2nd ed. Berlekey, CA: Peachpit Press, 2003.

Wolf, Patricia. "Brain-Compatible Learning: Fad or Foundation?" *The School Administrator*. American Association of School Administrators. December 2006. www.aasa.org/publications/saarticledetail.cfm?ItemNumber=7810. Retrieved October 17, 2008.

Wolfe, Don M. "Variety in Sentence Structure: A Device." *College English*, *11*, (7), April 1950, pp. 394–397.

World of Warcraft® End User License Agreement. February 2, 2007. www.worldofwarcraft.com/legal/eula.html. Retrieved October 15, 2008.

Wright, Lawrence. *The Looming Tower: Al-Qaeda and the Road to 9/11*. New York: Vintage Books, 2006.

Answers to Chapter Questions

Chapter 1 Answers

1. True
2. False
3. False
4. False—grammar's primary role is to establish patterns that allow us to combine words into phrases and phrases into sentences.
5. False—many, if not most, professional authors can't perform this type of analysis.
6. True
7. True, but their knowledge is subconscious—their conscious minds cannot access it.
8. True

Chapter 2 Answers

1. True
2. True—short-term memory would overload.
3. True
4. True
5. True
6. True
7. True
8. False—very specific rules govern the order of adjectives.

Chapter 3 Answers

1. False—the brain is designed for natural learning (i.e., finding patterns and interrelating them).
2. True
3. False—most students will not acquire the grammar of SWAE without guidance.
4. True
5. False—the brain is a social instrument. Natural learning occurs via many sources of input; interaction is a key one.
6. True
7. True
8. False—it is a collection of knowledge that you have acquired across time.
9. True

Chapter 4 Answers

1. False—an inquiry-based approach is first inductive and then deductive.

2. True
3. False—all learning, natural or rote, requires multiple exposures.
4. True—errors are a natural part of learning, so new ones are to be expected.
5. True—all dialects of English are rule-governed, logical, and efficient. The problem is not the language itself, but social judgments about what is "proper."
6. False—if all of the sentences in an exercise contain the error, then students do not have to see whether or not a sentence is erroneous before correcting it.
7. True
8. False—the logic behind conventions comes from processing requirements—what the listener or reader needs. This entire area is omitted.

Chapter 5 Answers

1. False—there are ways that allow students to access what they know subconsciously about grammar in order to resolve sentence management issues.
2. False—most words in English can function as different parts of speech, depending on how they are used in a given context.
3. True—context will allow the reader to understand the passage. However, apostrophes are expected in SWAE, so they are very important.
4. False—students have been using them for years by the time they get to your classroom. All you have to do is tap into that knowledge.
5. False—Grammar Wizard Tests clearly demonstrate that one's Grammar Wizard is well aware of this distinction.
6. False—errors are a natural part of learning new concepts.
7. True
8. False—they still need multiple, varied exposure across time in order to retain the information.

Chapter 6 Answers

1. True—let students figure things out whenever possible.
2. True (at a subconscious level)
3. False—if the challenge becomes too great, your brain will begin to allocate resources to protect you from a perceived threat.
4. True

5. False—a pronoun takes the place of an entire noun phrase. It relates back to a specific noun but cannot substitute for it unless the noun phrase is only one word.
6. True
7. False—plural nouns that do not end in an –s sound require –s.
8. False—a sentence can contain several "complete thoughts." Also, a fragment in context can, indeed, be a complete thought.

Chapter 7 Answers

1. False—understanding a structure requires receptive control; using a structure requires productive control. The former does not entail the latter.
2. True up to a point. Learning the names will help make students more aware of these structures when they read. However, they do not need to name a structure before they can use it in their writing.
3. True
4. True
5. True
6. False—research clearly supports their effectiveness as a learning device.
7. True—otherwise they wouldn't be able to read the material. However, this knowledge is receptive.

Chapter 8 Answers

1. False—the brain will always attempt to create a pattern to guide usage. However, that pattern may not be accurate.
2. True
3. True
4. True
5. True
6. False—if one or more items in the series contains a comma, then a semi-colon is used to separate the items.
7. True
8. False—it is possible for a hyphen to change the meaning of a phrase.

Chapter 9 Answers

1. True
2. True—but they may not know how to tell where one sentence ends and the next one begins.
3. True
4. True
5. False—*then* can float, so it is not a bridge.
6. True
7. False—comma usage is determined by the reader's need to know where to chunk.
8. False—it can cause readers to chunk erroneously, causing them to have to re-read the sentence.

Chapter 10 Answers

1. True, but that knowledge is receptive.
2. False—the presence of properly formed free modifiers is the key contributor.
3. True, because free modifiers normally begin or end with a voice comma.
4. False—it may sound boring or repetitious, but it does not have to sound childish.
5. True
6. False—context is the key determiner for placement.
7. True
8. False—legalese is a great example of a style that can easily confuse readers rather than impress them.

Chapter 11 Answers

1. True
2. False—it is expected in most business or academic areas, but it is no more logical or efficient than any other dialect of English.
3. False—SWAE is a register of English. Students have already acquired multiple registers; SWAE is another one to add.
4. False—commas can be used to achieve a rhetorical effect.
5. False—their usage is governed by context.
6. False—using overly fancy words sounds can easily sound pretentious.
7. False—errors are a natural part of learning. Congratulate the student for trying to use the new word and help him to understand the problem.
8. False—they usually already know the definition. Spelling is the problem, not meaning.

Chapter 12 Answers

1. False—structures are often movable. Placement then depends on the rhetorical effect the writer wants to create.
2. True
3. False—they can also be sentence interrupters.
4. False—passive voice is a very useful structure. However, they should not use it unless they can explain why they are using it; otherwise, they might easily overuse it.
5. True
6. False—very short sentences can be used as a powerful means of emphasizing a point.
7. False—they use them for rhetorical effect rather commonly. However, before students attempt to use them, they must first master sentence boundary conventions.
8. True

Index